The Common Vision

Studies in the
Postmodern Theory of Education

Joe L. Kincheloe and Shirley R. Steinberg
General Editors

Vol. 48

PETER LANG
New York • Washington, D.C./Baltimore
Bern • Frankfurt am Main • Berlin • Vienna • Paris

David Marshak

The Common Vision

Parenting and Educating for Wholeness

PETER LANG
New York • Washington, D.C./Baltimore
Bern • Frankfurt am Main • Berlin • Vienna • Paris

Library of Congress Cataloging-in-Publication Data

Marshak, David.
The common vision: parenting and educating for wholeness / David Marshak.
p. cm. — (Counterpoints; v. 48)
Includes bibliographical references (p.) and index.
1. Education—Philosophy. 2. Teaching. 3. Parenting. 4. Child development.
5. Steiner, Rudolf, 1861–1925. 6. Ghose, Aurobindo, 1872–1950. 7. Inayat
Khan, 1882–1926. 8. Waldorf method of education. 9. Sri Aurobindo
International Centre of Education (Pondicherry, India). I. Title. II. Series:
Counterpoints (New York, N.Y.); vol. 48.
LB14.7.M39 370'.9—dc20 96-41248
ISBN 0-8204-3702-6
ISSN 1058-1634

Die Deutsche Bibliothek-CIP-Einheitsaufnahme

Marshak, David:
The common vision: parenting and educating for wholeness / David Marshak.
–New York; Washington, D.C./Baltimore; Bern; Frankfurt am Main;
Berlin; Vienna; Paris: Lang.
(Counterpoints; Vol. 48)
ISBN 0-8204-3702-6
NE: GT

Cover design by James F. Brisson.
Cover art by Kumi Yamashita.

The paper in this book meets the guidelines for permanence and durability
of the Committee on Production Guidelines for Book Longevity
of the Council of Library Resources.

∞

Printed in the United States of America.

For Kalman and Goldie

In every age . . . [there are] scattered forerunners in the world.
They are those who are ahead of their time,
and whose personal action is based on an inward knowledge
of that which is yet to come.

Abbé de Tourville

CONTENTS

ACKNOWLEDGEMENTS

I thank two superb teachers without whose help I would never have begun the journey that has led to this book: Donald Oliver and Paula Klimek.

Many thanks also to Anna Peck and the then second graders at the Waldorf School in Lexington, Massachusetts, for sharing a part of their lives with me and helping me to learn about Rudolf Steiner's teachings; to the teachers and students at The Hollow Reed School in Boston, Massachusetts—particularly Rakib—for allowing me to learn from them about the teachings of Inayat Khan; and to the teachers and students at the Sri Aurobindo International Centre of Education in Pondicherry, India—particularly Paru Patil and Jugal Kishore Mukherji—for helping me to learn from them about the teachings of Aurobindo Ghose.

Special thanks to my friends and colleagues who read sections of this book while it was in progress and who shared their reactions to it with me: Gary and Donna Krasnow, Candace and Frank Burkle, Jayne and Stuart Fisher, Steve Wineman, and Peggy McNeill.

I am grateful to several generous educators who each read a chapter about which she or he had particular knowledge and critiqued the accuracy and clarity of my presentation in that chapter: Anna Peck, Jill Riedel, and Mrs. Lee LeCraw for the chapter about Steiner; Bill Moss for the chapter about Aurobindo; and Murshida Vera Corda and Aostre N. Johnson for the chapter about Inayat Khan. I'm also grateful to my colleague, John Chattin-McNichols, for reviewing my comments about the teachings of Maria Montessori.

Finally, thanks to Aostre N. Johnson for her helpful suggestions while I was completing the book's first revision.

THE EVOLUTIONARY CRISIS, THE COEVOLUTIONARY RESPONSE

At the end of the twentieth century, we find our lives entangled in paradox. Never before has human capability been so powerful, so productive, and so diverse. Yet never before has it been so dangerous, nor has it exacted so vast a toll from the health of the Earth's biosphere. Never before have hundreds of millions of people who live in "advanced" industrial cultures enjoyed such a high level of material wealth. Yet never before have billions of people lived in such extreme poverty and with such constant vulnerability to disaster. And never before have nation states had so much wealth that they could devote more than a trillion dollars a year to preparing for and making war, even without official enemies in most situations. The intensity of paradox that we experience is heightened by the richness and growing complexity of our electronic media. Never before have people throughout the planet, the poor as well as the rich, been connected to each other by such a powerful web of media. In the "global village" of pervasive radio and television and the exploding Internet, we can keep fewer and fewer secrets about the crises and contradictions of our times.

We struggle to make sense of these contradictions and, so far, most of us have largely failed to do so. Why? Because most of us have not identified the pattern that underlies and connects them all: the very paradoxical condition of our evolution as a species. Those of us who live within the technological culture have grown far more powerful than we are wise and compassionate, far more identified with our separation from each other, from our habitat, and from spirit than with our connections to each other, to the Earth, and to what we experience as "God."

To grapple effectively with our paradoxical condition—and to survive in our natural home as well as allow the survival of many other life forms on this planet—we must continue to evolve, particularly in our moral and spiritual dimensions. This book describes one critical means through which our species can

evolve: child raising and education. The way we raise and educate our young is the most powerful means we have to choose
consciously to evolve through and beyond our current crisis. We
can learn to nurture and educate our children in a way that differs
profoundly from the norms of "modern" culture. And as we help
our children to unfold into a more complete wholeness, we will
also encourage our own mental, emotional, and spiritual growth as
adults. Indeed, the more we unfold as whole beings, the more nurturance and aid we can give to our children.

What I will share with you in this book is a description of the
needs and potentials of children and youth from birth through age
twenty-one, a description based on a holistic understanding of
what human beings are and can become. This understanding is
founded on the insights of three early twentieth-century spiritual
teachers—Rudolf Steiner, Aurobindo Ghose, and Inayat Khan—
whose works articulate a *common vision* of human growth, wholeness, and evolutionary change. This *common vision* provides detailed responses to three key questions:

- What is the true nature of human beings?

- What is the course of human growth from birth through age
  twenty-one?

- Given this understanding of human growth, what are the desired functions of child raising and education?

This *common vision* of Steiner, Aurobindo, and Inayat Khan
provides a clear set of images of what constitutes human potential, wholeness, and growth throughout childhood and youth. It is
both holistic and integrative in character, describing the body,
emotions, mind, and spirit, and the systems of interactions among
them. This *common vision* of human becoming offers us a way to
collaborate consciously with the energies of evolution—as parents
and as teachers. It provides us with a template for a profoundly
postmodern way to raise and educate children. And it shows us a
path through the evolutionary crisis of our times—through the
work of conscious coevolution.

Chapter One delineates this *common vision* in detail, while Chapter Two briefly tells the life stories of Steiner, Aurobindo, and Inayat Khan. Chapters Three through Eight provide a detailed examination of the single vision of each of these teachers, with particular focus on their recommended methods for child raising and education and the ways that people have applied these purposes, principles, and methods in schools. Chapters Three and Four focus on Rudolf Steiner and the Waldorf School; Chapters Five and Six, on Aurobindo Ghose and the Aurobindo International Centre of Education; and Chapters Seven and Eight, on Inayat Khan and the Sufi Seed Centers. Chapter Nine details the specific ways in which the three single visions of Inayat Khan, Aurobindo, and Steiner both agree and diverge in relation to their descriptions of human nature. Chapter Ten explores the most important issue raised by differences among the three teachings and offers suggestions for applying these teachings, this *common vision*, today for the purpose of raising and educating whole children and youths and consciously participating in the coevolutionary process.

A COMMON VISION OF WHOLENESS

Three Visionary Teachers

For three men born into profoundly different cultures, Rudolf Steiner, Aurobindo Ghose, and Inayat Khan shared a strikingly related set of life circumstances and experiences.

- Rudolf Steiner was born in 1861 on the border of Austria and Hungary. Aurobindo Ghose was born in 1872, and Inayat Khan in 1882, both in India. Despite the differences in their years of birth, each of these men taught and published his major work at essentially the same time: from 1910 to 1924.

- Each of these men began his spiritual journey within a world religion, yet each rejected the exclusive claims to truth of that religious tradition. Instead each teacher synthesized the core truths of his religion of origin both with other spiritual traditions and with his own spiritual insight.

Steiner, born and raised within the nineteenth-century German culture, articulated teachings that related a Germanic Christianity, influenced by an explicit recognition of its roots in Teutonic paganism, to theosophy, a modern spiritual movement that found its primary sources in Hinduism. Steiner was also very familiar with the Western science of the late nineteenth and early twentieth centuries and brought its influence into his work as well. Aurobindo's teachings created a synthesis that drew on the Hinduism of his native India as well as an intimate understanding of European culture and its "religion" of science, which he had gained from the fourteen years he studied in England. Inayat Khan's influences included his family religion of Islam, his knowledge of Hinduism, his spiritual training in Sufism, and his years of experience as a spiritual teacher in the United States and Europe.

- In an era when communication and transportation technologies had not yet brought the many lands of this planet into their present proximity, each of these three men had a profound understanding of the cultures of both the West and the East. Each of them carried elements of Western and Eastern traditions into his teachings and joined these elements with his own personal knowing to create a vision that was both a synthesis of East and West and the expression of his own spiritual intuition. In a profound way, each of these men brought together East and West in his life and in his teachings.

- Their public lives all ended at essentially the same time. Steiner died in 1924, Inayat Khan in 1926. While Aurobindo lived until 1950 and communicated with his disciples through letters and appeared before them four times each year, he withdrew from public teaching after his "day of Siddhi" in 1926.

During the past two centuries, many spiritual teachers have talked and written about the nature of human beings. Yet only Inayat Khan, Steiner, and Aurobindo have informed this discussion with detailed descriptions of both the process of human becoming in childhood and youth and the desired functions of child raising and education. And these three men have given us essentially the same vision of human unfoldment within the same coevolutionary context, at the very same historical moment. (One other person, a doctor and educator, not a spiritual teacher, has offered a strikingly related vision: Maria Montessori.[1])

The Common Vision: A Guide to Coevolution

The teachings of Rudolf Steiner, Aurobindo Ghose, and Inayat Khan concerning human nature, human becoming from birth through age twenty-one, and the purpose and practice of child raising and education display a remarkable coherence. While these teachings are not identical, they are profoundly similar and congruent. As noted before and detailed in Chapter Two, each vision arises from a different cultural experience, different religious roots, a different mystical tradition and practice, and the personal genius and spiritual unfoldment of a different human being. Yet the larger designs of these three systems of knowledge constitute what is essentially a single music, and the great majority of the details play as notes that are identical to each other or in harmony.

There are differences among the three teachers' descriptions. Many of these differences are linguistic, but some are substantive. Other apparent differences are not disagreements at all but are descriptions offered by one teacher about issues or aspects not discussed by the other(s). Even with this complexity, there is no question that these three bodies of knowledge are describing essentially the same understanding of the universe and of the place of human beings within it. They constitute a *common vision* of human nature and human becoming from birth through age twenty-one that is holistic and integrative. This *common vision* includes and validates the learnings of the twentieth century developmental psychologies, particularly the work of Jean Piaget and Erik Erikson and their academic descendants, but extends far beyond them in scope.

Steiner, Aurobindo, and Inayat Khan also share a profound understanding of the evolutionary crisis that we have entered in "modern" culture. Each of them offers his teachings about human becoming, child raising, and education as a guide to coevolution, to our conscious participation in the evolutionary process, to our resolution of our current paradoxical crisis.

A Common Vision of Human Nature

According to Steiner, Aurobindo, and Inayat Khan, the most fundamental nature of human beings is that we are complex systems of energy that include several interpenetrated and interrelated sub-systems. One—and only one—of these sub-systems consists of energy in the form of matter. The others are purely energetic. Each sub-system exists largely but not exclusively on a different plane of being. The various planes of being are simultaneously separate and integral and range from the lowest plane, matter, to the highest plane, spirit. Each human sub-system is connected to and affected by every other sub-system. Thus, we are profoundly interdependent among all of our parts and with all other energies with which we interact.

Steiner, Aurobindo, and Inayat Khan differ somewhat in their identification and description of the various sub-systems of the person and their corresponding planes of being, as described in Chapter Two. Yet the common center that is shared by each of their descriptions of the human being is clear:

- **A physical being that exists on the material plane.** This being is the body of matter. It includes the vehicles of the five physical senses, the breathing and circulation systems, the digestive organs, and the trunk and limbs. The physical body also includes the body consciousness, the awareness that emerges purely from the physical body.

- **A life-force being that exists on the next higher plane, the plane of life-force or vital energies.** The life-force being exists on a plane of subtle energy that is of a higher and finer vibration than matter. This being consists of subtle energy that animates matter into the form of life. In the course of evolution, the life-force energy first manifested in plants, then in animals, and then in humans. It is part of what connects us with all other forms of life.

- **A mind or mental being that exists on the next higher plane.** The mental being operates on the next higher plane of being and includes the memory; the element of mind that receives sensory data and translates these data into thought forms; the element of mind that apprehends vibrations from higher planes and translates them into images; and the intellect, the seat of reason.

- **A spiritual being that exists on still higher planes.** Each person includes two levels of spiritual being. These levels of spiritual being embody the divine energy within the human person. It is this spiritual being that motivates personal unfoldment and the evolution of the individual—and the species.

In addition, both Aurobindo and Inayat Khan describe the ego as the false sense of self created in early childhood when the spiritual self identifies with the physical, life-force, and mental beings. The ego is illusory and distorted in relation to the spiritual being, yet it is a necessary step in the unfoldment of the person. The ego is required for survival until the spiritual being can unfold and establish itself within the consciousness. (Steiner does not mention the ego or anything like it.)

Finally Steiner, Aurobindo, and Inayat Khan concur that life on this planet is engaged in a process of evolution that is the unfoldment of spiritual energies that have previously been involved in lower levels of being. Humans are partially divine beings who are evolving toward greater divinity. All three teachers describe the task of human beings as the attainment of divinity or God-realization. Aurobindo and Inayat Khan note that humans are transitional beings within the evolutionary process like all others before us: when we have fulfilled our potential, the next level of beings will emerge from us and continue to evolve.

Steiner, Aurobindo, and Inayat Khan agree that the individual spiritual being is what experiences evolution. Steiner and Aurobindo describe the mechanism of this evolution as the reincarnation of spiritual beings. Inayat Khan both differs and agrees. He explains that each spiritual being or, in his terms, each soul, incarnates only once but can evolve in that incarnation. Then, as it returns to the spiritual plane, the soul leaves its impress on souls that are moving down to incarnate. This transmission is the mechanism of evolution that he describes in some of his writings. Yet paradoxically he notes elsewhere in his teachings that reincarnation is indeed a fact.

A Common Vision of Human Unfoldment: Birth to Age Twenty-One

In the broad outlines of their visions of human becoming from birth through age twenty-one, Rudolf Steiner, Aurobindo Ghose, and Inayat Khan share an even greater agreement than they do in their descriptions of human nature. While each spiritual teacher brings a distinct flavor to his descriptions, the details of these visions coincide to the extent that there are only a few important points of disagreement among them. Even these are more differences in emphasis than any sort of direct contradictions.

Their common vision of human becoming from birth through age twenty-one includes these elements:

- The process of human becoming from birth through age twenty-one is an unfoldment of inherent potentials that require proper nurture if the young person's nature is to evolve to the extent of its capacities. Thus, what is central in determining the becoming of the young person is her nature and her nurture in relationship to each other.

- Each child and youth is an organismic whole who contains within herself her own innate wisdom and motive force, her own *inner teacher*, to guide and power her unfoldment. This wisdom and motive force direct the child to unfold in a direction and at a pace that are appropriate for her development, if she is not coerced or compelled from them by adults.

- The unfoldment of the child and youth follows a course that is relatively consistent, regular, and foreseeable in its large outlines. Yet each individual unfolds at her own pace, which results in wide variations in the particular age when any given child experiences any particular step in her unfoldment; this process of unfoldment includes three major eras, each of about seven years in length:

    a. Birth through 6 years of age
    b. 6 through 12–14 years of age
    c. 12–14 through 21 years of age

What follows, drawn in broad strokes, is the *common vision* of human becoming between birth and age twenty-one described by Steiner, Aurobindo, and Inayat Khan. Within the articulation of this vision, I have included the elements of unfoldment and the needs for growth on which all three teachers agree. I have also brought in those elements and needs that any one of them describes, as long as they add detail to the *common vision* and are not contradicted by the writings of the other teachers.

THE FIRST ERA: BIRTH THROUGH 6 YEARS

In the first era, the child needs to direct her own activity as much as possible. She knows her experience as play, which is purposive to her. While her activity is more rewarding in its process than in its outcome, she needs the opportunity to experience a sense of completion about whatever she begins when she seeks such closure. She also needs to learn to satisfy her own needs as is appropriate to her age. The child who is free to direct her own activity will inevitably act in this way, for her inner wisdom will lead her to choose activities that meet her immediate growth needs.

In these years the child learns primarily by imitation. She perceives whatever is in her environment, including its physical, emotional, moral, mental, and spiritual aspects, and imitates these examples. As she learns through imitation, she does not gain from being taught rules or abstractions. What serves her unfoldment best is the provision of good examples that she can imitate: adults who are engaged in their own ongoing growth and who manifest truth-making, order, and spiritual opening as well as a calm and patient consistency in their behavior toward the child.

The young child also needs love, affection, support, and care of a high quality. When the child receives such nurturance, she experiences an interwoven happiness and trust and gains confidence in the fundamental goodness of life. This confidence evokes an inner joy and relaxation that provide her with even more nurturance.

The child needs to experience awe and reverence and to learn a feeling of gratitude toward the spiritual world for the wonders of the universe. She can best gain these experiences by participating with adults in rituals that evoke these feelings in the adults. The child will then learn them through her imitation of the adults' emotional and spiritual experience.

The first part of this era extends through the first two and half years of the child's life, when she belongs in the family. Each of these years has a powerful effect on the child's becoming, but all three teachers stress the critical importance of the first year in particular. While Aurobindo and Steiner describe the significance of the examples the child has in this year, Inayat Khan details the mechanism through which these examples influence the infant. At birth, Khan explains, the infant's soul, her spiritual being, is unfinished, like a photographic negative not yet exposed to light. The impressions that the child receives in her first year from her parents influence the completion of her spiritual being, either for the good or not.

In these years the child's primary growth tasks include learning to crawl, to stand and walk, and to speak and think. All of these tasks involve the exercise of her will, which must be allowed as much expression as possible without restriction from adults. The more the child can express her will in these years, Inayat Khan, Aurobindo, and Steiner strongly agree, the more powerful and spiritually open she will be later on.

Both Steiner and Inayat Khan note that the child's cutting of her first teeth is the outward manifestation of the initial unfoldment of her thinking.

In her third year the child first gains a sense of herself as a separate person, when what Aurobindo and Inayat Khan call the ego, the false sense of self, develops. Once her ego has evolved into consciousness, the child moves into the second part of this era, from about two and a half years of age into her seventh year.

In these years the child needs to experience what Inayat Khan calls "kingship": the freedom to follow her own initiative, and the absence of worry, anxiety, competition, and ambition. While the child benefits from experiencing social contexts beyond the family part of the time, she needs such contexts to be as free of competition and conflict as possible.

Steiner and Inayat Khan both specifically note the child's need for environments that allow unchecked movement and initiative, that encourage the child's fancy and imagination. She needs not to be directed to the learning of numbers or language but to be allowed to play according to her own inclination. The child's play is the expression of her spiritual being. The more she is allowed to express her spiritual being freely, the more she can evolve spiritually as she unfolds. The more she is directed into the learning of symbols in these years, the shallower and more materialistic she will become in later life.

The child also needs environments and playthings that are incomplete and open-ended. Such environments and toys require her to engage her imagination in completing them.

The child continues to learn primarily through the imitation of adults. She needs warmth and cheerfulness from adults as well as positive moral and spiritual examples. She also needs to learn from the example of nature, to be immersed in the rhythms and beauties of the natural world. In experiencing nature in this way, the child can discover another path that leads to awe, reverence, and gratitude. The more that the adults who guide her also experience these feelings in their own relationship with the natural world, the more the child will be open to learning from their example.

THE SECOND ERA: 6 THROUGH 12–14 YEARS

In her seventh year the child begins to move from the first era into the second. While she still lives within an ongoing stream of inner images and memories that are beyond her control, as part of this transition the child experiences a diminution of her will. Such an inner experience is confusing to the child. Before, she usually knew what she wanted to do; now she is sometimes lost, without motivation. This transformation often leads to inner conflict, expressed as restlessness or obstinacy. Only with her evolution into the second era of life can the child move through this conflict and confusion and enter a new quality of experience.

Steiner marks the beginning of the second era with the changing of the teeth, which is both a signal of and an element in the process of transformation. Aurobindo describes this transformation as the opening of the psychic being. Steiner teaches that this second era is primarily focused on the growth of the soul. Inayat Khan explains that with the beginning of this era, the child's inner conflict dissipates, and she grows calmer and more harmonious.

In this era the child learns best through joyous aesthetic activity: drawing, painting, music, dancing, movement, and so on. These years are a time when the child experiences compelling inner rhythms that she can best express through the arts. Yet the child does not benefit from any kind of artistic training now. Rather, what she needs is the opportunity for free expression of her own initiative through color, shape, pattern, music, and rhythm. This initiative flows from her spiritual being. When it is manifested through aesthetic activity, its expression helps the spiritual being to evolve. The child also needs to experience a regular rhythm in the course of her daily life.

With the growth of the adult teeth, the child begins to think, though in a very concrete manner, because her thinking is still fused with her physical body. It comes alive as a largely imageic process that is strongly influenced by her emotions. The child also begins to unfold a capacity for moral understanding.

Now the child needs to learn to write and read her native language and to gain competence in the initial understandings and skills of mathematics. Yet in this learning, too, she can be most fully engaged through the use of rhythm as a method of teaching.

As the child learns through her senses, feelings, and imagination in these years, she needs to be spared from theories and other abstractions that have little meaning for her. Instead she needs to experience stories and pictures that convey aesthetic and moral values, that she can visualize and take within herself for guidance and enduring meaning. She has the capacity to learn profoundly from stories of great and wonderful personalities from myth and history. Such stories evoke inner imagery, grounded in feelings of reverence and veneration, and arouse a spirit of emulation in the child's spiritual being that aids the growth of her character and moral nature.

Steiner teaches that the child's most powerful learning in these years results from her discipleship to an adult: a teacher by necessity of what that role demands, not a parent. In this experience of discipleship, the child can revere and emulate this teacher. From this relationship she can also learn about the bounds of natural authority. Both Aurobindo and Inayat Khan note that the child needs to experience teachers who embody integrity and nobility of character. But they do not mention the kind of intense relationship with a single adult to which Steiner gives so much significance.

In this era the child needs to learn good habits and attitudes, particularly patience, endurance, and perseverance. She needs to be encouraged to wait when necessary and to bring what she begins to completion. She also needs to continue to develop her relationship with nature, as her direct experience of nature supports her intellectual and spiritual unfoldment.

By the time the child has entered this second era, she has lost the clarity of will that directed her younger activity. She rejects imitation as "babyish" and seeks guidance from adults.

In the first three years of this era, the child needs to build on the gratitude to the spiritual world that was evoked within her in the preceding years in two ways. She needs to learn the will to love: first feeling this caring for a revered adult(s), then expanding its range to others and to nature. She also needs to learn her first ideals: respect for elders and the joy that flows from giving respect; self-respect; a sense of duty; and her first feeling of the divine ideal. During these years the child can connect her feelings of reverence for the natural world with her ideal of the divine, bringing feeling to that ideal and expressing it as her first experiences of worship.

The child's feeling for rhythm and her need to experience the world through rhythm are most intense in these first years of the second era. Her awarenesses are sensual and imaginative. She wants to interact with that which is alive, plants and animals, and that which is full of life, stories and pictures.

In these years the child is also engaged in grounding herself: developing a sense of her place in the family, school, and peer group.

Finally the child's memory awakens with the changing of the teeth and needs to be cultivated on a regular basis through rhythms of movement, tables, and rhymes.

At nine years of age, the child may experience an intense yet unformulated and unarticulated questioning of her respect and reverence for her elders. She needs adults to respond to this questioning not with fear or anger but with openness and love. At this time the child may also experience a new intensity in her social needs, seeking to be with her peers more and placing more import in their acceptance of her.

At ten years of age, the child enters the second part of this era. She begins to differentiate herself more profoundly from the world around her and to take on patterns of individuality that will be with her for the rest of her life. In this eleventh year of her life and through the remaining years of this era, she begins to discover what her strengths and proclivities are. She also has the potential to begin to discover her calling.

The child is very much open to knowledge in these years. She still can learn from stories of heroes and heroines, though the learning now takes place on a more complex level. She also begins to develop powers of concentration and needs to practice them through artistic and craft activities that require attention, patience, and coordination.

At eleven years of age, the child is ready to learn about cause and effect. Prior to this age, the less she interacts with this kind of reasoning, the richer the life of her spiritual being will be. Now she is ready to use her reason to observe cause and effect in the natural world and explore the relationships between them. She can also learn to classify, define, and discriminate what she perceives in nature.

At this age the child can extend her feeling for the divine and open to spiritual experience for the first time. Her feelings of wonder and awe for nature can take her beyond the boundaries of her physical being and bring her to a visceral awareness of the divine ideal both beyond and within herself. This kind of experience is an opening to the reality of spirit, though not the spiritual awakening to which she can come at the end of her youth. It is both a felt experience and a validation of spirit and an intimation of her potential for a more complete awakening later on.

In the last year or two of this era, the child's limbs and trunk begin to grow quickly. Her muscles enlarge and strengthen. She begins to develop an awareness of her sexual identity. What she needs now is not to be rushed into the world of adolescence but to be allowed to continue to unfold at her own pace.

THE THIRD ERA: 12–14 THROUGH 21 YEARS

The third era of childhood and youth begins with the onset of puberty and continues at least until age twenty-one. It is marked by dramatic growth and change in the physical body, which is the material aspect of a much larger transformation.

As this era begins, the youth starts to develop a more complete reason, which is dominated by independent, critical thought and the ability to work with abstraction. Her thinking is now based within her mind, not her emotion. She examines what lies around her with her growing but still inconsistent reason. She no longer accepts authority on its own terms but evaluates its validity, often choosing to question and challenge it.

The youth's inner life is vastly expanded as her thinking evolves. Both her new mode of thinking and her maturing feeling lead her to an increasingly larger awareness of herself and the world. As her inner life grows, the youth finds passion and delight in her ideas, much as the younger child experiences these feelings in her interaction with pictures and stories.

In these years the youth manifests her sexual characteristics and opens to sexuality and personal love. She also can experience the spiritual counterpart of personal love: a powerful caring for all living things expressed as an idealism bound up in imagination. As she learns about her own idealism, the youth both seeks people who share her values and continues to consider and explore her ideals to test their value to her as guides for her behavior.

The youth often experiences the third era, and particularly its first half, as a time of intense turmoil, struggle, and inner conflict. She gains the beginnings of adult comprehension and maturity but manifests these inconsistently. At times she is clear and responsible, at other times absent-minded, moody, and self-absorbed.

What the youth needs in these years is to explore both within—her feelings, passions, intuitions, thoughts, and questions—and without—her ideas and experiences and the people with whom she interacts. She needs the freedom to consider and think on her own, make her own decisions, experience their consequences, and learn from them. She also needs the help and support of adults who understand her inconstancy but who nonetheless respect her integrity and the demands of her unfoldment. The youth needs not criticism or repression from adults but support and appreciation of her positive qualities. She needs a consistent balance: firm and constant support and supervision, with gradually increasing freedom and responsibility. The young person responds positively to adult leadership that respects her. The youth also needs the experience of adventure: to explore beyond the world of family and school and to gain new learnings and new relationships.

The third era is naturally a time of self-absorption. In response to this tendency, the youth needs to be helped gently to think and feel beyond herself. She needs to learn about how things work in the practical world and to discover the contributions that previous generations have made to her culture. As she experiences this learning about the past, she needs to be engaged in imagining what her generation can do to make the world a better place. The youth also needs to cultivate a receptive, intaking attitude and to practice this regularly for short times to counter her natural imbalance between expression and receptivity.

In the first third of this era, the youth experiences an intense inconsistency over which she has little control. In the middle third, she begins to develop a center and needs to seek balance and increasing self-control. From fifteen years of age on, her major growth task is the development of her will, for it is the will that will direct and power her later spiritual awakening. She can work toward the unfoldment of her will through the practice of concentration and other will-related tasks.

In the final third of this era, the youth gains self-possession and clarity and finally becomes more of an adult than a child. In her twenty-first year, the young adult has the capacity to awaken to a conscious awareness of her spiritual being. This awakening brings her to an experience of the divine spirit within herself.

A Common Vision of Child Raising and Education

Since Steiner, Aurobindo, and Inayat Khan articulate a *common vision* of human becoming, of course their visions of child raising and education bear the same overall coherence. The three teachers describe the same purposes for child raising and education, which include the following:

- Helping the child and youth to grow with appropriate love, support, and structure so she can unfold into responsible, centered freedom.

- Helping the child and youth to unfold to her potentials in her various beings or sub-systems and all of their faculties; helping her learn to harmonize and integrate her sub-systems so they can work together; and helping her to gain a knowledge of herself and her various beings and faculties.

- In particular, helping the child's and youth's spiritual being to unfold, so that it can manifest as her *inner teacher* and express its innate wisdom for guiding her growth; helping the child and youth to follow the calling of her *inner teacher* within her spiritual being, which will lead her to meet her developmental needs.

- Helping the child to learn about the human condition, the worlds within and without, and the profound unity and interdependence of all things.

- Helping the child to evolve not only as an individual but also as a social person, a member of her community, nation, and species.

Steiner, Aurobindo, and Inayat Khan also articulate a profoundly similar set of principles to guide the practice of child raising and education. These principles are the following:

- The parent and teacher must apprehend the child and youth as a unified system, composed of physical, life-force, mental, and spiritual beings and their various aspects and faculties, existing on a path of life that includes the past, present, and future.

- The parent and teacher must provide the child and youth with both a safe environment and as much freedom as possible, so she can unfold according to her innate wisdom, her *inner teacher*. The parent and teacher must allow the child to unfold in tune with her own inner law, at her own pace.

- The primary external agent in the education of the child and youth is first the parent, then the teacher. It is the qualities of the parent and teacher that most affect the child and youth, not their skills or knowledge. The qualities that have the most positive impact on the child and youth are love and wisdom. Given this responsibility, the parent and the teacher must consciously attend to their own continuing unfoldment in an ongoing and consistent manner.

- The parent's and teacher's task is not to shape or mold the child and youth but to help, guide, and nurture her. The parent's and teacher's primary purpose is not to train the child and youth or impart knowledge but to help her learn to develop her own instruments, faculties, and capabilities. The parent and teacher also need to help the child and youth learn to recognize and validate her own inner knowing, her *inner teacher*.

These purposes and principles form the core of the *common vision* of child raising and education. When Steiner, Aurobindo, and Inayat Khan move beyond them to discussions of educational methods, there is both a great deal of agreement and considerable variation in their prescriptions. Most of this variation arises not from disagreements among them but from differences in focus. Indeed, taken together, the three separate descriptions of appropriate methods for child raising and education offer a richer and more complete understanding of what these processes require than any of the single visions alone.

The one significant area of apparent disagreement among Steiner, Aurobindo, and Inayat Khan in relation to educational practice is a critical one. It involves how the principle of providing the child with the freedom to heed her *inner teacher* is enacted in the school environment. Chapter Ten explores this apparent disagreement and clarifies it. In addition Chapter Ten considers the applications of this *common vision* of child raising and education in our families and schools today.

LIFE STORIES

Rudolf Steiner

When Rudolf Steiner died in 1924, he was a teacher and speaker known widely throughout western Europe. In the decades since his death, Steiner's contributions to our culture have not been eclipsed by the passage of time but, rather, have slowly gained a wider audience. His work has endured and may be more influential now than at any other time since his death.

Rudolf Steiner

Rudolf Steiner helped to invent and define eurythmy, a form of artistic movement that integrates spoken poetry and dance. He articulated a practice of bio-dynamic gardening, a sustainable method of agriculture based on harmony with the natural systems and cycles of the biosphere rather than an attempt to gain technological domination over them. He organized the Anthroposophical Society, which continues as a center for spiritual study in western

Europe, the United States, Australia, New Zealand, South Africa, and Brazil. He wrote about architecture, particularly the relationship between the structures people build and the lives they lead within them, and designed buildings that incorporated both sacred and secular space.

Steiner's most important contribution probably lies in the field of human development and education. For fifteen years Rudolf Steiner wrote and lectured about his vision of human becoming, particularly from birth through age twenty-one. He articulated a theory that is both profound and complex, that anticipated and still incorporates the work of developmental psychologists, such as Piaget and Erikson, and that extends into realms of human experience beyond cognitive and ego psychologies.

Steiner also articulated a theory and practice of education based on his vision of human becoming. In 1919 he founded a school, and he organized and supervised it until his death five years later. This school, called the Waldorf School because it originally served the children of employees in the Waldorf-Astoria cigarette factory in Stuttgart, Germany, provided the vehicle through which Steiner translated his educational theory into practice. It also became the model for what has grown into a worldwide network of several hundred Waldorf schools as well as a number of teacher training institutes.

Rudolf Steiner was born in 1861 in a small town on the border of Austria and Hungary. He studied mathematics and science at the Technical College in Vienna and, in 1891, received his doctorate from Rostock University. As a result of his work as a student, he was invited to serve as the editor of a portion of Goethe's scientific works. Although Steiner devoted much energy to this project both before and after earning his doctorate, he also wrote and published his own philosophical works and served as a teacher for many years.

From the age of seven, Steiner had experienced supersensible or spiritual realities beyond the material world as concrete and real. In his youth and early adulthood, he explored these planes and learned about their nature and meanings. By 1900 he had gained a good deal of control over his presence in these supersensible or spiritual realities. In that year Steiner first lectured publicly about his knowledge of supersensible realities, often focusing on the need for scientific research into the nature of these soul-spiritual planes. His lectures were well received, and he began to attract a following that viewed him as an enlightened spiritual teacher.

During his first decade of lecturing, Steiner was connected with the larger Theosophical movement of the time, which had a presence not only in western Europe but also in North America and India. From 1902 to 1912 Steiner headed the German section of the Theosophical Society and was an important voice within that movement. However, during the later years of this period, his disagreements with English leaders of the Society, particularly Annie Besant, led to a growing estrangement between him and the Theosophical movement. In 1913 Steiner broke with that movement and began to call his work not Theosophy but Anthroposophy, from the Greek *anthropos*, meaning man, and *sophia*, meaning wisdom. He also formed the Anthroposophical Society, centered in Dornach, near Basle, Switzerland.

Throughout the remaining decade of his life, Steiner continued to study supersensible realities through what he called "the science of the spirit" and to lecture about his learnings. He attracted thousands of interested listeners as well as many who were hostile and violent toward his ideas. Despite increasing ill health, Steiner continued to give lectures and direct the original Waldorf School nearly to the time of his death.

Aurobindo Ghose

The life of Aurobindo Ghose was marked by stunning reversals and seeming contradictions. Yet, when viewed as a whole, the course of his life was consistent and clear. Aurobindo was born in India into an upper-caste Hindu family but spent most of his childhood and youth studying in England. He was a leader in the movement for Indian independence for four years before he suddenly abandoned politics and gave himself entirely to a spiritual life. Aurobindo devoted much of his time to meditation and yoga for the last four decades of his life and never left his ashram in southern India. Yet he wrote with clarity and insight about modern European and American science, politics, religion, psychology, and education as well as about his own spiritual knowledge and his understanding of Indian culture, history, and needs.

Rabindranath Tagore, the national poet of India and a Nobel laureate, wrote of Aurobindo after meeting him for the first time in 1928:

> I could realise he had been seeking for the soul and had gained it, and through this long process of realisation had accumulated within him a silent power of inspiration. I felt that the utterance of the ancient Hindu Rishi spoke from him of that equanimity which gives the human soul its freedom and entrance into the all . . . I said to him: 'You have the Word and we are waiting to accept it from you. India will speak through your voice to the world.'[1]

Aurobindo Ghose

While Aurobindo was revered by many in his native land, the recognition of his wisdom and gifts stretched far beyond the borders of India. Romain Rolland, the French man of letters and Nobel laureate, described Aurobindo as ". . . one of the greatest thinkers of modern India, [who] has realised the most complete synthesis between the genius of the East and the West."[2] Pitrim Sorokin, the Harvard sociologist, explained that "Sri Aurobindo's *The Life Divine* and other Yoga treatises are among the most important works of our time in philosophy, ethics, and humanities. Sri Aurobindo himself is one of the greatest living sages of our time; the most eminent moral leader."[3] And U Thant, the third Secretary General of the United Nations, called Aurobindo "one of the greatest spiritual leaders of all time."[4]

Aurobindo Ghose was born in Calcutta, India, in 1872. His father, an upper-caste member who had received his medical training in England, both despaired of the decadence and degradation of colonial India and admired the energy and power of Victorian English culture. In 1879 he sent all three of his sons to England for their schooling. Aurobindo, the youngest child, lived first with the family of an Anglican minister, then entered boarding school, and completed his studies at Cambridge University. Although his father had instructed that his sons be taught nothing about their native land, in his late teens Aurobindo learned of the incipient movement for the liberation of India from the British empire and became involved in student groups that agitated for Indian independence.

Aurobindo returned to India soon after his graduation in 1893. When he first stepped onto Indian soil, he discovered within himself a deep, unshakable feeling of inner peace. He later described this experience as the first step in his spiritual awakening. Aurobindo gained employment in Baroda, first as a civil servant and later as a teacher and vice-principal at Baroda College. In the decade after his return to his homeland, he devoted himself to studying the languages and cultures of India. He also began a secret involvement in the movement for Indian independence.

In 1906 Aurobindo moved to Calcutta to become principal of the Bengal National College. Here his previously secret commitment to political work soon became public, as he began to provide leadership for the independence movement in Bengal. Aurobindo edited a newspaper that promoted independence, spoke publicly about the need for passive resistance to British rule, and participated in the organization of a secret revolutionary group that began to prepare for the possibility of armed rebellion in the future. Within a year Aurobindo had become one of the major leaders of the nationalistic forces throughout Bengal.

In 1908 the British colonial authorities arrested Aurobindo, charged him with treason, and imprisoned him in Alipore jail. Aurobindo spent an entire year in prison awaiting his trial. In this time he studied the *Bhagavad Gita* and the *Upanishads* and intensified his yoga and meditation practice. In 1909 he was tried and acquitted. Immediately after his release, Aurobindo returned to his political work, speaking widely and starting two newspapers.

Within a few months, however, Aurobindo received what he felt to be a divine command to abandon his political work and take up an entirely spiritual life. At once he left Calcutta and traveled to Chandernagore in French India. A short time later he moved on to Pondicherry, a hundred miles south of Madras on the eastern coast of India, where he remained for the last forty years of his life. Despite the urging of his former political associates on many occasions, Aurobindo took no direct part in the independence movement after 1910.

Aurobindo had begun his practice of yoga in 1904. He had searched for a guru for several years but, finding none, had taught himself through his study of the ancient Hindu scriptures. In 1907, with the assistance of Sri Lele, Aurobindo experienced his first of four major spiritual openings: *samadhi*, the experience of oneness between self and Brahman, the ultimate reality.

Prior to his imprisonment in 1908, Aurobindo's yogic discipline had focused on his work for the independence of India. While in prison, Aurobindo devoted most of his time to spiritual practice and study, and his sense of mission broadened from India's liberation to that of the entire planet. While in Alipore jail he experienced his second spiritual opening: a vision of Krishna as a living, personal God who brought a transformation of light to all who surrendered themselves to Him.

When Aurobindo received his message to abandon his political work, he realized both that armed revolt would not be needed to free India from British rule and that his own calling was no longer Indian independence but the larger, more profound work of teaching humanity about the next step in its evolution. Within hours of receiving this message, Aurobindo let go of the life he had known for more than a decade and traveled to Chandernagore.

Here he experienced his third illumination:

> . . . a vision of the supreme Reality as a multiform
> Unity, simultaneously static and dynamic, character-
> ized by silence and expression, emptiness and creativ-
> ity, infinite and yet composed of manifold forms.[5]

In this vision Aurobindo saw the Divine as both immanent in
all things of the world and simultaneously transcendent to the
world that humans know. He discovered the evolutionary need
not to reject any part of reality, as many previous Hindu mystics
had done, but to understand all of reality as divine and worthy of
liberation.

In his first decade in Pondicherry, Aurobindo lived with a
small group of followers who had come with him from Calcutta.
From 1914 to 1921 he edited *Arya*, a journal in which he published
in the form of serial articles most of what would constitute his
major writings, including *The Life Divine*, *The Human Cycle*, *The
Ideal of Human Unity*, and *Bases of Yoga*.

In 1914 Mira and Paul Richard, an upper-class French couple
who were traveling in Asia in search of a spiritual teacher, had
visited Aurobindo in Pondicherry. Both recognized him
immediately as their guru. Paul had stayed on and helped to
found *Arya* before returning to France to fight in World War I.
Mira continued on her journey to Japan but returned to
Pondicherry in 1920 to join Aurobindo as his student. Soon
afterward he recognized her as The Mother, his own spiritual
partner. He explained, "The Mother's consciousness is the divine
consciousness. There is no difference between The Mother's path
and mine; we have and have always had the same path."[6]

By 1926 Aurobindo's community of followers and students
had grown from a handful of people to several hundred members.
In that year Aurobindo experienced his fourth illumination: his
"Day of Siddhi" when he felt the Overmind, a higher spiritual
level of being than mind, descend into the physical plane of this
planet. Immediately after this experience, Aurobindo turned over
the responsibilities of administering this community, which soon
took the form of the Sri Aurobindo Ashram, to Mira Richard. He
retired into an almost complete seclusion for the rest of his life,

although he stayed very much in touch with the world through periodicals and letters and did appear in public on four occasions each year. He also kept up a voluminous correspondence with his disciples in the ashram.

While Aurobindo lived in seclusion for the final third of his life, he broke his silence on two occasions. During World War II he saw Hitler and the Nazi forces as the expression of pure evil in the world and appealed to all Indians to put aside their grievances with the British temporarily and to support them in the war against Germany. In 1947 India received her independence on August 15, Aurobindo's seventy-fifth birthday, and Aurobindo delivered a radio speech about the significance of the day and the event.

Aurobindo Ghose died in 1950. Mira Richard lived on until 1973. In those twenty-three years she guided the Ashram and its attempt to embody Aurobindo's teachings. By the late 1960s the community had grown to more than two thousand members from all over the world. In 1968 the followers of Aurobindo founded Auroville, a spiritually based "city of the future" near the Ashram, which has been recognized by the Indian government as an international city-state.

Inayat Khan

The story of Inayat Khan's life is stranger and more surprising than any fiction of a holy man bringing a mystical tradition from the East. Inayat Khan grew up in a Muslim family, yet he also was much influenced by Hinduism. All of the men in his family were traditional Indian musicians. By his twentieth birthday Inayat was playing the veena, an Indian stringed instrument, for the court gatherings of rajahs and maharajahs throughout India. Later, for four years, he was the disciple of a Sufi master who, on his deathbed, sent Inayat to the United States to bring Sufism to the West. With his cousin and brothers, Inayat played traditional Indian music to accompany the performances of famous "Oriental dancers," like Mata Hari and Ruth St. Denis, in both the United States and in Europe, all the while teaching of the Sufi path and gaining disciples. Inayat Khan devoted the last third of his life to traveling throughout Europe and the United States, lecturing, delivering radio addresses, and teaching those who sought him out.

Inayat Khan

In his sixteen years in the West, Inayat Khan, called Hazrat[7] by his students, brought the teachings and practices of Sufism into the lives of thousands of westerners. He inspired and directed the organization of an international Sufi movement and the inception of Sufi communities in many cities in western Europe and the United States, some of which have endured to this day. His teachings, gathered in the volumes of *The Sufi Message of Hazrat Inayat Khan*, offer a rich and complex, mystically based vision of human nature and human becoming.

Inayat Khan was born in Baroda, India, in 1882. His family was Muslim in its origins. His grandfather, the central figure in the extended household of three generations, was Maula Bakhsh, a musician of wide repute who was known as the "Beethoven of India." Inayat's grandfather and father both held tolerant views about religious differences and were influenced by Hinduism as well as Islam. All of the grandchildren in the house attended Hindu schools and interacted with Hindu children as equals.

As a child Inayat learned to play the veena. In his middle teens he began to teach at the Academy of Music in Baroda, soon becoming a professor. He sought to educate people about the musical culture of India, to help them see traditional Indian music not just as Hindu or Muslim music but as a rich synthesis of both cultures.

In his late teens Inayat traveled across India playing sacred music in the courts of regional rulers. He also gave talks about music and culture. Although he was favorably received by rajahs and maharajahs and offered rich rewards, Inayat Khan felt his efforts to be largely a failure because most people in the ruling classes experienced his music not as the religious inspiration he intended but only as entertainment. He felt despair because he saw this limited appreciation as a degradation of Indian culture.

For a number of years around the turn of the century, Inayat had experienced visions that he did not understand. Eventually, he felt called to seek a spiritual teacher. After a search of several long and often frustrating years, in 1903 he found Murshid Syed Mohammed Abu Hashim Madani, a Sufi holy man. Inayat spent four years as Murshid Madani's disciple, during which time he began the spiritual practice he continued throughout his life. In 1907, only a few hours before his death, Murshid Madani gave Inayat his final instruction. He told the younger man, "Go to the Western world, my son, and unite East and West through the magic of your music. God has given you great capacities, and a great task to fulfill."[8]

In the next few years Inayat continued to travel throughout India, giving concerts and talks. On one tour he went on to Ceylon, Burma, and what was then called Cochin China: Laos, Cambodia, and Vietnam. Finally in 1910 he felt ready to heed his late master's instruction, and he sailed to New York City with his brother, Maheboob, and his cousin, Mohammed Ali. A year later his youngest brother, Musharaff, joined them. For two years they alternated between living in New York for months at a time and journeying across the North American continent on performance tours for equally long periods. Sometimes they played a concert of Indian music accompanied by a talk about Sufism by Inayat. More often they accompanied "Oriental dancers" like Ruth St. Denis who could attract the audience that they alone could not draw. Yet even in those often unruly crowds, some individuals could sense a holy power in Inayat and would seek him out later as a teacher. In 1911 Inayat initiated his first American disciple into the path of the Sufis.

Inayat Khan and his family traveled to London in 1912 and then on to Paris, playing music for the dance performances of the infamous Mata Hari but also giving talks and attracting students. In this year Inayat married Ora Ray Baker, a young American woman who had followed him to Europe, and in 1914, their first child was born. They would eventually have two girls and two boys. Yet even as he became the head of a family, Inayat continued to travel and teach in many European countries, including Germany and Russia.

In these years Inayat struggled with adapting the traditional Sufi teachings into a form that Westerners could understand and experience. "He was not propagating a new religion, he assured them—but an ancient Wisdom which threw a light on every religion of the world. This embraced the eternal truths common to all great teachings whether Hindu, Buddhist, Zoroastrian, Jewish, Christian, Muslim, or some other."[9] He sought to help people see how all of the world's religions shared a common center. This commonality focused on the knowledge that there is only one God in the universe of which all the gods are partial manifestations, and that there is only one human religion and one fundamental religious law: do unto others as you would have them do unto you. As he taught, Inayat asked people not to abandon their previous religious identity but to expand its meaning, so they could see its oneness with all other religions. His aim in his teaching, he explained, was ". . . to spread the wisdom of the Sufis which hitherto was a hidden treasure . . . "[10] and make the experience of God-realization available to everyone.

For several years, Inayat resisted both giving a name to his teachings and starting an organization to promote them. Yet gradually he recognized the need for both. He called his way the Sufi path, a term derived from *safa*, meaning purified of ignorance and egotism. He explained that Sufism was not in essence an element of Islam but, rather, a much older mystical tradition that predated Judaism and Hinduism and that had found expression in every major world religion. In 1915 Inayat reluctantly founded the first Sufi organization, the Sufi Movement. Later he organized the Sufi Order, an inner school of mysticism for initiates.

Inayat Khan and his family spent the years of World War I in England. Inayat had written his first book—in English—in 1913, and he devoted a good part of his energy to other writing projects. His musical performances, which had become more and more infrequent, ended altogether by 1915, and the remainder of his time was devoted to teaching initiates.

Once the war had ended, Inayat began the last phase of his life during which he devoted most of each year to traveling throughout the nations of Europe, lecturing and establishing Sufi centers. He moved to France in 1920 and then on to Geneva, Switzerland, three years later, where he established the headquarters of the Sufi Movement. He journeyed repeatedly through Belgium, Holland, Italy, and the Scandinavian countries, always giving talks and teaching initiates. In 1923 and again in 1925 he toured the United States.

In 1926 Inayat Khan returned to India for the first time in sixteen years. He visited many shrines and holy places. Although he was only forty-four years old as the new year began, his picture shows the aged face of a man who seems at least two decades older. Inayat's exhaustive pace had worn down his body and sickened him several times during the previous six years. Each time he had aged noticeably, yet he had recovered. In February 1927 while still in India, Inayat Khan became ill again, this time with pneumonia. Within a few days, he was dead.

THE VISION OF RUDOLF STEINER

Steiner's Vision of Human Nature

In Rudolf Steiner's vision of human nature, we are energetic as well as physical beings, and our most profound identity rests in our spiritual elements. Each person is "the expression of a divine spiritual being that descends from purely spirit-soul existence and evolves here in physical-bodily existence between birth and death."[1] Each is a unique and inherently worthy being. We are necessarily neither good nor evil but have the capacity for both. We are partially divine beings who are struggling toward purer divinity.

In Steiner's view, human beings are systems that consist of one major and one minor set of sub-systems. The major set includes the four bodies that are parts of each person: the **physical body**, the **etheric body**, the **astral body** or **soul**, and the **body of the ego** or **spirit**. (All of Steiner's terms are explained below.) The astral body itself includes three of its own sub-subsystems: the three **faculties of the soul—willing, thinking,** and **feeling**. The minor set of sub-systems involves the combination of the four **temperaments** embodied in a person: **melancholic, phlegmatic, sanguine,** and **choleric**. All of the various sub-systems interpenetrate each other and are profoundly interrelated.

One element of what is central to this vision of the human being is that we consist of both sub-systems of matter perceivable by our senses and of sub-systems of energy that most people living in "modern" technological cultures do not directly perceive. Yet this energy is nonetheless real and powerful. The material sub-systems and the energetic sub-systems are all parts of us. In particular, the physical body is material. The etheric body, the astral body, and the body of the ego are energetic. These bodies occupy the same physical space, and they are all profoundly connected to each other. The four bodies are also interconnected with the faculties of the soul and with the temperaments. Whenever any one of these sub-systems changes or is affected by some force, every other sub-system is affected in some way.

Another key element in Steiner's vision is the belief that each human life embodies a dual process of personal unfoldment and species evolution. Unfoldment is the growth of the individual toward the manifestation of his full potential. Evolution is the same kind of growth for the human species. Humans as a species are evolving, even within historical time, not so much physically as energetically. Each individual unfolds according to his own personal path, and the sum of all personal unfoldment comprises the ongoing evolution of the species, toward divinity.

The purpose of evolution is the attainment of divinity, first by scattered individuals and eventually by the entire species. The task of each spirit-soul—the element of the person created by the joining of the body of the ego or spirit, from the spirit plane, with the astral body or soul, from the soul plane—is to reincarnate and join with a physical-etheric body again and again until that spirit-soul gains divinity. In this process, the spirit-soul strives to act as an *inner teacher* throughout the unfoldment of the person.

The four bodies of each person—Steiner's major set of sub-systems—include the physical body, the etheric body, the astral body or soul, and the body of the ego or spirit. Each interpenetrates and is interconnected with all of the others.

The physical body is the body of matter, the body known to our senses. We have its elements in common with the mineral kingdom. Not only is the physical body material, it is also conscious. As A. C. Harwood, one of the most widely known Waldorf educators, notes, "the whole human body, and not the brain alone, is a vehicle of consciousness."[2]

The etheric body contains **formative forces** that help to organize and shape the growth of the physical body as well as participate in the child's moral development. The etheric body is not material. Rather, it consists of energy, formative life-forces, that we have in common with the plant kingdom. (The plant kingdom, of course, also consists of matter; each kingdom includes all of the lower levels of being within its existence.)

The astral body or soul also consists of energy, the energy of the soul. This body contains the faculties of the soul—thinking, willing, and feeling—that make up our inner life. Thinking is a conscious activity that takes place through the physical vehicle of the brain and nervous system. In a profound sense, thinking is consciousness. It is our awareness of ourselves in the world. In contrast, willing is an unconscious activity. If willing surfaces to the conscious level, it does so only after the activity of willing has already occurred in the unconscious. Willing takes place through the physical vehicle of the limbs and the digestive system.

The third activity of the soul is feeling, which extends into both the conscious and the unconscious. Feeling takes place through the physical vehicle of what Steiner calls the rhythmic system: the heart and the lungs. Feeling includes pain and pleasure, impulses, cravings, and passions.

While the faculties of the soul can be described separately, in reality they are interpenetrated and interrelated. They are always interacting and often merging.

While we have the astral body in common with other members of the animal kingdom, the element of spirit and its manifestation as the body of the ego or the spirit is unique to humans. This is a third energetic body. This body descends from the spiritual plane to join with the astral body on the soul plane, thus creating the spirit-soul. At birth the spirit-soul joins with the other two bodies to create the whole person. It is the spiritual body within us that is divine and that works for our purification toward greater divinity.

In Steiner's vision of human nature, the temperaments—the minor set of sub-systems—are predispositions that are manifested both in the physical body and in the character of a person. Each individual includes aspects of all four temperaments. Many people are dominated by a single temperament, but others clearly manifest two or more. Also, a person's temperamental orientation can change during the course of his life.

The melancholic temperament is associated with an introspective orientation. Those who are primarily melancholic tend to be highly engaged with their own inner life and much inclined to thought and brooding.

The phlegmatic temperament tends toward stability and inertia. Those who are dominated by this temperament are usually pleasant and good-natured, well-balanced, but difficult to engage and often indifferent.

The sanguine temperament is associated with an extroverted orientation. Those who are strongly sanguine tend to be very active and dynamic yet often have difficulty in concentrating. They tend to be dominated by feeling, particularly because they enjoy the life of the feelings.

The choleric temperament is associated with swings between introverted and extroverted orientations. Those who are dominated by this temperament tend to be sturdy and energetic. Often they are leaders but sometimes are very one-sided and egotistical. They are also given to bursts of emotion.

Steiner's Vision of Human Becoming

In his vision of human becoming between birth and age twenty-one, Rudolf Steiner describes the unfoldment of and interplay among the sub-systems within the human being: the four bodies and the four temperaments. Steiner divides this period of twenty-one years into three dramatically different **epochs:**

• Birth through about the seventh year; the end of this epoch is marked by the changing of the teeth.

• About 7 years of age through about 13 years of age; the end of this epoch is marked by puberty.

• About 14 years of age through 21 years of age.

Steiner sees the overall process of unfoldment through these three epochs as regular, consistent, and predictable in relation to the path of unfoldment and the growth needs and potentials that correspond to each epoch. However, he notes repeatedly that while almost all children and youth move through the events of these three epochs of human becoming, they do so at their own pace. Thus, the following age parameters are generalizations, not absolutes. The experiences of many children and youths closely follow this generalized timetable for unfoldment, while the experiences of others vary considerably from the timetable.

FORCES OF UNFOLDMENT

Steiner explains that throughout these twenty-one years, human becoming is powered by three interrelated forces: the formative forces of the etheric body; the forces of awakening consciousness in the astral body or soul; and the forces of the body of the ego or spirit.

The formative forces work to organize and shape the physical body, starting with the head and moving downward. During the first epoch of childhood and youth, these forces direct the growth of the head and nervous system. By the time of the change of teeth in the seventh year, the child's head has reached almost its full size. During the second epoch, the formative forces work on the development of the rhythmic system, the heart and the lungs. By puberty the child's pulse, which had been almost 100 beats per minute at age seven, has slowed to nearly the adult rate. In the third epoch, and particularly at its beginning, the formative forces shape and energize the growth of the youth's lower trunk and his limbs.

The soul forces of awakening consciousness move from the opposite direction. During the first epoch of childhood and youth, these forces awaken the child's will, which is manifested primarily through the movement of his limbs. During the second epoch, these forces bring to life the child's feeling and imagination, which are centered in the organs of the rhythmic system. Only after puberty, at the start of the third epoch, does awakening consciousness reach the head, where it is manifested as independent thought.

The forces of the spirit also play a major role in human becoming. These forces are involved in guiding all of the processes of growth that take place in childhood and youth.

FIRST EPOCH

In the first epoch, from birth through the changing of the teeth in the seventh year, the child learns by imitation. He perceives what takes place in his environment—physical, interpersonal, moral, and spiritual—and, in his own way, imitates the examples he finds. As Steiner explains, "In his earliest years the child is one great sense-organ."[3] The child perceives not only the words and actions of those around him but their attitudes and feelings as well, and he imitates what he perceives. To a great extent, "the child becomes what the environment is."[4]

The growth of the physical body, including the internal organs, is guided by the interaction between the formative forces of the etheric body and the child's experience. In this epoch, the formative forces work to grow and shape the physical body into the form that is its potential. But the child's experience in his environment impinges powerfully on this process. The child is the perfect mimic, and all of his experience imprints itself on his physical form. So the organs grow and take shape as influenced by this interplay. The child who is loved and has good examples will be most able to grow toward manifesting his full potential.

The child of this epoch learns best from imitation; he does not understand or learn as deeply from rule-teaching or admonition. Nor should he be asked to learn other abstractions, such as reading or writing, before the change of the teeth. Although many children are capable of such tasks, the learning of abstractions in this epoch misdirects energy that is needed for physical and spiritual growth. Steiner explains that children who learn to read prematurely "age too early, are limited in their life of soul and spirit, and are predisposed to a materialistic outlook."[5] Children in this epoch often ask "why" questions. What they seek are not abstract explanations but stories and images that can help them to understand on their own terms that which they question.

Between birth and the change of the teeth, the child's physical body desires what is good for its growth. These desires are experienced by the child as pleasure and delight. The joy of the child helps the formative forces to shape the physical body—particularly the organs—to its proper form.

What the child needs from adults in this epoch are love, a high quality of care, and good examples. The main task of adults in addition to loving and caring for the child is the ordering and truth-making of their own lives, to be within and behave without as ethically and rightly as they can. For it is this being and behavior of the adults from which the child learns most: not only what the adults say and do, but also who they are in essence.

In addition, the child needs to learn gratitude to the spiritual world for the wonders of the universe. He learns to feel gratitude when the adults around him both experience such gratitude themselves and express it in rituals that involve the child. Then the child imitates the adults' gratitude, and such inner experience nourishes his soul.

Steiner's vision of human unfoldment offers not only the kind of discussion of forces and processes just summarized but also a detailed description of the child's unfoldment at each particular age, one that focuses on the child's needs for growth at that age. This description begins with birth, when the child's physical body emerges from his mother's womb and begins to be shaped by the formative forces of the etheric body and by the spirit-soul.

From birth to two and a half years, the formative forces shape the upper head, after which most of the growth of the upper head is completed. The child's major growth tasks during these years are learning to stand, walk, speak, and think. Learning to stand and walk involves the learning of the proper human orientation in the world, as manifested through an upright posture. Learning to speak follows from grasping and standing. The child teethes as he first develops rudimentary thinking processes, for these elements of unfoldment are connected to the forces of the spirit-soul and are simultaneous manifestations of the same energies of becoming.

As the formative forces are focusing on the upper head, the spirit-soul forces of awakening consciousness are centered on the unfoldment of the will and are manifested primarily in the movement of the limbs. In these years the child acts strongly from his own willing, resisting any will that seeks to impose on him from without. It is the child's crucial need to be allowed both to express his will and to accomplish the learning tasks of these years in his own way, according to his own timetable. Adults ought only to help gently and lovingly, guided by reverence. The child must learn to walk and talk by obeying the demands of his own inner law.

Around two and a half years of age, the child gains a sense of himself as an "I," a separate person. Now some of the formative forces go to work on the rest of the head and nervous system, while others move on to work with organs of circulation and breathing, the rhythmic system. In these years the child needs to live within his own special world of unchecked fancy and vivid yet uncontrolled memory. He needs environments and playthings that are not finished but are open-ended and that demand the use of his imagination. The child also needs the opportunity for unrestricted movement as well as a reservoir of warmth and cheerfulness in the adults on whom he depends.

From about the fifth birthday until the change of the teeth in the seventh year, the formative forces that remained in the head and nervous system complete their work. During the same period, the formative forces that had gone on to the rhythmic system move once again to work on the digestive system and the limbs. In these years the child who before had been largely a creature of his own will begins to become susceptible to adult influence. Yet before the change of the teeth, the child lives within an ongoing stream of pictures and memories that are beyond his control. The beginning of any mastery comes only in the next epoch.

SECOND EPOCH

In Steiner's vision, the second epoch of childhood and youth begins with the changing of the teeth and extends through the onset of puberty, roughly from 7 years of age through 13 years of age.[6] The loss of "baby teeth" and their replacement with another set is both a signal of and an element in a transformation within the child on several levels. The etheric body, until now lodged within the etheric envelope, is "born." The formative forces move on from their previous concentrations to new areas of growth. The child's thinking is emancipated from the body and achieves new forms. His capacity for feeling broadens and deepens, as does his capacity for moral understanding. Through much of this epoch, the child seeks legitimate authority in an adult whom he can revere and love and whose guidance he can follow. Most of these changes relate to the growth of the soul, the astral body. As the growth of the physical body dominated the first epoch, it is the growth of the soul that is central in the second.

When the etheric body is "born," it becomes involved in the development of character, habits, moral understanding and conscience, memory, and temperament. The etheric body is affected most powerfully by what the child sees with the eye of the mind, his inner imagery. When the child often experiences imagery that is founded in reverence and veneration for people he loves as well as for great figures in legend and history, his etheric body grows healthy and strong. It is at this time also that the child needs to learn good habits and practice them. Such practice must be based on artistic activity, such as stories, pictures, and songs, and cultivated through conscious repetition that is joyous. It is through joyous artistic activity that the child learns best in these years.

In the second epoch, one part of the energy of the formative forces remains within the physical body to shape the continued growth of the rhythmic system. This "heart of childhood"[7] is an age of rhythmical movement, as the child's outer behavior is one with his inner growth. The child needs the opportunity to express his rich life of rhythm in motion, language, and music. He also needs rhythmic regularity in his daily life, as manifested, for example, in regular meal, class, and bed times.

The remainder of the formative forces are released from the physical body and begin to work on the child's thinking capacity. With the growth of the adult teeth, thinking is freed from the physical body and comes to life as a soul faculty. The nature of the child's thinking is primarily pictorial. Although feeling is still bound up within the physical body, especially in the organs of the chest, it awakens more fully and strongly influences the child's thinking. His thought, penetrated with feeling, is dominated by the heart, because the forces of awakening consciousness are moving upward to bring awareness to the organs of the rhythmic system.

In this epoch the child needs to explore the relationship between thinking, located in the head, and willing, located in the limbs and lower trunk, and to learn a proper connection and balance between them. Because the center of the child's consciousness is in the rhythmic system, he can learn to create a harmony between thinking and willing through the experience of rhythmic activity in language, movement, and music.

In these years the child learns from his senses, his feelings, and his imagination. What defines the child's world most, particularly in the first years of this epoch, are the textures and boundaries of his imagination. He needs to be spared from theories and other kinds of abstractions, for they misdirect his energies for growth. Instead, the child needs to experience pictures and stories that convey aesthetic and moral values, from which he can learn inner values and inner meanings. The child needs to experience story as living pictures to be visualized and understood inwardly. He also needs to experience beauty in all forms, for aesthetic feeling awakens during these years and must be cultivated. His proper activity lies in the creation and appreciation of beauty in music, color, shape, and form. Also, memory awakens with the changing of the teeth. It is a soul activity that must be cultivated through the rhythms of movement, tables, and rhymes.

The most profound learning in this epoch can take place through the child's **discipleship** to an adult whom he finds worthy of his reverence. The child perceives the venerated adult with his inner eye and, finding the adult worthy, fills with spontaneous love both for this person, his guide, and for what this guide deems true and good. Steiner believes that educators need to fill this role, *for it is literally the work not of a parent but of a teacher.* Through this connection with his teacher, the child can learn a proper relationship to natural authority, which is not coerced but arises from the quality of the teacher as a person. The child needs both to experience an intimate relationship with such an adult and to see pictures and hear stories of the great and good people in history. These experiences of good people both in life and in story arouse a spirit of emulation in the soul of the child that aids his moral growth.

Finally, the greatest virtue the child can learn in these years is the will to love. If he has experienced gratitude to the spiritual nature of the universe previously, the child can transform this energy of gratitude into love for others, and for all things. He learns this best through the love he feels for his teacher, who can help the child learn to direct this feeling outward. The child needs to experience a sense of his connection to all that is around him. His inner faculty for wonder and reverence must be nurtured and cultivated.

Before the changing of the teeth, the child knows what he wants to do. He is guided clearly by his willing. Afterward he discovers a new experience of feeling lost, without direction. Yet the child consciously rejects imitation as a solution to this quandary, because imitation feels "babyish" to him. Instead his solution is to seek guidance from adults.

From the changing of the teeth through the ninth year, the child wants to experience all that comes to him through inner rhythms that correspond to his own rhythmic system. His awarenesses are not of thought but are artistic and sensual. He learns best from that which is alive—plants and animals—or full of life—pictures and stories. While knowing himself to be a person, the child is still one with the world in a profound way. And the things of the world—the winds, trees, clouds, and waterways—speak to him. The child's life of feeling and moral growth is focused in his devotion to a teacher. In this relationship, his love and trust grow.

Sometime in the tenth year, a great but unarticulated question may arise within the child, which he manifests as unusual restlessness. It is a question about the worthiness of his teacher. The child wants to know in some new way that this loved one is deserving of his reverence. When this questioning occurs, it is imperative that the teacher respond with special care and warmth.

In the eleventh year, the formative forces still moving downward through the physical body meet the forces of awakening consciousness moving upward. This meeting takes place in the rhythmic system within the chest. Now the child begins to differentiate himself from the world. What before was a harmonious melding of self and other is transformed into a separate ego living within an external universe. From this new awareness of self, the child often seeks a new basis for accepting authority from adults, one that requires more intense emotional involvement on both sides.

In the twelfth year, the child is ready to learn about cause-and-effect relationships. The less experience he has with cause-and-effect analysis prior to this age, the richer his life of soul and spirit will be. But now the child can handle rational concepts and needs to gain an understanding of cause-and-effect by becoming aware of these relationships in the natural processes around him.

In this year, the child also opens to the potential for religious experience. In such an experience, his wonder and reverence help him to extend beyond the boundaries of his sense of self and, for the first time, to be consciously aware of divinity in the universe and in himself.

In the thirteenth or fourteenth year, the child's muscles begin to serve the dynamics of his skeleton more directly. They grow and strengthen with the anticipation of adolescence. He is now no longer a child but a youth. Yet it is still important not to rush his unfoldment, because the youth needs the next epoch of his life to begin at its own pace.

THIRD EPOCH

The third epoch of childhood and youth, Steiner explains, begins with the onset of puberty and continues through the twenty-first year. The youth's puberty is marked by various physical changes that are material elements in a much larger transformation of his being. The focus of inner growth during this epoch is the unfoldment of the spirit, an inner opening that helps prepare for the possibility of spiritual awakening in the twenty-first year.

By puberty the forces of awakening consciousness have reached the head. Simultaneously the astral body, until now held within the astral envelope, is "born," and all the energies of the soul are awakened within the youth. These developments cause the young person's inner world to expand to a new level of awareness, which is dominated by independent and critical thought. Thinking comes now from the head, not the heart, and the youth can work with abstraction and theory. He enjoys ideas as younger children enjoy pictures.

With this growth, the young person becomes a complete being, a self who no longer accepts external authority on its own terms but gains the capacity for critical questioning and independent judgment. He begins to examine and often challenge all that lies around him, both large and small. While the choices he makes during these years are not always wise and this epoch involves the learning of good judgment, the young person needs the opportunity to think on his own, make his own evaluations and decisions, and experience and learn from their consequences. He needs neither control nor suppression but help and support, and he responds positively to leadership viewed as reasonable, valid, and respectful of his integrity. With such support from adults, the youth can develop a quality of thought, centered in moral judgment and religious feeling, that is clear and confident and that guides him to act within responsible freedom.

As the forces of awakening consciousness reach the head, the remaining formative forces guide the last spurt of physical growth in the lower trunk and limbs. At the same time, feeling is released from the physical body and becomes a soul faculty of its own. This liberation of feeling is manifested in the growth of the sexual characteristics of the young person. As part of the same transformation, the youth's etheric body takes on a form resembling that of the physical body of the opposite sex.

With puberty, the youth opens to sexuality and the power of personal love. The spiritual counterpart of these capacities is the potential for feeling an idealistic caring for all humanity and all living beings. In these years the coincident unfoldments in the soul activities of thinking and feeling breed intense idealism bound up with imagination. The youth longs to discover both people about whom he can care and, more important, ideals that can guide him. He searches for truth but usually experiences himself as meeting seemingly endless oppositions that give rise to a tumult of feeling. The struggle of the youth's search for truth rages on through the twenty-first year and often beyond.

In this epoch, the young person needs to learn about the social world in which he lives, about how things work in the practical world around him, and about how he can become skilled in contributing to the workings of this practical world. It is essential that his learning during this time include an ongoing connection and balance between head work and hand work. The youth also needs to learn about the contributions of previous generations to the culture in which he lives and to imagine and dream about how his own generation can make the world a better place for all.

The primary virtue that the youth can learn in these years is the will to do one's duty to self and others. If the young person has moved from gratitude to the will to love during the first two epochs of life, his soul will be filled with devotion to the good and true. In this epoch, this devotion will lead him to choose to do his duty from his own judgment and free will.

In the twenty-first year, the young adult can awaken to a conscious awareness of his spirit. Until this time his will is bound up within his body and can only be expressed physically, especially through his style of movement. With the end of this epoch and the beginning of adulthood, the will can be released from the body to become a soul faculty on its own. This freeing of the will can open the young adult to the spiritual reality within him and the universe. Given this potential for unfoldment, the major growth task of the youth from the sixteenth year on is the gaining of more conscious control of his will. It is this growth of will power that can nurture the young person's later spiritual awakening.

Steiner's Vision of Child Raising and Education

In articulating his vision of human becoming, Rudolf Steiner explains that the process of each child's unfoldment contains potentials for both health and disease. At every point within the process, the person's needs can be met, and he will grow toward wholeness and the responsible exercise of freedom. Or his needs can be unmet or blocked, leading to dysfunction and disease in the present or in the future.

The task of child raising and education is to help young people meet their developmental needs throughout childhood and youth. During the first epoch, parents have the primary responsibility for creating an environment in which the child's growth needs are met, because the child ought to remain primarily within the family or family-like settings before the changing of the teeth. The essential tasks of the parent are to understand the predictable processes of the child's unfoldment in these years, to create safe and developmentally appropriate environments in which the child can heed his *inner teacher* and express his needs through free play, and to work on the development of his own spiritual being so he can offer good example to the child.

In the second and third epochs, the teacher takes on much of the responsibility for the child's needs, both because the child spends considerable time in school and because the child needs a significant relationship with an adult outside his family. For Steiner, the key elements in schooling are the quality of the teacher's love and wisdom, and his capacity to know each child profoundly and support the child's *inner teacher*. He views teaching as a spiritual calling, a profession in which one accepts a significant share of the stewardship for the unfoldment of the next generation. The first qualification for teaching is the love of one's fellow human beings; the second, a thorough and profound comprehension of the nature of human beings and of the patterns and processes of human unfoldment. "Before anything else, one must acquire a fundamental knowledge of the human being . . . for it is only possible to educate when one understands the real being of man."[8] The teacher must not only understand this "real being" but must also believe in its inherent, organic wisdom, that is, the *inner teacher*: the child's capacity to unfold toward wholeness with the nurturance of love and respect. "If in education we coerce the impulses of human nature, if we do not know how to leave this nature free, but wish to interfere on our own part, then we injure the organism of the child for the whole of its earthly life."[9]

The third qualification for teaching is an understanding of pedagogy as an art based equally on feeling and thinking, not as a science. "Pedagogy is love for man resulting from knowledge of man."[10] The teacher learns what to do in school by knowing about the organism of the child. The teacher sees the child as a unified being consisting of physical, etheric, astral, and spiritual bodies and of all the interactions among the bodies. He looks into the complete being of the child with an eye to the present, past, and future. "In true methods of education it can never be a question of considering the child as it is at a given moment, but the whole of its passage through life from birth to death; for the seed of the whole earthly life is already present from the first."[10] Directed by this holistic vision, the teacher both guides the child and is interactively guided by his awareness of the child's *inner teacher*. The result of the teacher's pedagogical art is to influence the child's activities so that his experiences in school are continuous and congruent with the child's own ongoing process of becoming.

A key responsibility of the teacher is to be engaged in making himself worthy of the child's love and respect. Only by holding himself to the same standards that he advocates for the child can the teacher truly serve the needs of the child. If the teacher is not worthy of love and respect, he is likely to resort to coercion so that he can maintain order in the classroom, an action that inevitably harms the child.

Another responsibility of the teacher is to organize the learning activities so that the child fully experiences knowledge. Action must come before explanation, experience before understanding. All that becomes known must be felt as well. When the child learns to feel and to know from within in addition to knowing about, his learning is both informative and transformative.

Steiner recommends that schooling begin with the start of the second epoch of childhood and youth. During the first years of schooling, education must proceed from a center that is artistic and aesthetic. The child learns best from rhythm, music, imagery, color, and story. Any work of the intellect should flow from artistic feeling, for growth is liberated if the intellect is approached through art. In these years, the teacher must be careful not to ask the child to think in concepts too often, for the child is not ready to gain much from conceptual thinking. The teacher also needs to engage the child in systematic training of the memory through art and movement.

In the third epoch, the teacher needs to support the youth's growth as a critical and independent thinker, particularly as the youth begins to explore what freedom and responsibility mean. The teacher must also help the young person to extend his skills from the artistic to the practical, from the classroom to the world beyond. Yet this extension does not mean direct preparation for the adult work life. Rather, the child must grow up free of the demands of the economy and the state. The purpose of education is the nurturance of the whole person's growth. Healthy, moral, and fully unfolded adults will be able to contribute much more to the life of their culture than those who have been trained in school for specific work roles.

Steiner urges that each teacher stay with a class of children from first grade through eighth grade. Only with this continuity of relationship can the teacher know his students well enough to respond to their needs for growth and serve as a worthy exemplar for them. In addition the child needs a long-term relationship with his teacher if he is to experience the kind of "discipleship" to an adult that is critical to his unfoldment.

Finally, Steiner explains that the teacher should conceptualize each school day within a definite rhythm of activities. Each day should begin with a ritual of gathering and recognition. Then new ideas, especially in the academic subjects, should be presented in the **main lesson** in the morning. This lesson should be followed by rhythmical subjects, such as the arts, movement, and languages. The last activities of the day should be the practical arts, such as hand work and gardening. This kind of rhythm helps young people to experience congruence and continuity in their lives in school.

As I noted in Chapter One, Rudolf Steiner also articulated a detailed curriculum for the original Waldorf School. I have chosen not to review that curriculum here, because I do not want to draw attention away from the central principles and concepts that form Steiner's vision of human becoming and education. I believe that Steiner intended that the curriculum he created in 1919 serve as a guide for teaching in his own school at that particular historical moment, not as any sort of universal blueprint for education. Since Steiner espoused the importance of understanding evolutionary processes of all kinds, I am confident that were he to lead a school today, he would help to create a very different curriculum from the one he devised in 1919.

One aspect of that curriculum that I do want to highlight is Steiner's approach to the teaching of writing and reading. When Steiner developed his Waldorf School curriculum, most schools in Western Europe and in the United States expected children to learn how to read and write in first grade, just as they do today. Given Steiner's then unique comprehension of the developmental process, he understood that while many children could learn to read and write at this age, many others were not ready. What is crucial in terms of a child's readiness for reading and writing is not his chronological age but, rather, the status of his development. A child needs to have entered the second epoch before he can bring his best resources to the manipulation of language symbols.

In Steiner's Waldorf curriculum, children in first grade learn about language by hearing stories, acting out short plays, and creating drawings and paintings of letters and simple words. In second grade children move from drawing and painting letters and words to writing first sentences and then simple stories. They begin to read by reading aloud their own writing and then the writing of peers. Eventually they move on to reading books.

Of course, in our culture, some children come to school already knowing how to read and write or begin to do so in first grade. With Steiner's approach, these children would not be discouraged from these activities in any way. However, the level of skill development of these children would not dictate the curriculum or the expectations for any of their peers. Overall the goal would be that almost all children would read and write by the end of second grade, because by then almost all children would have entered the second epoch of childhood and youth.

Current Waldorf schools continue to draw on Steiner's original curriculum to a considerable extent, although some more than others. Chapter Four presents an introduction to some key elements of Steiner's original curriculum for second grade.

Steiner's Ways of Knowing

Rudolf Steiner sought to unite the scientific and the spiritual. He named his philosophical system *Anthroposophy*, his way of knowing *spiritual science*. Central to Steiner's vision of human nature is the description of humans not only as physical or material beings but also as beings that exist simultaneously on several different planes of energy. Since the material plane can be known by the senses and the other planes cannot, Steiner calls the energetic planes *supersensible*.

It was Steiner's belief that the whole human organism has the capability to act as a supersensible sense organ that can "perceive" the energetic planes. Yet such supersensible awareness, although a potential in all humans, is active only in those who seek it with reverence and discipline. A few are born with a greater opening to the energetic planes, but even they must choose to follow the path of spiritual awakening if they hope to gain access to these higher planes of being.

The purpose of the "science of the spirit" or spiritual science is "to rise by the development of hidden powers to the spiritual world, in the same way as the physiologist can use the microscope to descend into the world of the infinitesimal which the ordinary eye cannot see."[11] Material science is a way of knowing about the material plane, what we can perceive with our senses as well as whatever is a direct extension of what we perceive with our senses. Spiritual science is a way of knowing about the energetic planes through three different kinds of spiritual knowledge: the imaginative, the inspirational, and the intuitive.

Steiner explains that there are four elements to knowing with our senses: (1) the sensation of the object—the other, that which is known—that is perceived; (2) the image formed within our inner eye of the object; (3) the conception or idea formed within the thinking process from the image; and (4) the ego, the knower, the self that enacts all of these functions.

In imaginative knowing, only the final three of these elements take part in the knowing process. Rather than an image derived from sensation of an external object, the image of the object comes to the imagination through the etheric plane and becomes known through the imagination. In imaginative knowing, the ego begins to know that which is known, the other, by experiencing an identity with it. In this relationship, the knower and the known, the ego and the other, are in balance. For example, the knower is aware both of his own consciousness and simultaneously of the inner experience of what he is knowing: a plant, an animal, a stone, or whatever. Careful training is necessary to learn to distinguish between delusion or fantasy and images that convey genuine inspirational knowledge, that are valid experiences of identity with the known. The core of this training is the discipline of meditation.

Inspirational knowing brings the knower completely into the worlds of soul and spirit. The ego takes on a total identity with the other, the known, and in doing so, loses its initial sense both of itself and of the other. This absolute identity brings it to a higher level of being, that of soul and spirit. Here there are no images, only conceptions to be known by the ego. In this mode of knowing, inspiration offers an impression that the ego forms into an ideal. In this way of knowing, the knower completely loses his consciousness of self and instead experiences the known from within on the levels of soul and spirit.

In intuitive knowing, only the ego, the witness of self, is present, but it knows itself both as an individual consciousness and as the divine consciousness. Its awareness is of oneness with all else. Intuitive knowing is the knowing of the soul and spirit of everything from within and without. Intuitive knowing is what is often called cosmic consciousness.

Steiner explains that his knowledge of human nature and human becoming results from his own personal path of spiritual awakening. It is a path on which he cultivated, over several decades of his life, the following qualities and capacities:

- inner reverence for and devotion to truth higher than human existence;
- inner tranquility gained through the discipline of meditation;
- control of the inner flow of thought;
- conscious initiative in action;
- freedom from prejudice;
- deep and ever-renewing faith;
- inner balance.

Steiner maintains that the path of spiritual development is open to all who choose it not for reasons of selfishness but from genuine devotion to the divine. The knowledge of human nature and human becoming revealed along this path is regular and consistent, he argues, and can be examined by reason just as knowledge revealed through the procedures of material science is. These regularities and consistencies are the discoveries of spiritual science.

Thus, Steiner calls his way of knowing a science because he believes that any human being can engage in the same process of knowing that he has. Anyone who does, Steiner maintains, will find the same qualities of reality and the same knowledge that he has discovered. These qualities and this knowledge can be examined by reason and evaluated according to common scientific standards of proof, particularly replicability. In fact, Steiner urges others to pursue the study of spiritual planes and knowledge with a scientific spirit and method so that they can both affirm his discoveries and add to them.

A DAY IN THE LIFE
OF THE SECOND GRADE
AT A WALDORF SCHOOL

Welcome to a day in the life of the second grade at the Waldorf School in Lexington, Massachusetts: a day of song and rhythm and story and color, of children whirling in motion and etched in concentration; and a day in the life of their teacher, who works from a model of education articulated by Rudolf Steiner but who brings her own gifts to her work as well.

I spent this day at the end of March with the second grade, watching and listening and sensing, taking notes and tape-recording. Although these six hours contained a myriad of detail that no written report could ever reproduce, this series of verbal snapshots captures something of the feeling of this day, of its texture and flow, of the little things as well as the large.

One day like and unlike any other.

8:16 A.M.

Noam is the first to arrive. He has twinkling eyes, shiny black hair, and a sharp giggle. He's quick with curiosity or silliness one moment, patient and meticulous the next. Anna Peck leaves the blackboard, where she was touching up a chalk drawing of St. Patrick standing above a tangle of green snakes, and comes over to greet him. "Good morning, Noam," she says, shaking his hand as she bends toward him to bring her head closer to the level of his.

"Good morning, Miss Peck," Noam replies, smiling, before he wanders off into the coatroom. When he emerges twenty seconds later, he spies me sitting in the corner and skips over to say hello. During the next few minutes, other children enter the classroom:

Ananda, who is bright and playful, a leader and a thinker; Heidi, a good-natured and friendly child with a taste for athletics and music; Marston, a quick learner with an equally quick temper just beginning to settle down; Terra, graceful, artistic, and very, very quiet. And others: Jeremy, Eric W., Sarah, Eric N., Jed. Miss Peck stands by the classroom door to greet each one, shake a hand or share a hug, say good morning, establish a connection for this new day.

As they emerge from the coatroom, the children drift comfortably across the room. The classroom is large with the kind of high ceilings that are common in old school buildings. Beautiful wood floors, large windows across most of one long wall, chalkboards across two others, and the fourth wall covered with an array of the children's work. The school building dates from before the First World War, an old public elementary school no longer needed by an aging town and, so, available for purchase by a private school.

The children move easily in and out of small groups, talking and playing and laughing. Some look out the window at the trees' first buds, while others sit on a rug and work with pattern blocks.

8:32   A.M.

A hand-rung bell clangs out in the hallway and echoes down the stairs. Miss Peck takes a few steps into the hall and looks for any of her children who might be straggling. Anna Peck is a young woman in her mid-twenties. She has blond hair and a comfortably pretty face, clear and firm and solid, with the slight tracings of age lines just beginning to take root on her forehead. Her eyes are vivid. They grab your attention and hold it as she speaks to you. She has the look of a pioneer woman. And her strengths as a teacher are her strengths as a person: imagination, love, patience, forgiveness, and a willingness to be open, to touch her students profoundly and to be touched by them. She has taken on their nurture and their education for eight years—for teachers in a Waldorf school take a class from first grade through eighth grade—and it is no small responsibility.

Anna has had only a few years' experience in the classroom.

She is still learning her craft and her art. At times she's anxious about her inexperience, about not knowing enough or not being certain of the best way. But there is no doubt about her path: she is on her way toward artistry, toward excellence.

Finding none of her charges in the hall, Miss Peck returns to the classroom, closing the door behind her. She asks the children to move to their desks and stand behind their chairs. Some hear her and begin to go at once. Others, absorbed in their play, require a second request. So she repeats her direction. It takes a minute, but then each child is standing quietly behind a chair and looking ahead into the center of the circle of desks. Just as Miss Peck gives Sarah, a graceful and clever girl, the matches to light the morning candle, the door opens. Gretchen walks in slowly, wide eyed and smiling, a big box in her hands. At once there's a flurry of excited voices: "What is it?" "What's that?" "It's a butterfly, isn't it?"

"No, it's not," Gretchen announces. "It's a caterpillar. My mom found this caterpillar in our backyard." And all the children rush over to see for themselves.

"Hey Gretchen, see if you can find a stick and lean it up in the box for it," Eric N. suggests. "They like to live on sticks."

8:36 A.M.

"Stand very tall and quiet," Miss Peck says in a soft voice. "Very straight and tall, like oak trees." The children stand in silence. Then Sarah strikes a match and lights the candle sitting on her desk. Miss Peck begins the morning invocation, and the children readily join her.

The sun with loving light makes bright for me the day.
The soul with spirit power gives strength unto my limbs.
In sunlight shining clear I reverence, O God,
The source of human strength which thou as gift of grace
Hast planted in my soul, that I may love to work and
Ever seek to learn. From thee stream light and strength.
To thee rise love and thanks.

The ritual of beginning the day moves on with a Mexican

morning song sung in Spanish, Miss Peck sounding the first note and the children's reedy voices joining her. Eric N., the tallest boy in the class and already well coordinated and strong, sings with an energy that lifts his voice over all the others. Now all of the children are engaged, their eyes and limbs alive with music, as they weave into another song.

> All things bright and beautiful,
> All creatures great and small,
> All things wise and wonderful, the lord God made them all.
> Each little flower that opens, each little bird that sings,
> He made their flowing colors, he made their tiny wings.
> All things bright and beautiful,
> All creatures great and small,
> All things wise and wonderful, the lord God made them all.

8:44 A.M.

The children have gathered at the far end of the room, standing in two lines that face each other. Miss Peck establishes the rhythm of clapping, and the children join in: first, clap your left hand with your partner's, then your right, then clap your own thighs and both hands together. And now they start to sing as they clap: "Oh, ho, the laughing bug, lives down in the valley-o." The song tells a long, nonsense story, and the children sing and clap with intensity, finding the rhythm and staying with it. From time to time, some of them lose it and then focus on getting back in step with their partners.

"Left, right, legs, clap. Left, right, legs, clap!" They're all chanting together now and starting to count aloud. "One, two, three, four." All the way to one hundred, then back down to zero.

8:52 A.M.

Miss Peck asks the class to form two lines again. When they do, she designates one line as the English, the other as the Romans. Immediately, several boys complain about their status. "I want to be English!" Jed yells. "I wanna be Roman!" Eric W. demands. For nearly a minute the children discuss the issue, and then gradually the lines form. Miss Peck stands silently to the side and waits until the children are ready.

"Now, Romans, you go first," she reminds them.

"Have you any bread and wine, for we are the Romans?" one line sings. "Yes, we have some bread and wine," the other line replies, "for we are the English." It's a long and intricate responsive song and game in which both sides symbolically enact meeting, conflict, battle, and death. The children know most of the words and act out the story as they sing. Of course, the part they like best, giving themselves fully to its drama, is the fighting and dying.

At the end of the game, some of the children talk about what it might be like to die in a real battle. "I bet it would really hurt," says Jeremy.

9:02 A.M.

It takes the children a couple of minutes to calm down from the excitement of the game. Miss Peck gives them time to talk and laugh, to let their excitement drift away before she gently yet persistently begins to gather them in a circle, standing left shoulder to right shoulder with their partners. They begin to sing, "Old bald eagle sail around, daylight is come." And they move around the circle in an old folk dance. Jed isn't happy with this choice of song, so he throws up his arms in disgust and goes to sit in the corner of the room. The two lines of children weave in and out around the circle. Then two of the children lift up their arms into an arch, and everyone else ducks under them, swaying and singing. And the dance goes on into another round.

In this dance, as in all other activities, Miss Peck joins in with the children. When they need her to guide them, she leads. When they don't, she becomes a part of the group. Just because she's the teacher doesn't mean she can't enjoy herself like everyone else.

Toward the end of the dance, Jed returns to the group and takes up the steps with a surprising enthusiasm. "You go ride the old gray mare, I'll ride the roan. You get there before I do, just leave my gal alone!"

9:09 A.M.

Miss Peck models the counting rhythm once, and then the children join her. Stamp your left foot, then your right, hit your thighs with both palms, raise your left hand, then your right, snap your fingers and clap your hands high as you say "Seven!" Then on through the rhythm again and again, announcing each multiple of seven up to eighty-four, then back down to zero. Then the eights up to ninety-six, and back again. And finally the nines, all the way to ninety-nine!

9:16 A.M.

Each child stands behind her or his own desk. Ananda and Noam push each other playfully, then settle back into calm attention as Miss Peck eyes them from the front of the room. When everyone is ready, she asks the children to take out their blocks and place them in the ready position between their right inner arms and their right sides. The blocks are wooden, about six inches by two inches by an inch. Miss Peck waits until all the children have followed her lead before she balances her block flat atop her head and asks her students to do the same. They all reach up, setting block on head, except Terra, who is mysteriously upset and sits silently at her desk, her face in her hands. Miss Peck walks down to her and whispers in her ear, but Terra does not reply.

Now Miss Peck leads the children, blocks balanced more or less securely on their heads, through the recitation of a poem with a series of accompanying movements. First left arm out, then right, then both arms way up high and turning all the way around. Jed's block is the first to crash to the floor. He snatches it up and, with surprising deftness, returns it to its perch. Once more the class recites the poem with its movements.

The earth is firm beneath my feet.
The sun shines up above.
And here I stand both straight and tall,

All things to know and love.

Now the wooden blocks are tumbling like thunderclaps in a hectic storm. Blocks fall and crash, and without hesitation the children pick them and try again. Eric N. has kept his aloft almost the whole time so far. His face is beaming through his concentration. When the poem ends, the class counts aloud to one hundred by fives, then back down to zero. And now most of the children are holding their balance effectively, tuning in to their own sway and flow and learning to compensate.

In a final exercise, Miss Peck directs the children to rise onto their tiptoes, then sink down onto flat feet, then back to their tiptoes. "I'm on my tippy toes," Jed yells excitedly, his block solidly on his head. Then the children slide down onto flat feet for the last time. And slowly they walk around the outside of their circle of desks, lifting their legs high and stepping very consciously as they move, wooden blocks balanced more and more securely on their heads. Terra is looking up and watching them intently.

9:23 A.M.

The children sit on their desks, their wooden flutes held between their right arms and sides. In the far corner of the room, Heidi and Jeremy are still discussing the fate of Gretchen's caterpillar. "We're waiting for everyone to be ready," Miss Peck says softly as she gazes at the two children. Reluctantly Jeremy and Heidi walk away from the caterpillar and come to rejoin the class.

"Bring your flutes up now," Miss Peck says, "and get your fingers ready."

"My fingers are all ready," Eric W. replies in a chirpy voice. Miss Peck plays eight notes from a song, and the children repeat it after her. They go through it again, then a third time. The first run-through is ragged. But, by the third, the children are playing in unison. Then Miss Peck plays the next bar, and the process is begun again. Now everyone plays both bars together. And the melody of the song begins to take on its own life.

"Can we play it again?" Sarah asks, children nodding their assent all around.

"Yes," Miss Peck replies. And so they do, twice more through the entire sixteen notes. Then Gretchen asks Miss Peck to play thewhole song. And the children listen, satisfied, as she weaves the song's melody through the room.

9:32 A.M.

Miss Peck waits for each child to stand straight and calm, to be present and centered. Marston is leaning over his desk. Jeremy and Heidi are turned around and talking. Miss Peck continues to wait without speaking. She has already given the direction twice. As the seconds tick by, Marston ever so slowly pushes himself upright onto his feet, and Jeremy and Heidi finally notice the silence around them and come to attention.

"Straight as a spear I stand," Miss Peck begins when all are finally ready. And the children join her at once both in words and in the corresponding movements. "Strength fills my arms and legs. Warm is my heart with love."

"Good morning, second grade," Miss Peck sings to the class. It's time now for another ritual, the beginning of the main lesson.

"Good morning, Miss Peck," the children sing in response. Then Miss Peck starts at one point in the circle and sings each child's name as if it were a question. "Marston P.?"

He replies in song, "I am here," and sits down in his chair.

When they are all seated, Noam asks urgently, "Will you tell us more of the story, Miss Peck?"

"Yes, I certainly will, Noam. Yesterday we were hearing about St. Patrick, but we didn't find out what happened to him in the end."

"Oh goody," Gretchen exclaims. And Miss Peck begins to tell the story that she had begun the day before.

"Now when Patrick struck the Druids' idol at Cronculach, it crumbled into pieces. And the winds carried the dust to the very farthest corners of the world. And the word spread throughout all of Ireland that the Druids' most sacred and powerful idol had been destroyed." Miss Peck speaks quietly, yet her voice and features are animated with the feeling of her story. The children follow the flow of her language with precision, often faintly echoing phrases or words that catch their imaginations. "Now all the people of Ireland were afraid because they had worshiped this idol for so very long, and all of their magic and mystery were gone. But Patrick was free to go about Ireland as he wished and tell the stories of the one God."

"And tell all the people?" Eric N. asks.

"Yes, that's right."

"Go on, Miss Peck," Sarah urges. "Now we're getting to the best part."

Miss Peck tells the story of the Irish people's confusion in the face of these startling events. Should they hold on to their old Druid ways or learn the new ones of Patrick's Christianity? Now Patrick went on to the Druids' second most holy mound and struck it down. And snakes appeared by the thousands and thousands.

"Patrick had called out all the snakes in the land," Miss Peck is saying as the children's eyes bulge with the enormity of the image. "And Patrick said to the snakes, 'It is no longer right that you should be here in this land, for I have come to bring a new way of life to these people. The old way has to change, so you must follow me.'" And she describes how Patrick mesmerized the snakes and led them down to the sea. "And from that day unto this, there are no more snakes in all Ireland!"

Miss Peck pauses, looking around the room expectantly. "Except," she notes dryly as the children start to grin, "Patrick did meet one more snake that hadn't been caught." She goes on to tell how Patrick tricked the last wily snake into climbing into a wooden box by asking him just to see if he could fit within it. "And when the snake slipped inside, Patrick closed the lid and shipped him off the island on the high waves." Now the room fills with the children's chortling of delight.

"He wasn't so smart," Eric W. says in the middle of his glee.

"But there must be more snakes in Ireland," Marston bursts out when the room finally begins to quiet. "There must be."

10:04 A.M.

When all the children are standing tall behind their desks, the class sings to mark the end of the main lesson. The children's energy is high, and their song is loud and spirited, at times raucous.

Tis a gift to be simple, tis a gift to be free,
Tis is a gift to come down where we ought to be.
And when we find ourselves in the place just right,
It will be in the valley of love and delight.
When true simplicity is gained,
To bow and to bend we will not be ashamed.
To turn, to turn will be our delight,
Til by turning, turning, we come round right.

When they finish, Miss Peck claps her hands five times, stamps her feet twice, and claps four more times. "Who can tell me how many?"

Ananda raises his hand first. "Eleven," he says. "Five and two and four."

"Yes," Miss Peck replies. "You're excused." Ananda heads off into the coatroom for his snack, and Miss Peck starts to clap again for the others.

10:08 A.M.

The children sit at their desks, eating their snacks of fruit and crackers and raw vegetables. Miss Peck sits with them and drinks tea. It's her chance to catch her breath. The children talk mostly of Gretchen's caterpillar as they eat, weaving a fabric of conversation that includes everyone as it jiggles and jags all across the map of the topic. Sometimes two or three children break off into their own discussion, but the larger fabric always draws them back.

Eric N. is the first to finish his snack. It's warm and sunny outside, and he's in a hurry to be there. "May I be excused?" he asks. Miss Peck nods assent and smiles, and Eric takes off for the door. Within three minutes, everyone has followed him.

10:23 A.M.

Morning recess brings the whole school together. In a community of a little less than one hundred people, including students and teachers, everybody knows everyone else by name. And children from first grade on up through seventh mix and mingle all across the field and the playground. The younger children tend toward kickball, the older ones toward soccer. Others play on the swings and slides, while some farsighted souls wander on the edge of the field and study the birds in the marshland across the railroad tracks. It's a beautiful spring morning, more like early May than late March. And the children and teachers alike are enjoying the luxuriance of the sunshine.

10:45 A.M.

The members of the second grade, cheeks flushed and eyes bright, stand quietly behind their desks as Miss Peck greets Mrs. Weiland, another teacher in the school, at the door. The two women exchange handshakes and greetings. Then Miss Peck formally gives over her class to their French teacher.

"*Bon jour, mes amis,*" Mrs. Weiland says to the children when she arrives at the front of the room.

"*Bon jour,* Madame Weiland," they respond in unison. And for the next twenty minutes Mrs. Weiland takes the children on a nonstop expedition through a whirl of games and songs, all spoken or sung in French. The lesson culminates with a high-spirited game of "Simon Says," in which Marston and Ananda duel to the very end, with Marston falling one false move behind.

11:08 A.M.

"What in the world is that?" "The book of what?"

"It's called *The Book of Kells,*" Miss Peck explains.

"The book of cows?" "The book of kettles?" "What are kettles?" "No, silly, kells." "Well, what are kells?" "They're not cows!"

"All right, second grade," Miss Peck interjects firmly into the outburst of half a dozen excited voices. It's the first time she's raised her voice all day. "I think we are ready to begin." And the children fall into a hush. Miss Peck waits another few seconds to let the silence settle in. Then she begins to explain that one of Patrick's main interests was teaching people how to read and write. "Now, much later after Patrick, there lived a monk named Columba at the monastery at Kells, and he also loved to read and write. He particularly loved to write."

The class is listening with fascination as Miss Peck describes how books were made in Columba's time. The monks had to collect swans' feathers for quills and tan sheep hides for parchment. Her voice is rich with her feeling for history as she relates the intricate details of the way parchment was made. Then she goes on to describe how Columba made ink from berries and stones. "The book that he wrote, or some people say he wrote, is something that you've probably read. It's called the Gospels."

"Do they have that book still but, uhmm, the writing's made out of paper?" Eric N. asks.

"Yes, they do." She brings out a copy of *The Book of Kells* and, holding it open and aloft, describes how each page was handwritten and decorated with an extravagant array of drawings, how even the letters themselves were like paintings. She walks slowly around the inner circle of desks, giving each child an opportunity to examine the pages carefully.

When everyone has had a chance to look, Miss Peck gives each child a piece of paper two feet by three feet. "It's your sheet of parchment," she says as she turns to the chalkboard. "All look up here now," she requests and points to the lines she had written on the board earlier. "This is St. Patrick's prayer. I'll read it aloud, and you read it along with me to yourself."

I bind myself today
To the virtue of heaven.
Light of sun.
Brightness of Moon.
Splendour of Fire.
Speed of Lightning.
Swiftness of wind.

Depth of sea.
Stability of Earth.
Firmness of rock.

"If you were a monk working with Columba, you would say to yourself, 'I wonder what I can draw so that people who don't know how to read will be able to understand the words?' Because the pictures in the book were often clues and hints to what the words meant. How might you draw this line," Miss Peck asks, pointing to Light of Sun, "so it would be like the way Columba did it in *The Book of Kells*?"

"You could make a sun next to it," Marston replies quickly.

"Or you could write all the words in yellow," Heidi suggests.

"And have, uhmm, like rays of sun coming out from the words," Sarah adds. Miss Peck goes on to the next line, and the next, eventually eliciting the children's suggestions for each line in the prayer.

"Now I'd like you to imagine that your paper is *The Book of Kells*. I'd like you to write each line in St. Patrick's prayer. Write each line in your own way but like the way we've talked about it. Now I want you to write very carefully. But you don't have to hurry at all, because we have today and this afternoon, and we also have tomorrow. Do you know that sometimes it took months for someone just to finish one page?"

"A month is just four weeks," Eric W. comments as the children turn their attention to their own papers. Miss Peck goes to the board and, for a few minutes, works on illustrating the prayer in colored chalk. The children write and draw intently. Some use Miss Peck's version as a model while others heed their own imaginations. Miss Peck insists that they draw quietly for twenty minutes and then allows them to talk if they wish. Some discuss their illustrations and compare work. Others go on in focused silence.

11:50 A.M.

Gretchen has discovered that her caterpillar is missing. She's looked all over the room for it, but it doesn't seem to be anywhere. "I hope I can find him," she says a little plaintively. "I think he'll show up. He's got nowhere else to go."

11:54 A.M.

Miss Peck asks the class to put their crayons away and bring their
papers to her. "Lunchtime," Jed sings out, and a few other children echo his call. Several children bring their papers to her desk
immediately and rush to get their lunches. Others continue to
work. Miss Peck gives them another minute and then patiently
reminds them of her instruction. Now Terra and Noam, the last
ones drawing, reluctantly surrender their papers.

When the children are all in their seats, Miss Peck asks them to
fold their hands and be silent. They need almost a minute for everyone to calm down and join in the mood for grace. Miss Peck
waits without speaking until all are ready, and then she begins the
song.

> For health and strength and daily bread,
> we praise thy name, O Lord.
> For health and strength and daily bread,
> we praise thy name, O Lord.
> For health and strength and daily bread,
> we praise thy name, O Lord.

11:59 A.M.

Lunchtime is much like snack, children sitting at their desks and
eating while they talk of their pictures and their sandwiches and
giggle about caterpillars and butterflies and funny names. As some
of the boys finish eating, they suddenly grow more raucous and
wild. Miss Peck encourages them to clean up quickly and go outside where they can run and yell as much as they wish. Heidi runs
out to the field with the flock of boys, but Sarah, Gretchen, and
Terra eat more slowly. When they are done, they take another
quick look for the missing caterpillar and then saunter outside.

The sun is even warmer now, and the playing field seems bus-
ier: a game of kickball, a round of freeze tag, and a large game of

soccer. There seem to be fewer children wandering around or playing on the swings and slides. But perhaps the wandering ones have already rambled farther away.

12:48 P.M.

"Teacher, can I sit next to him?" "You can sit next to me if—" "I want to sit next to—" "Can I sit next to you?" It takes a minute, and then the children are gathered in small groups of their own choosing. They are working on drawings of their own design. Noam is creating a bright and stunning series of multicolored patterns; Marston, a huge castle stretched out over four large sheets of paper taped together; Terra, a bright yellow and red circular design that looks like a mandala.

As the children draw, Miss Peck reads aloud to them. "When Toad found himself in a dank and noisome dungeon and knew that all the grim darkness of the medieval fortress lay between him and the outer world of sunshine, he flung himself full length on the floor and shed bitter tears and abandoned himself to dark despair. 'This is the end of everything,' he said. 'At least it is the end of the career of Toad, which is the same thing. Of popular and handsome Toad, of rich and hospitable Toad.'" A ripple of giggles slips out from Noam and Gretchen, Sarah and Eric N. "'How can I ever hope to ever be set at large again, who has been so imprisoned so justly for stealing so handsome a motor car in such an audacious manner?'"

A few of the children have begun to talk about their pictures. Miss Peck has ignored their voices for a bit. Now, as their conversation grows louder, she stops reading and waits. Yet their discussion goes on. After half a minute, Eric N., frustrated with delay in the story, says pointedly, "You're wasting our time." The children look up quickly and then fall into silence. And Miss Peck begins to read again.

"'How can I ever hope to ever be set free after I have bestowed upon such a number of fat, red-faced policemen such lurid and imaginative cheek—' That means he was very sassy to them." And she continues to read the sad, funny tale of Toad, the jailer, and the jailer's daughter who liked animals.

1:11 P.M.

Miss Peck goes into the hall to talk with Miss Magrisso, the fifth grade teacher who teaches handwork to the second grade. In her absence, the girls gather and talk quietly while the boys engage in an excited conversation. Each comment trips over the end of the ones that came before it. "Sucker is not a swear!" "A sucker is an animal." "No, it isn't!" "Suckers are!" "No, they aren't—" "I bet he means—" "Yes, they are. They live in marshes and places like, uhhm, in Africa." "Suckers are not swears." "Who said they were?" "There's no such thing as an animal called a sucker." "Yes, it's called, uhhm, bloodsuckers." "Bloodsuckers, huh?" "Yeah, well, that's an animal." "It's an insect." "Yes, it is. It's an animal." "A bloodsucker is like a worm." "Except it's red." "Nooo!" "Yes!" "It's not red." "It's red when it has blood in it." "Yeah, but it's not red." "It just looks like a worm." "Oh, here comes Miss Magrisso!"

1:14 P.M.

The children stand behind their desks as Miss Magrisso leads them in the opening blessing.

> May our hands complete our tasks with patience.
> May our work be done with care.
> May our fingers work as friends together.
> May I my laughter share.

When the class is seated, Miss Magrisso passes out the crocheting projects that the children are working on. Ginny, a student from the fifth grade, begins to read aloud from *Charlotte's Web*, a book that the children have chosen to hear. Some of the children are working on potholders, others on pouches and scarves. As they receive their work and needles, the children begin eagerly, pausing only to giggle at the story. Their hands move the needles with high concentration, in and out, in and out, their eyes intently focused. Then someone laughs, and all of the children's eyes shoot up for a moment to inspect the pictures in the book. Then they're right back to work. Miss Magrisso moves easily among the children, sharing a word of praise here and lesson and a pat there.

1:48 P.M.

Miss Peck returns to the room as Miss Magrisso asks the children to stop working. "The time always goes so fast," Marston says.

1:58 P.M.

The children have returned to their renderings of St. Patrick's prayer. Miss Peck calls up one child at a time to sit on her lap and read. First Noam, then Eric W., then Jed, Heidi, and Sarah. Gretchen is still looking for her caterpillar. Miss Peck notices her search and asks her to return to her drawing. "I'll help you look for it later," she promises.

2:18 P.M.

Marston, Ananda, and Heidi have finished their illustrations. They give Miss Peck their papers and go to the back of the room. There they sit on the rug and play "Concentration" with a deck of playing cards. It's an evenly matched game.

2:26 P.M.

Miss Peck asks everyone to look for the caterpillar. For a minute they all do. They search everywhere in the room, but it's nowhere to be found. "He must've gone away when we weren't looking," Gretchen says finally and resigns herself to the loss.

2:29 P.M.

The second grade has lined up by the classroom door. They are struggling to keep themselves calm—no talking, no pushing, no jokes—because they all want to go outside immediately. Miss Peck recognizes the difficulty of their task and opens the door. The children hustle down the stairs and outside, this time racing to the front of the school.

In the fall they had planted bulbs that are beginning to send their first shoots above the ground. The children loosen the soil with their hands and dig shallow rows around the bulbs for planting nasturtiums, marigolds, and impatiens. Miss Peck gives each child a small batch of seeds and guides the planting, directing the children first to mix the seeds with sandy loam and then to pour the mixture along the rows. They cover the seeds with soil, and Noam, Eric N., and Gretchen fetch small buckets of water with which to wet the planting. It's very absorbing, exciting work.

"How long will the flowers take to be beautiful?" Eric W. asks.

2:48 P.M.

Miss Peck gathers the children on a grassy spot about ten feet distant from their row of flower seeds. A soft spring breeze has arisen from the west. The sky is still a sharp blue, without haze or clouds. "Are there any thank yous for today?" Miss Peck asks.

"Thank you for doctors," Heidi says.

"Thank you for the seeds," Eric N. offers.

"Thank you for my caterpillar," Gretchen says a bit wistfully.

There is a short pause. "Thank you for trees and new leaves," Sarah contributes.

"Thank you for funny things," Eric W. says.

Now there's a longer silence. Finally Miss Peck begins the song for closing the day. The children sing with an enthusiasm tempered by the tiredness that comes from a full day of activity.

I see the moon, and the moon sees me.
God bless the moon, and God bless me.
There's grace in the cabin and grace in the hall,
And the grace of God is over us all.

When they finish singing, they all join hands around the circle, and Miss Peck says in a clear and musical voice, "Thank you for the day." Then, one by one, each child comes to her, shakes her hand or shares a hug, and says goodbye. "See you tomorrow!"

Steiner's Vision of Education: In Practice

Many of the educational principles and practices that Rudolf Steiner describes are illustrated in this single day in second grade. Steiner's vision of the role of the teacher, the role of the child's *inner teacher*, the rhythm of the day, the focus on the child learning through his senses, his feelings, and his imagination in the second epoch, the aesthetic and artistic core of all activities for children at the start of this epoch, the grounding of all intellectual work in the aesthetic and artistic, and the holistic approach to memory are all embodied in Miss Peck's classroom.

• **The role of the teacher:** In this classroom Miss Peck plans the activities and guides the children through them, basing her planning on the Waldorf curriculum, her awareness of these particular children, and her own knowledge, insight, feeling, and intuition. She leads with clarity and direction fused with a gentle yet focused attention on each child. Her awareness of and sensitivity to each child guides her judgment as she responds to their behavior. For example, when Jed distances himself from the group, she knows to give him space to experience his feelings rather than intervene, because she understands his need to withdraw and then return to the group according to his own timing. In considering her actions in the classroom this day, it is crucial to recall that Miss Peck has already taught these children for nearly two years and that both she and they expect her to teach them for six years to come. This kind of longevity of relationship produces both profound knowledge of and feeling for the children by the teacher and a powerful commitment between each child and the teacher.

• **The role of the child's *inner teacher*:** The *inner teacher* makes itself evident in the children's actions and expressions, particularly in their art work. During this day, Anna Peck's respect for and heeding of each child's *inner teacher* is evidenced in the way she attends to each child's expressions and inclinations and, as much as she can, tries to make room for and support these expressions. She also works to pay attention to her own intuition in relation to each child's needs and directions for growth.

• **The rhythm of the day:** The day starts with a ritual of beginning: candle lighting, silence, and song. These activities focus the children's attention in the present and engage their energy and enthusiasm for this day of school.

The next group of activities engages the class in song, story, and number through the means of rhythmic movement, to be followed by activities that focus on balance and concentration and then on playing music.

The next segment of the day is the main lesson: listening to the story of St. Patrick, feeling its richness, and "living" it through inner imagery. This is followed by snack, recess, and the French lesson. Then there is a return to the context of the main lesson in the discussion of Columba, *The Book of Kells*, and the making of a book. This is followed by a focus on expression in the children's writing and illustrating of Patrick's prayer. This lettering and illustrating gives the children an opportunity to bring their own feeling and imagery to this story. Next come lunch and recess.

The afternoon is devoted to more work on the children's illustrations, the hand work of crocheting as the children listen to a story, the planting of seeds, and a closing ritual.

The pattern of the day places the intellectual work in the morning, followed by expressive work. The afternoon is devoted to practical, hands-on activities. The repetition of this pattern provides each child with a desired regularity in his daily life. While the content of the various segments of activity changes from one day to the next, the child knows that the segments and their order will continue for the most part in a predictable and comforting pattern.

• **In this epoch the child learns from her senses, her feelings, and her imagination, not from abstractions:** Most of the activity of this day engages these three aspects of the child. Indeed many engage all three simultaneously. When there are abstractions to be dealt with, they are always grounded in the concrete and the aesthetic.

• **The aesthetic and artistic core of all activities for children at the start of the second epoch, and the creation and appreciation of beauty**: Joyous, aesthetic activity is at the core of the second grade day. Much of this activity involves the rhythms of motion, language, and music. Examples of these activities include the many songs; the "laughing bug" clapping game; the "English/Romans" and "old bald eagle" dances; counting by multiples; the French lesson; and the writing and illustration of Patrick's prayer, which also involves the creation of beauty.

• **The grounding of all intellectual work in the aesthetic and artistic, and in the concrete**: All intellectual work begins with and is grounded in the concrete and the aesthetic. For example, counting by multiples of seven, eight, and nine engages the children in the correct number of body contacts for the number with which they are working, first seven snaps, slaps, claps, then eight, and so on. The French lesson is grounded in games and songs, so that all of the abstractions of French words are given both a concrete context and an aesthetic character. The writing of Patrick's prayer is grounded in the illustration of each line.

• **A focus on pictures and stories that convey aesthetic and moral values, not on theories and abstractions**: The focus of the American version of the Waldorf curriculum for second grade in history and literature includes Celtic and Aesop's fables, the legends of saints, local folklore, and Native American stories. The story of St. Patrick is intended to engage the children in terms of both aesthetic and moral dimensions. The pictures in *The Book of Kells* extend the expression of these dimensions.

• **The holistic approach to memory**: This approach to memory training is best exemplified in the counting by multiples activity. The integration of movement, body contact, rhythm, and spoken numbers is a multimodality approach to memory that grounds the ideas—the numbers—in the sensory experience of the game.

This was one day in the second grade, a day of song and rhythm and story and color, of children whirling in motion and etched in concentration. One day like and unlike any other.

THE VISION OF AUROBINDO GHOSE

Aurobindo's Vision of Human Nature

Aurobindo Ghose's understanding of human nature is informed by his conception of the universe as consisting essentially of consciousness that is expressed on many different planes of being. Consciousness is "the fundamental thing in existence . . . not only the macrocosm but the microcosm is nothing but consciousness arranging itself."[1] The planes of being are "linked in graded continuity from the lowest matter to the highest spirit."[2] These planes include the **material plane**, the **vital plane**, the **mental plane**, the transitional spiritual planes of **higher mind, illumined mind, intuitive mind,** and **Overmind,** the **Supramental plane,** and the **divine consciousness.** (All of Aurobindo's terms are explained below.)

Aurobindo's vision of human nature describes us as "divine being(s) in an animal and egoistic consciousness."[3] Each person is a unique individual, "a self-developing soul."[4] We are partially divine beings who are evolving toward greater divinity.

Human beings are dynamic systems that consist of five major sub-systems: the material or **physical being;** the **life** or **vital being;** the **mental being;** the **psychic being** or **soul;** and the **spirit.** In addition, most humans include an **ego,** which is not a being or sub-system as such but is a necessary yet ultimately transitory construction of identity.

Each of the five sub-systems includes several or many elements within it. Each exists primarily on its own plane of being. Yet because the various planes of being are integral, not isolated from each other, these sub-systems interpenetrate each other and are profoundly interrelated. Whenever one sub-system changes or is affected by some force, every other sub-system is affected in some way.

Aurobindo's description of human nature is profoundly rooted in his conception of the evolution of consciousness as the central process in the existence of the universe. This evolution is a dual process: the emergence of consciousness from its involved state in matter into higher planes of being, and the simultaneous descent of spirit into the material, vital, and mental planes to aid the evolution of consciousness. In all cases, the next higher level of being is involved in the one below it. Through evolution, "life appropriated matter and transformed" it.[5] Then mind appropriated life and has transformed it, first into animals and then into humans. As consciousness has evolved, each new unfoldment is always wider, richer, and more complex and powerful. "Evolutionary ascent is not by the negation of that which is lower, but by its complete appropriation and integration into a higher-level experience."[6]

Central to Aurobindo's vision of human nature is the understanding that evolution does not stop with humans. We are transitional beings. as were all that have preceded us. We openly embody the mental plane as well as the vital and material, yet latent, involved within us, is the Supramental. In the next step in evolution, the Supramental will appropriate mind and transform it.

At this stage in the process, the mechanism of evolution is the individual soul, each person's connection to the Supramental and her potential for bringing forth that plane of being within herself. "There is an outward visible process of physical evolution with birth as its machinery . . . there is, at the same time, an invisible process of soul evolution with rebirth into ascending grades of form and consciousness as its machinery.[7]

Aurobindo teaches that evolution has itself reached a radically new stage in its unfoldment. In this century for the very first time, the beings that evolve—ourselves—have become conscious of the process of their evolving. With this awareness as guidance, humans can consciously choose to participate in evolution, to bring the energy of their will to organize their consciousness and, through spiritual discipline, learn to manifest the Supramental in this world. For in the movement from the mental to the Supramental, the primary medium of change will be consciousness, not matter.

SURFACE AND HIDDEN ASPECTS

Each of the first three beings—the physical, the vital, and the mental—has a **surface** aspect and a **hidden** aspect.

> The part of our nature of which we are normally conscious is our surface personality, consisting of the (material) body, the (surface) vital and the (surface) mind. But behind this superficial consciousness there exists a far greater, deeper and more powerful consciousness which is in constant touch with the universal planes of Mind, Life and Matter. This hidden consciousness influences and governs us without our knowledge.[8]

Each of the three hidden aspects consists of three elements that exist on separate sub-planes within their particular plane of being:

1. A subconscient element that works below the level of the outer aspect, that retains impressions of all experience in a concealed and unexpressed form. The content of these subconscient elements is often expressed in dreams and in neurotic behavior.

2. A subliminal or inner consciousness that, though located on the same sub-plane as the surface consciousness, exists behind the surface aspect. Each inner consciousness is larger, more plastic and free, and more powerful than its surface counterpart. The inner consciousnesses of the physical, vital, and mental beings all have their own **inner centers** or **chakras**, which are located on a subtle energetic level within the person.

3. A higher element that is connected to the superconscient and gives each being access to the higher planes, beginning with the Higher Mind and going upward. This consciousness is the source of intuition and inspiration, which can be known through each of the three lower beings.

PHYSICAL BEING

The physical being includes the body of matter, of flesh and blood, and the physical consciousness, which has both a surface and a hidden aspect. The inner center of the physical being's consciousness is located within the base chakra at the bottom of the spine.

VITAL BEING

The vital being is "the life-force acting in its own nature (through) impulses, emotions, feelings, desires, longings, ambitions, and so on."[9] The vital being is also the seat of the instincts. It is integral with the physical being and occupies the same "space," although on a higher plane of consciousness.

The vital being contains four parts, each of which has a particular realm of function. Each part interacts with the vital's subconscient element and includes its own subliminal consciousness and inner center. But only the emotional vital and mental vital interact with the vital's superconscient consciousness. These four parts are the following:

1. The lower vital is "occupied with the small desires and feelings such as make the greater part of daily life, that is, food desire, sexual desire, small likings, dislikings, vanity, quarrels, love of praise, anger at blame, little wishes of all kinds."[10] The lower vital is located around the spleen chakra, which is the seat of the inner center of this part of the vital being.

2. The higher vital is the "seat of the stronger vital longings and reactions, that is, ambition, pride, fear, love of fame, attractions and repulsions, desires and passions of various kinds."[10] It is also the seat of anger and jealousy. The higher vital is located from the navel up to the heart, and its inner center is within the solar plexus chakra.

3. The emotional vital is the "seat of various feelings, such as love, joy, sorrow, hatred, and the rest."[10] It is also the seat of hope and pity. The emotional vital is located in the area around the heart, and its inner center is within the heart.

4. The mental vital gives a mental expression by thought, speech, or otherwise to the emotions, desires, passions, sensations, and other movements of the vital being. One of its purposes is to look toward the future: to plan, to dream, to imagine what can be done. The mental vital is located from the heart up to the throat, and its inner center is within the throat chakra.

MENTAL BEING

The mental being is "a faculty for seeking knowledge."[11] Yet "mind is only a preparatory form of consciousness. It is an instrument of analysis and synthesis, but not of essential knowledge."[12] The mind often perceives a part of some knowing that it can apprehend as the whole.

Aurobindo elaborately describes the limitations of the mental being.[13] Yet with the same breath he stresses the mind's spiritual nature. Human reason is a function of the divine, not an antagonist to it. For it is "the mission of mind to train our obscure consciousness to enlighten its blind instinct, random intuition, vague perception till it becomes capable of a greater light."[14] The mental being thus plays a central role in the training of the other beings as well as in the development of its own capacities. In addition, the mind is needed to critique spiritual experience, to clarify it and detect errors caused by the influence of emotion or imagination.

The mental being consists of four elements:

1. **Chitta** is a passive memory, which acts as a reservoir of all past mental impressions. It is the subconscient element of the mental being.

2. **Manas** receives sensory data from the five outer senses,

translates these data into thought-sensations and thought-impressions, and conveys them to buddhi, the intellect. These thought-sensations and thought-impressions are the material of thought, not thought itself.

Manas is also the seat of the sixth sense, the inner sense, which receives subtle images from the higher levels of being within the person. Such perception through manas is the mechanism of ways of knowing such as telepathy and clairvoyance.

Manas can distort the data it receives from the outer senses when the mind lacks training and is affected by strong emotions or interference from previous associations or habitual ways of being. Since manas acts both as a translator for and a channel to buddhi **and** as the sense organ of the sixth sense, distortion is even more likely when it is called upon to enact this dual function, that is, to perceive subtle images from higher levels of being, translate them into thought-impressions, and convey them to buddhi.

3. **Buddhi** is the seat of the intellect, the real instrument of thought. It orders and disposes what is acquired by manas and transmitted to it.

Buddhi is composed of the faculties of the left-hand mind— reasoning and logic, analysis and criticism, distinction and comparison and inference—and the faculties of the right-hand mind— creativity, imagination, observation, vision, memory, and synthetic judgment. The left touches only "the body of knowledge" and serves the right, which has access to the soul and is the "master of knowledge." Aurobindo stresses the need for the equal development of both the left and the right minds for the mental being to be whole.

The subliminal consciousness of the mental being is part of buddhi. Its inner center is located in the forehead chakra.

4. The **higher faculties** are the superconscient element in the mental being. When developed, these faculties can give access to the Higher Mind and generate "sovereign discernment, intuitive perception of truth . . . direct vision of knowledge to an extent often amounting to revelation."[15] These faculties are imperfectly developed in most people, although one example of their power can be seen in the mental expression of human genius.

The crown chakra is the pathway to the higher faculties, which are located in the energy field above the physical head.

EGO

The ego is not a being. Rather, it is a distorted reflection of the psychic being and of the spirit as conveyed through the consciousnesses of the physical, vital, and mental beings. The ego plays an important role in unfoldment. Its function is to protect the person by giving her a clearly felt though ultimately illusory sense of a center within herself until she learns about her true center within the psychic being. Once a person's psychic being manifests itself and establishes itself in her consciousness, the ego is no longer needed.

PSYCHIC BEING

The psychic being or soul is a spark of the divine that has individual identity and is immanent within us. It is inherently pure and has a profound connection to the truth-consciousness, The psychic being is located "behind" the heart chakra, as it is more inward than the chakras.

> It is our inmost being . . . its power is not knowledge but an essential or spiritual feeling. . . . [It} supports all others, mental, vital, physical, but is also much veiled by them and has to act upon them as an influence rather than by its sovereign right of direct action.[16]

Because the psychic being is centered behind the emotional vital, it is particularly vulnerable to distortion from the "desire soul," the egoistic expression of the emotional vital. A major task of spiritual growth is to learn to discern between the expression of the "desire soul" and the psychic being.

The psychic being experiences individual evolution. The

outer and inner aspects of the various beings convey their growth to the psychic being, which, in turn, conveys that growth from one incarnation to the next.

Aurobindo explains that the psychic being can emerge and manifest itself consciously only ". . . when there is a complete stillness in the being. There can be a decisive emergence in which the being separates itself from thought and sees itself in an inner silence."[17] Within this inner silence, the psychic being is

> an inherent, intrinsic, self-existent consciousness which knows itself by the mere fact of being, knows all that is in itself in the same way, by identity with it, begins even to see all that to our mind seems external in the same manner, by a movement of identity or by an intrinsic direct consciousness which envelops, penetrates, enters into its object, discovers itself in the object.[18]

SPIRIT

The spirit is a grain of the universal, the infinite divine. The spirit is transcendent of us, yet we have access to its expression through the psychic being. The spirit is immortal. It is outside the evolutionary process, yet it supports the unfoldment of the psychic being and helps to convey the evolutionary growth from one rebirth to the next.

Aurobindo's Vision of Human Becoming

Aurobindo describes human becoming between birth and age twenty-one as a process of unfoldment in which the person's innate potential seeks to emerge and grow. Each newborn child is an organismic whole that contains within it a developmental urge toward growth and self-mastery. This urge originates within the person's psychic being and is the manifestation of the divine consciousness seeking to propel the evolution of the individual and, through the individual, the evolution of the species.

Aurobindo discusses the nature of the developmental urge and the person's innate wisdom for seeking growth tasks that are appropriate for her particular stage of unfoldment. Although he suggests that there are regular stages of unfoldment that most humans experience in their first twenty-one years, he does not detail them in any of his writings.

However, a description of these stages, based on the vision of Aurobindo, can be found in the writings of three of his most intimate associates: Mira Richard (known as "The Mother" at the Sri Aurobindo Ashram), who came from France to join Aurobindo's community in 1920 and whom he later announced as his spiritual partner and successor; Pavitra (P. B. Saint-Hilaire), also of French origins, who was a long-time student of Aurobindo, a resident of the ashram, and, from its inception in 1952 almost until his death in 1969, the director of the Sri Aurobindo International Centre of Education, the school at the Ashram; and Narayan Prasad, also a long-time student of Aurobindo and resident of the ashram who for many years edited *Mother India*, the journal of the Aurobindo Ashram. This description of the stages of human unfoldment emerges from a study of each of these authors' writings about education and Aurobindo's teachings. While no single author presents a complete vision, a synthesis of their discussions of growth and development offers a description that is coherent, internally consistent among the three authors, and clearly derived from the vision of their teacher.

THREE AGES OF CHILDHOOD AND YOUTH

The vision of human becoming that Richard, Pavitra, and Prasad articulate includes three ages of childhood and youth:

- Birth through 6 years of age
- 7 through 12–13 years of age
- 13–14 through 20 years of age

The **first age** is a time marked prominently by the child's need to direct her own activity. In the first three years, the child belongs to the family. In the next three, she needs to reach out into larger social contexts. What is consistent through most of this age is that the child knows her experience as play, that is, self-directed activity that is purposive and more rewarding in its process than in whatever it achieves.

Around the age of 7 years, the psychic being awakens in many children[19] and brings the beginning of the **second age** of unfoldment. In this age the child begins to think but only in a concrete manner. Her locus of interest shifts increasingly away from the family and toward the school and peer group.

At 7 through 9 years the child is engaged in the task of grounding herself, of gaining a sense of her place in her family, school, and peer group. At 8 through 9 years she experiences a new intensity of social needs that continues into the teens. She wants to be with her peers more, to be engaged in activity with them and accepted by them. At 10 through 12 years the child begins to take on the patterns of individuality that will be hers throughout the rest of her life. This is also a time in which she has the potential for beginning to discover her calling on this planet.

At 12 or 13 years the child unfolds into the **third age**. This growth is marked by the youth's development of a more complete reason, including the capacity to work with abstraction, and by her new awareness of her own inner life. In this age the youth seeks freedom to explore both within—her feelings and passions, thoughts and intuitions and questions—and without—ideas, people, and experiences. She seeks freedom and adventure. It is a time when she wishes to explore the world beyond the family and school and to establish new relationships with it. This age is also a time when the youth brings energy and passion to her investigation of the meaning of life.

THE CHILD'S NEEDS FOR UNFOLDMENT

Along with this scheme of unfoldment, Richard, Pavitra, and Prasad detail a number of developmental needs that must be met for a child to grow toward health and wholeness. When these needs are not fulfilled at all, the growth of the child is thwarted or stunted. When these needs are not met directly, the child may try to meet them in other, inappropriate ways, thus generating distortions in her character. Behaviorial signs of such distortion include restlessness, irritability, instability, and mischievousness.

The first need of the child, particularly in the first age, is the experience of an interwoven trust and happiness. "The very central character of the child consciousness . . . is confidence in life, the surety that nothing can baulk the fulfillment of life's purpose, the trust that overrides all setbacks and stumbles."[20] When this confidence, this trust "that knows that needed things will come,"[21] can flourish within the child, it brings the experience of happiness. Such happiness is not constant laughing or shouting or clapping but, rather, is "first of all relaxation, a liberation from tension of all sorts, an expansion of the being in silence and peace. Then comes a mute joy, a smile, the effulgence of a sweet presence within, a look of friendliness towards the world."[22]

This kind of trustful happiness plays a significant role in the child's life, for it is both her primary need and a sign that no other important needs are being neglected. Among these other needs are the ones listed below. Each is important in all three ages though in different ways in each age.

- The child needs to grow in all of her beings as is appropriate to her stage of unfoldment.

- The child needs to grow in freedom and independence according to her own inner calling, the expression of her soul or psychic being. This need does not require adults to accede to the child's every wish, for every child expresses desires, whims, greeds, and so on that are not needs. What it does demand of adults is a profound respect for the child's expression of herself and a willingness to accept that expression as it manifests itself, not to try to mold or shape it to meet the expectations or desires of the adults.

- The child needs the security of knowing that her growth will not be hampered by or interfered with by adults. She needs to know that she will not be compelled to do things for which she is not ready.

- The child needs support, affection, sympathy, and love, particularly on the soul level.

- The child needs to be given the opportunity to complete that which she begins. Her behavior is purposive. When she becomes engaged in an activity and gives attention to it, she wants to experience a sense of completion in relation to that activity before she moves on to something else.

- The child needs to experience beauty in people and in her environment. She also needs to experience gratitude, awe, and reverence.

- The child needs to learn how to satisfy her needs herself. She needs to learn how to take responsibility for her expression of a need, accept the consequences from her attempts to meet her needs, and learn from these experiences.

Aurobindo's Vision of Child Raising and Education

The description of Aurobindo's vision of the purposes and practices of child raising and education presented below is based primarily on the works of Aurobindo. It also includes reference to the writings of Mira Richard, Pavitra, and several other students of Aurobindo who lived within the Aurobindo Ashram and taught at the Centre for Education. This vision refers primarily to the needs of school-age children and youth in the second and third eras, but it also offers some insights into the needs of younger children.

INTEGRAL EDUCATION

The process of education that Aurobindo described and that his students sought to implement at the Ashram school is called **integral education**. The integrality refers both to the understanding of reality as a series of integral planes of being and to the nature of humans as immensely complex systems composed of various interrelated and interpenetrated sub-systems or beings. Although these sub-systems exist primarily on different levels of being, they are profoundly integral with each other. The term integral education also speaks to the purpose of education: helping the various beings and their faculties unfold according to their potential and learn to work together for a common purpose, a purpose that is conveyed from the spirit through the psychic being. Such "harmonisation and integration of the divided and wayward energies of the human child . . . must be essentially an inner fact of life, not primarily one of behaviour. The inner fact alone will be able to produce the right outer behaviour."[23] The focus of integral education is first on the inner unfoldment of the child and then on the relationship between the child's inner life and her actions.

Aurobindo explains that the development and harmonization of the child's various beings is best nurtured by helping her psychic being to unfold as well as supporting the growth of her other, lower beings. The child's psychic being can be apprehended by the teacher through her own psychic being. It can also be known through the expression of the child's developmental urge, for this urge is the direct manifestation of the psychic being. This inmost being "is essentially marked by the quality of wholeness and has the power of integration."[24] In its capacity to "guide the other members of the personality . . . the psychic influence is the greatest friend of the teacher in the work of guiding . . . "[24] the child.

The psychic being, then, is a powerful *inner teacher*. In a profound sense, ". . . the child, with the tremendous motivating potential within, is his own teacher. The nurture of the child means this actualization of the inner motivating potential through the careful nurture of the developmental urge."[25] This insight calls upon adults to respect, not suppress, the child's developmental urge.

The *inner teacher* is manifested as the child's curiosity, urge for exploration, aspiration for achievement, and pursuit of excellence. "It is never by external compulsion that a child acquires interest, the key of all learning, but by finding within herself a security, a sanction, an authority from her own nature and the law of her own being."[26]

When the inner teacher is unheeded or neglected, the child's unfoldment is inevitably limited and/or displaced from the course of its potential.

> The suppression of this inner urge due to family up-bringing leads to perversion of curiosity into purposeless prying, exploration into frivolous activities, aspiration for achievement into ruthless competition which encourages foul means, and pursuit of perfection and excellence into devastating ambition for status and power.[25]

Aurobindo summarizes the purposes of education by explaining that young people need to learn to "think for themselves, change their consciousness, evolve their true personality in an integral way, live the truth which they discover."[27] Yet education must focus not only on the individual but also on her relationship to her opportunities and responsibilities as a member of her community, nation, and species.

THREE PRINCIPLES PLUS ONE

To elucidate his conception of learning and teaching, Aurobindo offers three guiding principles:

1. "The first principle of true teaching is that nothing can be taught. The teacher is not an instructor or a taskmaster, he is a helper, a guide. . . . He does not actually train the pupil's mind, he only shows him how to perfect his instruments of knowledge and helps and encourages him in the process. He does not impart knowledge to him, he only shows him how to acquire knowledge for himself. . . . He does not call forth the knowledge that is within [the learner]; he only shows him where it lies and how it can be

habituated to rise to the surface."[28]

2. "The second principle is that the mind has to be consulted in its own growth. . . . He [the learner] himself must be induced to expand in accordance with his own nature."[29] The teacher must help the child learn to recognize, validate, and heed her own *inner teacher.*

3. "The third principle of education is to work from the near to the far, from that which is to that which shall be."[30] Each person is born to a particular place and time, a particular family and culture. Education needs to respect this uniqueness in every individual's life and not uproot the child from it. The child needs to learn about her own people and culture as well as about other peoples and cultures throughout the world.

Pavitra adds a fourth principle to this list: "The educator should always remember that he should not try to act upon the child, nor upon the needs, but upon the environment of the child. . . . A child's needs are always satisfied by the child himself; the educator must only place the child in conditions where this satisfaction is possible."[31]

FORMS OF TEACHING

To clarify these principles, Aurobindo describes three forms of teaching. Direct teaching, the conveying of information, is sometimes appropriate but generally of limited value. Its practice needs to be carefully organized so it does not violate the principles described before.

Teaching by the example of the teacher's own behavior is a much more effective method. It does not compel the child in any way but offers her a pattern from which she can choose to learn. Example communicates with the child on all levels, including the physical, vital, mental, and psychic. Aurobindo notes that the child will learn from the example of the teacher's behavior whether such learning is intended or not. Given this inevitability, it is particularly important that the teacher understand her power as a model to the child and strive to embody a coherence between what she advocates and how she acts. As Richard emphasizes, "To say good words, give wise advice to a child has very little effect, if one does not show by one's living example the truth of what one teaches."[32]

The most powerful method of teaching is what Aurobindo calls influence, "not the outward authority of the teacher . . . but the power of his contact, of his presence, of the nearness of his soul to the soul of another, infusing into it, even though in silence, that which he himself is."[33] Influence involves a link between the divine element of the teacher, her psychic being and soul, and that of the student. It is an interaction not of matter or mind but of spiritual energy on a higher plane of being. Through influence, a teacher can help the child to evolve by sharing her own spiritual energy with the child, thus supporting and nurturing the *inner teacher* and divine element within the child.

GUIDELINES FOR TEACHING

Aurobindo describes the practice of education both in terms of specific, practical guidelines for parents and teachers and in terms of the kinds of growth and learning needed by each of the sub-systems or beings of the person. In their practice of education at his ashram over five decades, Aurobindo's students have employed their teacher's guidelines and, from their experience of such use, have clarified and elaborated upon them.

The guidelines that Aurobindo offers include the following:

- Invite the child to begin her academic studies when she is 7 years of age. Before that time she should be in an environment that is designed for play. Beginning the learning of academic subjects too early can interfere with the child's unfoldment.

- Treat girls and boys equally in all activities.

- Know that the focus of education is the actualization of the child's inner potential, the manifestation of her personal capacity for evolution. Education is not the acquiring of mental information. Such information is useful when it relates directly to the accomplishment of another appropriate goal. It is not a goal in itself. When the acquiring of information does not take place in the context of another goal, such activity wastes the child's energy and hinders her growth.

- Understand and respect the child's unfoldment, and invite her to participate in environments and activities that are appropriate to her stage of unfoldment. For example, for children who think in concrete terms, offer stories, images, and parables rather than abstract concepts.

- Organize the learning environment and activities to suit the present needs of the child, not some set of projected future needs. At the same time, understand that education is for the unfolding and evolving soul of the child and the future in which she will live, not for the past or even present society.

- Organize the learning environment to function as "a student activated classroom ecology."[34] Invite "the spirit of freedom to permeate the entire atmosphere of integral education."[35] "Activate a climate of curiosity, discovery and free progress —through living situations of self discovery rather than the acquisition of knowledge."[36] Interact with the child so that you "suggest and invite, never command or impose."[37] Richard calls this kind of approach to education the free progress system. "It is free because it encourages each one to break the limitations of the past and to open to an exploration of new future possibilities."[38]

Within a free progress system of education, the child can and must learn about freedom and discipline: not one or the other but both in relation to each other. The teacher can help the child's learning best through the example of her own free and disciplined behavior: her calmness, evenness, and orderliness woven together within a joyous spontaneity. She can also aid the child's learning by helping her channel her freedom through participation in groups, classes, and individual instruction as appropriate to her needs and by providing her with feedback about her behavior and with helpful guidance.

Another key to the child's learning about freedom and discipline is her involvement in the practice of a spiritual discipline. It is the teacher's responsibility to provide appropriate instruction and support.

The teacher must guide and help the child as she learns freedom with discipline, discipline with freedom. If necessary, the teacher must intervene to protect the child from herself or to protect others from her actions. For example, harmful disorder or chaos are not acceptable conditions in the learning environment.

• Invite the child to set the pace for her own learning.

• Help the child to learn by appealing to her natural characteristics.

> Every child is a lover of interesting narrative, a hero-worshipper and a patriot. Appeal to these qualities in him and through them let him master without knowing it the living and human parts of his nation's history. Every child is an inquirer, an investigator, analyser, a merciless anatomist. Appeal to those qualities in him and let him acquire without knowing it the right temper and the necessary fundamental knowledge of the scientist. Every child has an insatiable intellectual curiosity and turn for metaphysical enquiry. Use it to draw him on slowly to an understanding of the world and himself. Every child has a gift of imitation and a touch of imaginative power. Use it to give him the ground work of the faculty of the artist.[39]

It is the teacher's responsibility to organize the learning environment in such a way that the child's own characteristics motivate her to learn. The teacher's role, once the environment is created and the tools for learning are at hand, is not to teach directly but to help the child move in whatever ways her *inner teacher* impels her.

- Give responsibility, power, and meaningful roles to the child as is appropriate to her level of unfoldment. For example: tutoring younger children; cooking, cleaning and maintenance; leading games and sports.

- Invite the child to discover and experience reverence, so that she can experience moving beyond the narrow identity of her ego consciousness. The teacher can best involve the child in this by sharing her own feelings of reverence and by creating activities through which the child can join with her and others in experiences of reverence. The teacher can engage the child in experiencing gratitude in the same way. Gratitude brings a sense of connection to the universe—"a state of consciousness wherein one is aware of one's relation with God"[40]—and is a power in itself. Its experience evokes a sense of peace and well-being for both teacher and student.

- Help the child "to develop his instruments of knowledge with the utmost thoroughness . . ."[39] and help her to gain a mastery of her native language, which will be the medium for much that she learns. Once she has developed her instruments of knowing, she can learn and grow in whatever directions her *inner teacher* carries her.

- Invite the child to learn about one subject at a time in depth, both as a whole in itself and in the ways it relates to other subjects.

EDUCATING THE SUB-SYSTEMS OF THE PERSON

Aurobindo and his students describe the education of the **beings** or **sub-systems** of the person in considerable detail. They explain that one of the teacher's overriding goals is to help the child and youth become conscious of the physical, vital, mental, and psychic elements within herself. As the child learns about the elements of which she consists in a way that is appropriate to her stage of unfoldment, she can make more sense of her inner and outer experience and strive to direct and discipline her own energies.

As the beings of the human person are interrelated and interpenetrated, so must their education be interrelated and coordinated. In guiding the growth of a child, the teacher must be as conscious as she can of the various relationships among the child's beings and the ways in which these interactions affect her unfoldment.

PHYSICAL BEING

Aurobindo describes the physical or material being, the physical body, as an agent and partner in the spiritual unfoldment of the child. It must be treated with respect and care and helped to awaken its physical and conscious potentials. The purposes that motivate the education of the physical body are to help its own faculties unfold and evolve to their potential and to help the child learn to integrate and harmonize these various faculties. The methods of training must be organized and disciplined. As Richard explains, "Of all the domains of human consciousness, the physical is the one most completely governed by method, order, discipline, procedure."[41]

Aurobindo and Richard discuss the education of the physical body in terms of seven categories, as follows:

1. **A sound and fundamentally healthy body**: To grow into health and well-being, a child needs physical activity each and every day. At the Sri Aurobindo International Centre for Education, physical education is the only mandatory activity for children and youth—and for adults! For at least one hour each day, people from 6 years to 75 years and up are involved in games, gymnastics, movement, dance, swimming, team sports, and other physical activities as appropriate to their age.

Another aspect of this category of physical education involves nutrition and self-care. The child needs to learn to eat according to her needs and no more, to follow the guidance of her body consciousness in regard to food and not to make eating the expression of cravings or greed. The child also needs to learn a conscious awareness of her body's condition through which she can monitor its well-being and seek care when she needs it.

2. **The education of the senses**: The child needs to develop full and right use of her six senses both for their own capacities and for their roles in the development and functioning of other beings. The senses are important to the life of the physical being because they play such a central role in the gaining of information that the physical consciousness can use to guide the unfoldment and life of its own being.

The senses are also crucial to the functions of the vital being. Education of the senses provides "the basis for vital education by enabling the child to appreciate and create the harmony of colors and forms and the rhythm of sounds."[41] The training of the senses engages the child in developing her aesthetic sense and feeling, which relates to moral education and the training of the will, as discussed below.

Education of the senses is fundamental as well to the growth of the mental being. The senses provide the material that manas forms into thought. Training of the senses helps the child learn to use her senses with clarity to gather sensory data from the world. It also helps the child to train her manas to transmit thought-sensations accurately to her buddhi and to receive clearly and transmit accurately the subtle images of the sixth sense, through manas.

In the training of the senses of sight, hearing, smell, touch, taste, and manas in its sixth-sense function, clarity and accuracy depend on the learning of awareness and sensitivity. These qualities, in turn, require the child to learn the skills of attention and concentration. Attention means to bring all awareness into the here and now of the senses. "Concentration is to bring all the scattered threads of consciousness to a single point."[42] Richard explains that both of these capacities "can be developed exactly like muscles"[43] through practice.

One kind of practice involves the child in the careful observation of nature, followed by the drawing and/or describing of what she has perceived. "The practice of imitation by the hand of the thing seen is of use . . . in noticing the objects of sense and in registering accurately what has been seen. Imitation by the hand insures accuracy of observation. This is one of the first uses of drawing, and it is sufficient in itself to make this subject a necessary part of the training"[44] of the senses. Another kind of practice engages the child in experiencing and creating rhythm, symmetry, and beauty. A third kind involves her in attending to more than one sense at a time and learning to bring her powers of concentration to two or more objects in the same moment.

One obstacle to effective functioning of the senses is the lack of their conscious use by the child. "The student needs to be accustomed to catch the sights, sounds, etc. around him, distinguish them, mark their nature, properties and sources, and fix them in the chitta so they may be always ready to respond when called for by the memory."[45]

Other obstacles to effective sensory function are nervous energy, emotion, and interference from previous habitual ways of being and associations. The child can learn to calm and purify her nervous system through the practice of breathing exercises. She can learn to discipline her emotions by gaining skills for calming and centering herself.

The child can remove interference from past habits and associations by learning to stop her inner dialogue. In the inner dialogue, chitta bombards buddhi with an onslaught of old impressions and memories that interfere with the clarity of the child's senses. Only by pacifying chitta and halting the inner dialogue can she free herself from these habits and associations both to perceive with complete accuracy in the present and to achieve a clarity of intellect within buddhi. The practice of a spiritual discipline is the way in which the child can learn to achieve this cessation of the inner dialogue.

3. **The awakening of the body consciousness**: The child needs to learn to recognize and honor the intuition of her body consciousness, expressed as instincts and inner body knowing. The body consciousness is often obscured or dominated by the consciousness of the vital or mental beings. To awaken the body consciousness and help it evolve to its potential, the child needs to be informed about the nature of this part of herself. She also needs

practice in becoming aware of her body consciousness and guidance in relation to this practice.

To be clear and open, the body consciousness needs discipline. To discipline her body consciousness, the child needs both to discipline her physical body and to heed the knowing of her body consciousness when she becomes aware of it. Mastery of the body consciousness can evolve within the child through her experience of perceiving it, acting according to its wisdom, and experiencing the consequences. When the child learns to discipline her body consciousness, this center will be able to enact its own role and harmonize its activity with that of the other beings without being overwhelmed by the vital or mental.

4. **Discipline and self-mastery**: The child needs to learn discipline and control of her physical body. As noted earlier, such self-mastery helps the body's consciousness to unfold and evolve. Discipline of the physical body also aids the child in the development of strength, dexterity, endurance, and grace.

Self-mastery of the body helps the child to develop confidence in her abilities and courage in her actions. It also assists the development of the will.

The child can learn discipline and self-mastery through participation in movement, dance, gymnastics, and team sports.

5. **Strength and fitness, with dexterity and control**: The child needs daily involvement in activities such as movement, dance, and sports, which help her to grow strong and fit while developing her coordination, dexterity, and endurance. The goal is a physical being that incorporates strength with suppleness, power with control.

6. **Grace, beauty, and harmony**: The child needs to learn harmony among the parts of her physical body and grace in their movement. "In every human being there is the possibility of establishing a harmony among the different parts of the body and different movements when the body is in action. . . . The human body that undergoes a rational method of physical culture from the beginning of its existence can realise its own harmony and thus be fit to express beauty."[46] The child should aspire to beauty not to

please others or gain fame but "for the love of beauty itself."[46] Beauty in the grace and harmony of the physical body is the manifestation of a spiritual value, "for beauty is the ideal which physical life has to realize."[46] The experience of harmony in the physical body also relates to moral education, as discussed below.

7. **Relaxation**: "To know how to relax the muscles and nerves is an art which should be taught to children even when very young."[47] The learning of such skills gives the child greater control over the energies of the body. It also helps her to learn about her own inner rhythms and to discharge negative energy and replace it with positive energy when she needs to do so.

The child's participation in individual athletics and dance and in team sports furthers the unfoldment of the physical being as described earlier. It also plays an important role in the education of the vital being. Dance, movement, gymnastics, and other individual athletics aid the development of the will. Team sports help the child to learn cooperation and fair play and can contribute to her moral education.

VITAL BEING

The vital being is the seat of the life force, of power and energy, of emotion and dynamism, and of appetites and desires. Richard explains that "the vital in man's being is a despotic and exacting tyrant. It is a master that is satisfied by nothing and its demands have no limit."[48] This quality of the vital being makes its training "the most indispensable"[48] aspect of the child's education, for an untrained vital being fills the child with wild and chaotic impulses, emotions, and desires that severely obstruct her growth.

The aim of the education of the vital being is "to become conscious and gradually master of one's character."[49] Aurobindo explains that this process of education must focus on two tasks: the training of the vital energies for the building of character and will, that is, moral education; and the education of the aesthetic sensibilities of the child. These two aspects of the vital being are interrelated, and so are the paths of their training. Also the successful education of the vital being depends on the concurrent education of the physical and mental beings.

MORAL EDUCATION

Most philosophies of moral education address the negative characteristics of the vital energies—the potentially limitless wants, appetites, and desires and the great power of emotions such as fear, hate, and jealousy—by advocating suppression, coercion, asceticism, and/or abstinence. While offering some control over the harmful potential of the vital being, each of these strategies in some way limits or violates the vital being's positive potential for unfoldment and thus hinders the growth of the child as a whole person.

Aurobindo describes a different kind of approach to moral education that relies on awareness, sublimation, inaction, and transcendence and that includes the following elements:

- Helping the child first to learn to become conscious of her desires and impulses. Helping her become conscious of her emotions in the same way.

- Empowering the child by helping her will to awaken and become focused, so she can use it to direct her desires, impulses, and emotions.

- Helping the child learn to sublimate the energy of her vital being through aesthetic and sensuous expression.

- Helping the child learn when it is appropriate just to be silent and refuse to act in any way.

- Helping the child learn the practice of a spiritual discipline through which she can learn to transcend the desires, impulses, and emotions that she does not choose to enact.

"The child must be taught to observe himself, to note his reactions and impulses and their causes, to become a clear-sighted witness of his desires, his movements of violence and passion, his instincts of possession, appropriation and domination."[50] The child can learn this skill of self-observation through her first steps in the practice of a spiritual discipline. Such practice can help her learn to witness her inner and outer self. The more conscious she can become of her vital expressions from the vantage of her own inner **witness consciousness**, the more effectively she will be able to direct, sublimate, and eventually transcend them when she evolves to levels at which she is capable of these actions.

What can help the child and youth gain these inner capabilities along with her development of a witness consciousness through spiritual practice is the unfoldment of her will. Within its energies, the vital being includes an aspiration to the perfection of the divine. This aspiration can be awakened in the child and then manifested as will, the inner capacity to act in alignment with one's conscious and centered choices. Will plays a major role in many positive qualities that the child needs to develop, including endurance, resourcefulness, truthfulness, courage, respect for others, and loyalty to duty.

The teacher can help the child develop her will by sharing the example and influence of her own clear will. The development of the will is also aided by activities that require attention and concentration, for example, handicrafts and fine arts as well as disciplined physical activities. Aurobindo stresses that the unfoldment and empowerment of the will depends upon ongoing practice, on "methodical and progressive exercise."[51] Pavitra notes that the free progress system of education creates a learning environment in which the child's will is awakened and in which she is engaged in the exercise of her will in an ongoing and continuous way.

Once the child has begun to gain power through her will, she can learn to sublimate her vital energies through aesthetic and sensuous expression. An important capability of the aesthetic faculty, if well developed, is the purification of the emotions and desires. The child can learn to purify her vital energies through her conscious enactment of sublimation by the expression of these energies in dance, music, painting, poetry, and other artistic forms.

The child and youth can also learn the willed power of choosing to be silent and not act in any way, to witness her desires or wants yet choose not to move toward their fulfillment.

In the next step in her moral education, the practice of a spiritual discipline can help the child and youth learn to transcend the emotions and desires that she does not wish to express. Rather than suppressing them or even sublimating them into aesthetic forms, the practice of such a discipline can help the person learn to experience her desires and emotions fully within herself, without acting upon them in any way, and then move beyond them toward a clear, inner space. Such a discipline can help her purify and refine her emotions and desires as she chooses.

Central to this systematic approach to the education of the child's vital being is the ongoing attention and involvement of the teacher. The teacher must bring an evolved will of her own to this task, capable of persistence and endurance. The teacher must also engage the child's heart and psychic being in this process by becoming the child's ally, her moral guide. Yet she must teach only by suggesting and inviting, never by commanding or imposing. Part of her responsibility is to offer the child a moral example through her own actions. She must also provide the child with heroic moral figures from literature and history whose stories can inspire the child to emulation.

Even given the experience of the best education of her vital being, it is inevitable and necessary that the child will commit moral errors. What is important is how she is treated once she has committed such errors. For her to learn from these experiences, she must not be scolded or punished, if possible. Scolding breaks the calm of the teacher who scolds, and scolding and punishment arouse fear in the child, which interferes with her growth. Instead of scolding, the teacher should point out the child's error to her calmly and give her an opportunity to try again. Richard suggests, "When a child has made a mistake, see that he confesses it to you spontaneously and frankly; and when he has confessed, make him understand with kindness and affection what was wrong in his movement so that he should not repeat it."[52] Scolding is to be used only with a clear and definite purpose when such an action is indispensable.

Aurobindo emphasizes that moral growth comes through the

experience of freedom to make mistakes and learn from them. Only with this kind of experience can the child find the higher law and divine influence within herself that ultimately bring all moral evolution. If the child has "bad qualities, bad habits, bad sam-skaras (associations), whether of mind or body, he should not be treated harshly as a delinquent, but encouraged to get rid of them. He should be encouraged to think of them not as sins or offences, but as symptoms of a curable disease, alterable by a steady and sustained effort of the will."[53] To be guided by this insight, the teacher needs to see the child's negative qualities, habits, and associations as characteristics that she can help the child to change. She must view each child as worthy of her care and effort and genuinely expect each child to evolve morally.

Finally, in her concern with moral education, the teacher must be careful not to reject unformed virtues as faults. "The wildness and recklessness of many young natures are only the overflowings of excessive strength, greatness, and nobility. They should be purified, not discouraged."[53]

AESTHETIC EDUCATION

The second task in the training of the vital being, the education of the child's aesthetic sensibilities, is both based upon and interwoven with the education of the senses. The education of the aesthetic sensibilities involves "the cultivation of discrimination and the aesthetic sense, the capacity to choose and take up what is beautiful and harmonious, simple, healthy, and pure."[54] From an early age, the child must learn to "add artistic taste and refinement to (the) power and precision . . ."[54] of her senses. With the guidance of the teacher, she must learn to appreciate and to "love beautiful, lofty, healthy and noble things, whether in nature or in human creation."[54]

With intentional training of the sensibilities integrated with that of the senses, "the sense organs may be so cultivated as to attain a precision and a power in their functioning far greater than what is normally expected of them."[54] They can achieve a subtlety and power that can, in turn, enrich the child's sensibilities.

The education of the child's aesthetic sensibilities has several powerful effects on her moral unfoldment. Aurobindo explains that an

> . . . indispensable activity of the sense of beauty is the powerful help it has given to the formation of morality. We do not ordinarily recognize how largely our sense of virtue is a sense of the beautiful in conduct and our sense of sin is a sense of ugliness and deformity in conduct.[37]

As noted previously, such training of the child's aesthetic capabilities helps her learn to sublimate her vital energies and express them through the arts. A developed sense of aesthetics also positively influences the mind, because the child's appreciation of beauty and harmony in the outer world brings habits of this quality to her mental activity.

A third result of this kind of education involves its effect on the psychic being. When the child learns to appreciate beauty and harmony in the world, she experiences joy in response to them. This quality of joy is largely spiritual in nature. Its experience helps both to bring out the psychic being within the child and to bring the child to a greater awareness of her psychic being.

MENTAL BEING

The purpose of the mental being's education is to train its various faculties to unfold to their potential and learn to work together harmoniously. These faculties include the following:

- **The faculties of expression**: The child must develop her faculties of expression first through the mastery of her native language and then through the learning of other languages. The learning of languages, particularly at a young age, helps the mind to unfold and avoid rigidity in its forms.

- **The faculties of memory**: The child can develop her memory through daily practice of its skills. She must not be asked to remember information by mindless rote but be engaged in challenges to her memory that arouse her curiosity and enthusiasm. One kind of practice involves asking the child to notice and remember similarities and differences that she observes in the natural world around her. Such practice can also help her to develop a scientific outlook.

- **The faculties of observation**: The child needs to learn to bring all six senses into play when she is engaged in mental knowing. She must also learn to bring attention and concentration to her observation when such is appropriate.

- **The faculties of discrimination**: The child needs to learn to compare, contrast, and differentiate. She must learn to bring all of her senses and her faculties of observation into play to help guide her as she discriminates.

- **The faculties of concentration**: The child must learn the skills of attention and concentration and cultivate the habit of receptivity. This learning requires ongoing practice and relates to the training of the faculties of observation, the training of the senses, and the learning of discipline by the physical body.

- **The faculties of inner silence**: Through concentration training and the practice of a spiritual discipline, the child can learn to to quiet the mind's inner dialogue and gain mental silence.

- **The faculties of imagination**: By opening herself to her inner silence, the child can experience her imagination. She must learn to be conscious of her mental imagery and gain an appreciation of its potential as a source of inner knowing, as an ally to her will, and as an opening to experiencing the soul in things, the spiritual life that pervades the world.

- **The faculties of intuition**: By practicing the inner silence, the child can open herself to intuitive knowing from the higher planes of being. Some of this knowing will come through the imagination, while other aspects will flow through different vehicles. The child must learn to recognize her intuitive knowing and discriminate it from less valid images and understandings.

- **The faculties of will**: While the will is primarily a vital function, it does include a mental component. The child must learn to bring her mental energies into alignment with her will and avoid the inner conflicts that arise when the mind and will have different purposes.

- **The faculties of judgment**: The child must learn to know and trust her inner judgment. She can learn this quality of discrimination about her judgment by comparing her judgment with that of others and learning from her experience both of being "right" and being "wrong." To gain this discrimination, the child must also learn not to be attached to the results of her judgment: to judge correctly but not take pride either in the accuracy of her judgment or in whatever results from it. Another part of this task involves the child in learning to step away from her own judgment in a disagreement with another person for the purpose of exploring that person's view of things. The more she can learn not to be attached to her own judgment, the more her mind will be able to appreciate the genuine complexity of the world as well as the limitations of her own mental judging. One mental skill that the child can learn to aid her judgment is the drawing of analogies. Another related skill that she can learn is knowing when it is appropriate not to judge but only to be silent and attentive.

- **The faculties of reason and logic**: The young person needs to learn to use her capacities for reason while recognizing their limitations. She must learn to infer from facts and evaluate her inferences, to deduce and induce, and to move from example to rule and from rule to formal science. The young person needs to gain experience in approaching ideas and problems from various directions. A part of this involves her learning to see and appreciate points of view opposite to her own. The young person also needs to be engaged in learning to synthesize apparently contradictory views by expressing a thesis, exploring its antithesis, and eventually articulating a synthesis that unites the thesis and antithesis on a higher level. These kinds of experiences will help the young person to develop a richer, more supple way of thinking. They will also lead her to discover the relativity of reason and the ways in which reason can be employed to support contradictory views. Eventually this understanding of the relativity of reason and logic will help to motivate the young person to search for a more profound knowing within her psychic being.

For the education of the mind, the teacher must engage the child in a naturalistic way, always drawing on the child's own interests and curiosity. The child needs first to apply her mental faculties in relation to physical things. According to her own unfoldment, she can move from things to words and concrete ideas, and much later, on to the abstract. Aurobindo stresses that it is the teacher's responsibility to nurture the evolution of the child's mind, not hurrying it but respecting its own developmental timing while seeking to widen and enrich the child's thinking at every particular stage of her growth.

The training of the mind is very much dependent on the training of the physical and vital beings. The mind needs its freedom to choose for itself, to explore and discover its own truth. Yet the physical and vital beings can easily confuse or misguide the mental being. The mind can experience genuine freedom in its unfoldment only if the physical being is disciplined and the vital being is clear, ordered, and fulfilled.

A specific way in which mental education is related to physical and vital education involves the child's development of the qualities of expansion, wideness, complexity, and richness in all of her mental life. When the child is engaged in the training of her senses and her aesthetic sensibilities simultaneous to her mental education, she can much more readily develop these qualities. A rich, complex, and expanded thought requires an aesthetic component that can only unfold when the child is encouraged to connect the physical, the vital, and the mental. In addition, as noted above, the child's development of her aesthetic sensibilities, her appreciation of beauty and harmony, brings these kinds of qualities into her mental life as well.

Another aspect of mental education focuses on the child's learning the strengths and limitations of the mental being. The mind does not formulate essential knowledge. It receives such knowledge from higher levels of being and articulates it. In its ability to receive and articulate knowledge, the mind's greatest power is the skill it can gather for learning. The task of educating the mind, then, does not involve the accumulation of information. Rather, it centers on the child's learning how to learn: how to gather old knowledge, how to find out new knowledge, and how to apply both kinds of knowledge to specific situations. A related aspect of this learning is the child's need to discover the unique nature of her own mind, for mental capacities vary greatly among individuals.

PSYCHIC BEING AND SPIRIT

Psychic education, the education of the soul or psychic being, involves the person's knowing of the divine immanent within herself. Spiritual education, the education of the spirit, involves the person's complete surrender to the transcendent divinity. Psychic education must precede spiritual education, as the education of the psychic being prepares the person for the education of the spirit. Most people younger than 21 years of age are not sufficiently unfolded to be directly engaged in spiritual education, but every child and youth has need of psychic education.

The teacher is the key to the process of psychic education. She must be aware of the psychic being within the child and know its inherent goodness, light, and love. To gain this awareness and knowledge, the teacher must be engaged in her own spiritual practice and thus in nurturing her own psychic and perhaps spiritual beings. The most powerful teaching she can give to the child is through her influence and her example as these relate to her own psychic and spiritual life. Empowered by her own spirituality, the teacher can invoke soul qualities in the child's consciousness and behavior.

The young child is often very open to her own psychic being and frequently expresses soul qualities—love, truth, beauty, nobility—in her words and actions. When adults disregard or belittle these expressions and/or draw the child into an experience of schooling that focuses only on narrowly defined mental faculties, the child learns to mimic the adult attitudes and distance herself from these soul energies. As Richard notes, "I have known children who were much more conscious of their psychic being at the age of five than at fourteen, and more at fourteen than at twenty five."[55]

It is the teacher's responsibility to encourage and validate the child's expression of psychic qualities. She must also teach the child about the psychic plane. "From the very earliest age the child must be taught that there is a reality within—within themselves, within the earth, within the universe, and that himself, the earth, and the universe exist only as a function of this truth."[56] In these ways, the teacher can help the child to nurture and expand her openness to her own psychic energies.

In addition, there are three other practices through which the child can grow more aware of and open to her psychic being:

- From an early age, the child needs to learn and practice a spiritual discipline through which she can learn to quiet the mind, experience the inner silence and the witness consciousness, and grow more and more open to her psychic being.

- The giving of oneself freely to the service of others opens one to the psychic being. Through her own actions, the teacher needs to show the value of service to the child. Then, helped by her teacher's example and influence, the child can choose to give service to others and, by this gift, open more to her psychic being.

- The arts are another way of opening to a consciousness of universal harmony and unity, to a perception of the divine. Experiencing beauty and harmony through artistic expression and experience can also help the child to know and explore her psychic being.

In their discussions of psychic education, Aurobindo and his students distinguish spiritual teaching from religious teaching. For them, religious teaching means the instruction, and often the indoctrination, of the child in a system of religious belief that is specific to an historical tradition and that usually claims primacy for this tradition over other religious teachings. In contrast, spiritual teaching, which in this context refers both to psychic education and the education of the spirit, recognizes the essential validity yet partial truth in all religious traditions but helps the child to transcend such traditions and discover that which is divine through her own experience. Richard notes that

> religious teaching belongs to the past and halts progress. Spiritual teaching is the teaching of the future—it illumines the consciousness and prepares it for the future realisation. Spiritual teaching is above religious and strives towards a global Truth. It teaches us to enter into direct relations with the Divine.[57]

The education of the five beings is a lifelong task, not only a work for childhood and youth. But the quality with which this work is carried out through the first two decades of life has an extremely powerful effect on the person's unfoldment. The education of the physical body begins first, soon after birth, and continues when the vital education commences. "These phases of education succeed each other in a chronological way following the growth of the individual. This, however, does not mean that one should replace each other but that all must continue, completing each other, till the end of life."[58]

Tasks of the Teacher

According to Aurobindo's vision, the qualities of the teacher—who she is as a person, how she organizes the learning environment, and how she behaves as she interacts with her students—are the most important factors in education. The teacher must be on the same path of unfoldment as that which she seeks for her students. "The teacher must himself progress if he wants the students to progress, must not remain satisfied either with what he is or what he knows."[59] She must be striving to unfold in each of her beings: to create a strong and supple physical body, a harmonious vital being with a clear and powerful will, a developed yet calm mind that can enter the inner silence, and a soul that has emerged as a living fact within her person.

The teacher must seek to make her personality "integral, marked by wide sympathies, and deep central selfhood."[60] As much as she can, the teacher must try to be what she wants her students to become, for as Richard explains, "you cannot ask of a person what you cannot do yourself."[61]

The first task of the teacher, then, is to tend to her own unfoldment. As she does so, the teacher becomes a worthy example for her students, and they in turn love and admire her. "The [child's] love of a teacher is of a more creative kind, inspiring respect and admiration."[62] Such love can powerfully motivate children and youth to model themselves on the example of their teacher. In addition, as the teacher gains knowledge of her own psychic being, she can help her students open to their psychic reality and discover their inner guidance.

The second task of the teacher is to approach and organize her teaching so that she is always a learner as well as a teacher. "Each teaching needs to be approached with dual purpose: the desire to teach and equally the desire to learn."[63] The third task of the teacher is to be genuinely and profoundly available to her students when they seek her out for help, support, guidance, influence, and evaluation.

The fourth task of the teacher is to create, organize, and maintain a free progress learning environment that is appropriate for the growth of her students. To accomplish this, she must have "the ability to see and think as a child in a given situation . . ."[64] and to create an environment that "awakens curiosity and inquisitiveness and provides an incentive to the growing child."[64]

The final task of the teacher is to "organize and maintain the good will of the students. For this purpose the teacher must carefully observe the behaviour of every student and detect any sign of boredom, fatigue or restlessness, any hitch in the normal functioning in the class. He must find the cause of the disturbance and remove the obstruction."[65]

When the teacher can accomplish each of these tasks, she will interact with and cooperate with her students on every level of their being. Her guidance of them will meet the criteria of true teaching, for the most profound purpose of teaching is to act as evolutionary energy, to help the child know her true self and evolve.

The Learning Environment and Curriculum

The learning environment and the curriculum compose the second most important factor in education, although they are dependent on the first because they are created by the teacher. Aurobindo and his students conceive of the learning environment and the curriculum as two different aspects of the same whole. In a profound sense, the environment for learning is the curriculum.

The child's "foremost need . . . is that his environment should be well supplied with all kinds of objects suited to his stage of development. . . . Their aim is to satisfy an immediate and actual need of the child, not a future need as anticipated by the parent or teacher."[66] The desired qualities to be embodied in the learning environment are richness, diversity, appropriateness, and the right degree of order. "An environment which is ill-organized or too rich causes often in the child a feeling of insecurity and bewilderment."[67]

One curricular element that Aurobindo stresses is hand work. Such experience fosters the education of the child's physical body, her emotions, and her will and helps the child to learn attention and concentration. Children and youth also need to be engaged in practical work in an ongoing way, so they learn the dignity of work, of doing things with care and skill, and gain a sense of what they can contribute to others and themselves.

Academic subjects are also of great importance and can be effectively learned within the free progress system. Such learning can be encouraged both by providing the learning environment with subject-oriented materials and resources that are appropriate to the child's level of unfoldment and by guiding the child toward the exploration and manipulation of these materials and resources. The teacher should encourage the child to explore one subject at a time. To begin with, she can help the child to focus on a subject's nature as a whole system. For example, mathematics is a system of relations. History is a systemic record of evolution. Ecology is the system of the physical environment. Physical science is a system of the nature of the physical plane. The teacher can also encourage the child to explore the interrelationships among the elements of a subject and, as appropriate, the ways in which subjects interconnect. For example, geometry directly relates to design and eventually to art.

In the learning of academic subjects as well as that of others, the teacher must stay in her role as a guide and helper. She must help the child to open to her own inner guidance and support and assist the child in following this guidance wherever it leads her.

Aurobindo's Way of Knowing

Aurobindo Ghose knew the worlds of spirit and of science. He understood, celebrated, and, in his view, practiced the scientific method. And for five decades he engaged in the practice of yoga and meditation and gained access to the wisdom that these experiences offered.

Aurobindo's primary access to knowledge was through his own spiritual path, his yogic and meditative practice, and the illuminations that they brought to him. His unfoldment carried him to four major spiritual realizations: his experience of samadhi in 1907; his vision of Krishna in the Alipore jail in 1908; his "vision of the supreme Reality as a multiform entity"[68] in Chandernagore in 1910; and his "day of Siddhi" in 1926. He learned about the nature of human beings, the process of human becoming, and the purposes and practices of education from these experiences but also from his daily meditation and yoga. As he explained, "I had only to write down in terms of the intellect all that I had observed and come to know in practicing yoga daily."[69]

Yet each experience of spiritual insight Aurobindo subjected to the consideration of his reason, to what he saw as a scientific evaluation. Gabriel Monod-Herzen, a French physicist, explains:

> That which Aurobindo announces and describes is not a theory which pleases him or which is to him personal: it is the truth he has experienced. This is precisely the scientific attitude and Sri Aurobindo knew this, since he himself said that his room was his laboratory. There he tried everything, and verified it before offering it to us.[70]

But how can the difference between science as a public activity and the seeming subjectivity of spiritual practice be reconciled? "When, if ever, does personal experience which is unique and individual reveal truth that is universal and valid for all men?"[71] Aurobindo explains that the individual's inner experience does convey universal truth when his "personal consciousness has been thrown open to become a recipient of the Divine and an instrument for communicating its influence."[71]

According to Aurobindo, an individual consciousness that is in touch with the divine energy is marked by four qualities:

- A profound and pervasive coherence and harmony brought into personal experience and human relations;

- The ongoing experience of learning and expressing truths through the individual consciousness that are recognized by others as well as the individual as universal;

- The ongoing experience of a unifying joy within, not a pleasure from the gratification of the senses but the experience of joy that arises within the spirit from an inner harmony; and

- The "union with the Divine reveals the possibilities or potentialities of the individual consciousness. . . . Spiritual union enables man to overcome egocentric desire and purpose, and hence to eliminate causes of conflict between man and man."[72]

Reason and scientific attitude are helpful for evaluating spiritual knowledge, but the ultimate claim to validity for Aurobindo's kind of knowing lies not with the intellect but with its own identity, as Aurobindo explains:

When it is claimed, therefore, that "coherence and harmony," "universality," "joy," and the disclosing of "the possibilities of personality" are characters indicating the truth of genuine spiritual experiences, we are aware that these lack the clarity of scientific explanations. Nevertheless, the fact that experience of the Divine does infuse these characters into human experience brings to those who enjoy them convictions of its truth.[73]

6

A VISIT
TO
THE SRI AUROBINDO ASHRAM

Pondicherry lies one hundred and six miles south of Madras on India's eastern coast along the Bay of Bengal. From the mid-nineteenth century through the early 1950s, it was a French-ruled colony within British-dominated southern India. Since then Pondicherry has been a district within the Indian nation. By Indian standards, it is a midsized city, with the urban core and its outlying villages home to about half a million people.

The Sri Aurobindo Ashram is the most notable institution in Pondicherry. It consists of about four hundred structures throughout the area, and its central buildings and courtyards dominate a forty-square-block area to the northeast of the city's commercial center, between the seasonally dry canal and the Bay. Other buildings and grounds are spread through the district. The facilities of the Ashram include the Main Building, with offices and a courtyard in which the graves of Sri Aurobindo and Mira Richard are located; the several buildings of the International Centre for Education and its various sports facilities and playing fields, which are used not only by students but by all of the Ashram members; archives and a library; essential services such as maintenance, electricity, water, and sanitation; farms, a granary, and rice, cooking oil, and flour mills; industries such as a paper factory, a foundry, a sheet-metal works, and an automotive shop; craft shops such as weaving, batik, marbling, and incense making; print shops; several health care facilities, including an allopathic or Western scientific medical clinic, a homeopathic clinic, an Ayurvedic or traditional Indian medical clinic, and a nursing home; several dining halls and kitchens; various dormitory, hostel, and other lodging facilities; and many guest houses for visitors.

In 1985 the Ashram community consisted of about two

thousand people, about four hundred and twenty of whom were children and youths enrolled in the International Centre. This community included many Europeans and some Americans, although the great majority of Ashram members were Indian natives from all the different regions and peoples of India.

The Ashram is really a city-within-a-city, one that functions at essentially "modern" standards of living in terms of hygiene, diet, and culture, although without the "modern" propensity for the acquisition of material goods. People do have personal property, but these goods tend to be limited to relatively small amounts and items, such as clothes and books and bicycles. Ashram members display generally good health and high vitality, and many members of the community are in their seventies, eighties, or even nineties. The quality of life and good health enjoyed by Ashram members are particularly striking in contrast with the poverty and disease that rule the lives of so many of those living in Pondicherry outside the Ashram.

The Ashram has only a few proscriptions: no criminal behavior; no use of alcohol, drugs, or cigarettes; and no sexual behavior. As a duty, everyone must contribute to the work and livelihood of the community. Also, everyone who is younger than sixty-five must take part in daily physical activity, because Aurobindo taught that physical wellness is an important element in the whole of spiritual unfoldment. Beyond these few rules and duties, the Ashram demands no fixed behaviors from its members, either in terms of material duties or spiritual practices. As Aurobindo taught, each person's life and spiritual practice is her own responsibility. As Paru Patil, the Registrar of the International Centre of Education, explained to me, beyond these few rules, "nothing is ever imposed upon anybody, nothing. Even when Mother and Sri Aurobindo were there and they were the accepted masters of the Ashram, they never imposed anything. This yoga is a free yoga, that everybody has to find his own path of development, his own rhythm of development."[1]

Many members live collectively in dormitories and hostels and eat in dining halls. Others live in private residences. Everyone works several hours each day, usually three or four: cooking, teaching, gardening, cleaning, editing, farming, or whatever her or his work responsibility is. For Ashram members, the amount of work expected from each leaves considerable time for reflection, study, meditation, social life, and other activities.

In keeping with the spirit of personal freedom and responsibility as taught by Aurobindo, there is no demand that people believe any particular doctrine or dogma. People come to live at the Ashram because they are drawn to the teachings of Sri Aurobindo and Mira Richard. But once they have come, they remain personally in control of and thus responsible for their lives and their spiritual growth. Of the several dozen people with whom I conversed, all share considerable agreement in terms of their worldviews and orientations, but they also express differences that are clearly the products of free choice and expression. Unlike many other ashrams, the Aurobindo Ashram is not a closed community but an open one.

This Tuesday morning in mid-October I arrive at the main building of the Ashram's International Centre of Education on Marine Street, park my bike, and enter the gate. The main building is a two-story stucco structure built along the four sides of an entire city block. The stucco is painted gray, with white trim. Brownish water stains mar the paint here and there on the outer wall. The main gate into the complex is lined with bike racks, filled with hundreds of bicycles.

The inner area of the complex includes one large courtyard and two small ones as well as an arm of the building that extends into the yard, the teacher's room, open on two sides. All the windows in the structure are open as well, a reflection of the year-round warmth of southern India. Each courtyard is attractively decorated with stone walks, trees and flowers and shrubs, and grassy areas. The large courtyard is particularly beautiful in its design, featuring a round marble lily pond, with a trellis above it rich with red and white flowers and deep-green vines; an oval brick stage and platform before a large grassy area; and several borders with many flowering bushes and trees in bloom.

I walk to the Registrar's office and after announcing myself to her secretary, sit in an outer office area that opens both to the large courtyard and to one of the smaller ones. As I wait, I notice that almost all of the men who pass by are wearing shirts and pants. A few elderly men are dressed in traditional clothing. Many of the boys wear shorts and shirts. Others wear trousers. Some of the women and girls wear dresses, while others are clothed in saris. Everyone wears sandals on their feet out of doors and leaves them by the door when they enter a building. To the side of every entrance I see dozens and dozens of seemingly identical sandals placed neatly in rows. On the walls in each room that I can see are pictures of Aurobindo and of Mira Richard.

I walk into one of the smaller courtyards to look at a bed of flowers, and through an external window I see a small brown goat drinking from the gutter in the street outside. A few feet beyond the goat a white-haired woman in a torn red sari sits in the shade on the sidewalk next to a sleeping man. Farther up the block a woman sells fruits and nuts from a cart. Beyond her stand a few of the ubiquitous bike rickshaw drivers and their vehicles.

As I return to the waiting area, the class period ends, and dozens of children and youths of various ages pour out into the large courtyard. The feeling in the air is one of excitement. The faces I see amid the rush are alert and vibrant.

In a few minutes I am called into the Registrar's office. Paru Patil, the Registrar, greets me and asks me to sit across from her. I have already corresponded with Miss Patil about my visit. Now I remind her of my interests, and she welcomes me to the Centre and reminds me of the school's rules for visitors. Many people come to the Ashram each day who wish to observe classes in the school. Although observation was allowed in earlier years, eventually the teachers agreed to bar visitors from their classrooms because the number of visitors had grown so large that such observation had become disruptive to the learning process. Only the kindergarten continues to allow visitors. However, I was welcome to talk with teachers and with secondary and college students and to observe in the kindergarten.

I ask Miss Patil to tell me a little more about her responsibilities. The Registrar is not a director, she explains, but really more of a coordinator. While the school was started and guided for many years by Mira Richard and then had a director for some years after her death, now its direction comes from the collaborative effort of its faculty and registrar. Miss Patil tells me that she came to the Ashram as a child in 1945 and was a student in some of the first classes in the school. From 1952 to 1970, she was a teacher of French and English literature. In 1970, she began to serve as an aide to the registrar and then moved into that position several years later. She is a stately woman in her fifties, about five feet four inches in height, whose jet black hair is beginning to whiten. She wears a purple-and-white sari with a white top. Her presence conveys dignity and a keen intelligence. Her smile is warm and open, and her gaze is piercing yet not uncomfortable.

This year the Centre has 420 students, Miss Patil explains. They range in age from 3 to 21 years. Almost all of them have been brought here by their parents, because the parents are students of Sri Aurobindo and Mira Richard. And most of them began their educations at the Centre before they were 6 years of age. They come from all over India as well as from Europe.

There are 115 teachers in the Centre, she continues, and classes are no larger than ten students at most. The Centre is housed in four buildings: this one, a similar complex across the street, the kindergarten building two blocks away, and the college program a block from the kindergarten.

I ask about the structure of the school, and she explains that that there are four sections: three years of kindergarten, with children from age 3 to 6; five years of the primary program, called "The Future," with children age 6 through 12; three years of the lower secondary program, called "Progress," with youths from age 12 through 15; three years of the higher secondary, called "Towards Perfection," with youths from age 15 through 18; and three years of the higher or college program, called "Knowledge," with youths from age 18 through 21.

Miss Patil also describes the daily schedule for children and youth older than kindergarten age: classes from 7:45 A.M. to 11:30 A.M.; a break from classes until 1:40 P.M., with this time used for eating lunch and a variety of artistic, craft, and other activities; classes from 1:40 P.M. to 4:45 P.M.; and physical education activities from 5:00 PM to 6:00 P.M. There is no homework for the time beyond school hours. All of the school work is done during the day.

We talk about whom I might interview and when I can visit the kindergarten. When we have arrived at a tentative schedule, she agrees to make the arrangements for me. I thank her for her help and ask if I can come and interview her at the end of my visit. "Of course," she replies.

Two days later I stand in the courtyard of the kindergarten building at 7:40 A.M. Some of the children have already arrived and are romping around the courtyard in the morning light, skipping and singing and climbing on the bars. Others arrive as I survey the building, a two-story stucco structure much like many others in the Ashram complex, and its adjacent yard, partly paved with stone, the rest covered with a grassy lawn, part of which is filled with an array of playground equipment and a sandbox. The beach is only a block away to the east, and when I look in that direction, I see a large flock of gulls flying lazily northward.

The kindergarten has three classes, organized by age. Each has about fifteen children and two teachers. At 7:45 A.M. the teachers, all women dressed in colorful saris and seemingly in their late twenties and early thirties, call the children into the building to begin the school day. The middle and oldest groups gather in a circle on a rug before a large portrait of Mira Richard. These children are 5 and 6 years of age. The teachers greet the children warmly and then engage them in a minute of silence. All of the children sit quietly, most with evident concentration. Then one of the teachers leads the group in a morning invocation that all speak together. They talk in French, so I cannot understand the content of what is said, but the feeling tone is clear: a sense of togetherness, of communion.

As I soon discover, all of the kindergarten classes are conducted in French, except for lessons in other languages such as Sanskrit. Indeed I learn later that instruction in science, mathematics, and French literature are conducted in French throughout all age levels of the Centre's program. Other subjects are conducted in English. Students also take classes to support and further develop their proficiency in their native Indian language, their "mother tongue," such as Hindi, Tamil, Oriye, and the dozen other major languages spoken in India.

At the end of the invocation, the older group leaves, and the teachers gather the middle group in a circle and engage the children in a spirited group conversation. What becomes evident to me quickly, partly because I cannot understand the meaning of the words spoken and so must focus on the structure of the discussion, is that this is a language lesson in the form of a conversation. The children are animated and vocal, and mostly they wait their turn to speak, although some burst out of turn in their enthusiasm. When such an outburst takes place, the teachers gently remind the child to wait and go on with the discussion.

After about twenty-five minutes the teachers involve the children in two minutes of silent concentration. Eleven of the children are immersed in their own silence. The other four play with their toes, fidget, or look around the room or through the open area to the courtyard. As I follow their gaze, I notice for the first time that an entire side of the room is open to the courtyard, allowing the breeze from the Bay to find its way inside. The room is high-ceilinged, as are all the classrooms and offices I visit in the Centre. One wall of the room is covered with shelves and cupboards full of picture books, wooden construction materials, and art supplies. Toward the end of the period of concentration, a girl gets up quietly and heads off to the bathroom. Evidently there is no need to ask permission.

At the end of the two minutes, the teachers engage the children in an art project, and I move from this room to one across the hall, so I can observe the youngest group. There are fourteen children in this class, all 4-year-olds now although many of them were 3 when they first came to school. The class has two women teachers. As I enter, a man with an angular face and deep black, curly hair is beginning a lesson in a language that I don't recognize but later learn to be Sanskrit. He wears a white shirt and shorts and tells a story with many sound effects that the children are called on to repeat. Then he adds hand and arm motions, coordinated with the sounds. One little boy turns away from him, and after a minute the teacher moves to the boy and engages him in one of the movements. The boy smiles and turns back to the group. The story goes on for nearly twenty minutes, with the teacher maintaining the children's involvement throughout. Eventually the hand and arm movements evolve into a variety of whole body postures, which I recognize as evocations of various animals but which also look like yoga positions. Then the positions evolve into a kind of dance. The teacher and children snap their fingers, walking forward and backward in a circle, and repeating a chant. Soon they are all running around in a wild finale, and then at a signal from the man, they launch into exquisite collapses onto their mats. The Sanskrit lesson is over.

Now it is almost 9:00 A.M., and I move on to the oldest class, where I watch the children intently work on paintings and drawings of scenes they saw in a trip the previous day to an Ashram farm not far away. Some of the scenes seem to be realistic, while others are primarily imaginary. All of the art work is vivid and rich with color, and the children stay engaged in their art throughout the half hour that I observe them. The teachers move easily around the room, responding to requests and offering support and encouragement.

A few minutes before 9:30 A.M. the teachers engage the children in cleaning up their art materials. The pictures are carefully placed on a shelf, and the children move out into a back corner of the courtyard to join the other groups for a snack and a few minutes of quiet time, followed by nearly an hour of free play in the courtyard.

A little after 10:30 A.M. the teachers call the children back into the building. During the final hour of the morning I move from class to class and watch a wide array of activities, including games, art activities, songs, conversations, and a pantomime. Mostly the children are in small groups.

At 11:30 A.M. the program ends for the day with a ritual closing similar in structure to the beginning. As I sit outside afterward and wait for my appointment with Kala Patel, I reflect on my morning's observation. On the whole, I recall, the children were all engaged and active throughout the morning. There was a feeling of familial relationship within each group, and the children were comfortable and happy within that feeling. Yet they were not "perfect." When a child misbehaved, one of the teachers got her attention to put an end to the unacceptable behavior and then drew the child back into the group or activity. There was no scolding or punishment.

Kala Patel arrives a few minutes later, and we sit in the shade in the courtyard of the kindergarten building. Miss Patel is a woman who looks to be in her late fifties or early sixties. She wears a sparkling white sari with a blue-flower pattern on its edges. Her forehead is smooth skinned, but deep lines under her eyes give an indication of her age. Miss Patel's face is sandy brown in color. Her eyes are clear and lively.

I ask Kala Patel to tell me something about herself. "Well," she replies, "I'm here since 1946, and with children I started working in 1954. For the last five years I'm not teaching. I don't have direct contact with the children, but I look after the kindergarten sections."

As she describes what this role involves, it becomes evident to me that Miss Patel's work includes supervising and supporting the active kindergarten teachers. "Can you tell me about the approach you use in the kindergarten?" I ask.

"It's what I call the motherly approach. That is, feeling and understanding what the child is feeling, and also feeling love for the child, love to work with children. Now maybe some gents can do this, but here the lady teachers have done this. And also our lessons are not prepared, there is not a syllabus. The teacher is free to have her own imagination. One aim is to make the child more or less fluent in French, to understand, and then, in the second and third years, to speak. The younger children can't express that much yet, but they do imbibe a lot of different ideas and things. They can't express that much in their mother tongue either. But they are always receiving. The teacher is always talking to them. The more you talk to the child, the more the child imbibes."

"Yes, I noticed that this morning," I say.

"So that is the main technique of teaching French, talking with the children all through the morning: in the groups, when they drink water, when they are resting, on trips. The teacher uses conversation as the medium of instruction."

"When a child first comes here, what is her or his experience usually like?"

"Well, it is different for each child. With some children, they get adjusted in two or three days. Some take a month or even longer. But, we don't hold them, keep them all together. In the beginning, they are in the courtyard. So, they are free. And the teacher will sit with a few of them and start playing with those who are quiet and want to work, who want to be in school. And the others are left to observe. After awhile, though it may take some days, the children come to join the teacher on their own. That way the child doesn't feel forced or have a fear of school."

When Miss Patel speaks about children, her face becomes even more animated, and her eyes sparkle. "Our aim for our children," she goes on, "is their all-around development, not just learning the language. So part of that development is their collective life with each other. Very often in the beginning, they have little quarrels, and they hit each other. Some children have a natural habit of hitting. Not that he wants to hit, but he has got a tendency to hit. So, we slowly try to eliminate all these things, try to see that they don't learn to tell a lie and make stories just to defend themselves. See, children do this to defend themselves. See, he has done something wrong, and, out of fear, he tells a lie. Now, we are conscious that these things are not developed. We never ask the child why you have done this. When you ask why, there is always a reply, always a plea. We just tell them, if you have a quarrel, say they're sorry and then I embrace or kiss them and we let them go. Those who are very loud or very naughty, we ask them to sit down quietly if they can't get controlled. So, you see, we don't ask them to explain. The child is not conscious really of telling a lie or stealing. It's impulsive in the child at this age. So we try to eliminate the child's fear, and they become spontaneous. Whatever the truth is, they can come and speak if they are not afraid that they'll be scolded or punished. Then children will come and say, 'I have done wrong but I have said sorry.' This is the frankness that comes if there is no fear. We are firm with them, but we don't throw anger on them. This helps to build their character to be truthful and straightforward."

I ask Miss Patel about some of the language instruction activities that I observed, and she explains, "We don't teach reading or writing. These children are too young for that. But what we do is preparation. Like, we take paper strips and write each child's name on a strip. We may write each letter in a different color. Then we show the name to the child as you show a picture of a flower or a cat or a dog. Immediately he says, 'this is a flower or a cat or a dog.' So they look at the paper strip, and you say it aloud, and the child knows the word as his name after a few times. And so they can learn each others' names, too. They don't know the letters, they know the words. So next time when we ask, pick up your name, they know it right away. And then slowly we work with the letters. All the names starting with "s" or "r" or "p," and then through all these sorts of games, they are made aware of the letters. So then we use flash cards with words for things that are all around, like table and chair and book and so on. We hold up the flash cards for the objects and say, now put this card for book on the book. And we play all kinds of games with them. And eventually they know the letters and are ready to start to read when the time is right.

"In the same way, we prepare for writing. They are given free writing and drawing, so to prepare their finger muscles, drawing with chalk, crayons, work with paint brushes, to use the fingers in the same way all the time. It is exercise. They learn to write their names, but they don't start writing really until they go to the primary classes.

"Let me tell you about a way we teach the French. In the beginning, we make the movements for the words, like I'm running, I'm walking, I'm jumping. If I only sit and tell the word, the child has no idea. These are only abstract words. So when they are first learning French, we do the movements for the word and we have the children do the movements as they say the word. And the teachers speak only in French. It takes about two months, and then the children can grasp the whole spoken language. We do the same thing with Sanskrit then.

"You know, we start with French in the kindergarten because French and English are our two mediums of instruction here in the Centre. We found that it's easier for children to learn French first and then go on to English. If you teach them English first, then it's more difficult for the child to go on to French."

"I know that Sri Aurobindo talks about the *inner teacher*," I say. "How does the kindergarten call forth the *inner teacher*?"

"Well, first there must be love for the child. That is the main principle to it. It is the love that helps the best in the child, the inner, to come out. And you know, we have tried some experiments in previous years. Gave the children full freedom, because some of the teachers wanted it. But Mother (Mira Richard) has said if you recall, til the age of 7 the child's mind is not developed. The child doesn't have reasoning. So when you give too much freedom, he goes with the natural instinct of—say, monkeys." Miss Patel laughs at the image, as do I. "Following it here, following it there, they sometimes don't know what to do. So after all our experiments, we came to what it is now. From quarter to eight until nine thirty, they are in a class with a teacher. Then they have an hour to let out all their energy, all their likes and dislikes, and shouting and running. In the the last hour they are more subdued. And the teacher has them in more liberal activities, like painting, playing games. But, you know, even with this schedule, the teacher must have a kind of flexibility. If she prepares her program but the children may have seen a circus or some animals, and their minds are full of those ideas, she must be able to drop her idea for the moment and let the children speak, let them express. She must be able to change her program, too. You see, we don't want to subdue the child or pressure him. We give him free scope in this way to bring in his ideas. If they come bubbling with ideas, the teacher can then concentrate on what the child is saying, can give him the freedom to express and follow along with him, and can get the whole class involved.

"So, you see that this is a very delicate thing. The teacher must have a kind of intuitive understanding of the children, to let them be creative, let him choose his activity if he is restless. Let's say a child is disturbing the class. Give him a chance to choose his activity, to work out his feeling in that, and you'll see the atmosphere change. He will sit quietly, or he will choose something. He won't disturb others. But when we try to impose our ideas on the children, the children become restless.

"Then this comes back to our whole approach: approach with love. It changes the child. He can get confident when he knows he has love. Teaching is not important at this age. It doesn't matter if he learns a hundred words or fifty. It's the whole growth of the child that matters. Each child comes with his own capacity. The teacher must have a general visualization of the growth of the child. Our aim is the growth of the child. All can't grow and grasp the same. But each can grow in his own capacity. And growth is our purpose here."

As a final question I ask Miss Patel to tell me about where the kindergarten children live in the Ashram. She explains that many of the children and youths in the primary program and above live in dormitories and hostels, with the supervision of monitors who are graduates of the Centre. Others live with their families. The children in kindergarten, in contrast, must live with at least one family member. For a child to enter the kindergarten, a family member—usually the mother, a grandmother, an aunt, or someone else from her family—must come to Pondicherry and take up residence, so that the child can live in a household with that person. In some situations, the whole family will move to Pondicherry. But usually only one family member comes. "So, from 11:30 A.M. until 4:30 P.M., the children have their own lives, their own routines, with their mothers or whoever. You see, it's not advisable for the young child to be separated from a family member. Somebody from the family needs to be there. It's often a sacrifice for the family, but someone has to come to be with the child. Then, at 4:30 P.M. the kindergarten children come back to the courtyard for an hour of physical activity. Sometimes they have races, or go to the beach to run, or whatever. But mostly they are on their own. You see, we have created an environment here so they can climb, jump, run, you know. So it is a natural expression."

In the early afternoon on the following Monday, I meet Dilip Mahtani outside the Registrar's office. He leads me through the small courtyard, out a door and across the empty street, and through a gate into the adjacent school complex. Then we go through another courtyard and into a large, airy classroom.

Dilip Mahtani appears to be in his late thirties. He's about five feet, ten inches in height. He wears a white shirt and tan trousers. His face is youthful, set off by his thick, wavy brown hair with only the slightest traces of gray, and by a thin brown mustache. He speaks clearly and directly.

"I came here when I was 9," Mr. Mahtani tells me. "I joined the school, had most of my education here, and then I joined as a teacher. So, I've been teaching since fifteen years now. I teach young children, ages 8 and 9, and older students, too, ages 15 and 16. They're at the end of the secondary program. My subjects are physics and mathematics. Astronomy, too."

"Can you tell me about your goals as a teacher?" I ask.

"There are two goals. One is the inner goal. The other is the outer goal. With the inner goal, you understand the development of the child, his latent faculties whatever they may be, the flowering of all his capacities, a growth in self-understanding. And the outer goal is acquiring certain techniques, capacities, languages, you understand? These are the two types of goals, and they complement each other. Like an attempt to teach English is a means of trying to help the child to understand himself, to develop himself.

"The inner goal, it's much more subtle. The self-understanding of the child, that whole thing is somewhat difficult for a teacher to do, because it depends a lot on his own self-development and his own self-understanding. It is the inner growth of his own being which helps him to evoke a similar growth in the child, you understand? What is termed by The Mother and Sri Aurobindo the psychic being. So the teacher's own development in some spontaneous way, it communicates a similar growth to the child."

"Let me come at this from another angle," I say. "As I look around this classroom or the other rooms I've visited in the last week, it looks very much like a good classroom in a school in the United States."

"Yes, I can believe that."

"So what makes this school different?"

"The inner approach. Because the community here in the Ashram is dedicated to certain ideals, and we believe that the major work is being done from inside, not from the outside. What I do in my classroom is the best I can. The results, the important results, are due to some inner force that is working, you understand? We believe that the force is working, and we experience the working of that force."

"How do you experience that force?"

"I'll tell you how. There are days when one is more open to one's inner self. On those days, things work out perfectly in the classroom. You've got the right idea, the children are happy, and things just go right. Because of that inner opening. On other days, you may have planned your class exactly as you would have previously, but you aren't so open. And things don't work out as they should. And you know what the cause is? It's not because you didn't plan rightly or enough. The reason is because you yourself were not open."

"Can you tell me how you work with the child's *inner teacher*?" I ask.

"The *inner teacher* is the psychic being," Dilip responds. "There are many different elements in a human being, different levels of being. The innermost one is the true guide. And one attempts to contact that—"

"Is it a conscious contact or—"

"It is not a fully willed contact, by which I mean that one doesn't have full control over one's inner movement. So, I can't say that Monday, I've got something to do, so I must have that contact. It's the result of an aspiration. But there's some movement on the other side also. When the response is there, then things are fine, Otherwise, well, we go on to do our best. But having the awareness of seeking, that makes a tremendous difference, because as a result of that aspiration, one does get the response."

"How do children feel about this kind of contact?" I ask. "Are they aware of it?"

"They are spontaneously conscious of that element," Dilip responds. "All children, all over the world. And that's why, if you look at them, you feel a certain purity. Because the mind and the other elements are not yet developed. Only when the other elements get developed does that part of us get covered up."

"Can you tell me about what roles freedom and discipline play here in the Centre?"

"We believe in external freedom to a large extent, but there must also be inner discipline. Also, outer discipline, to a certain extent, because most of us don't have strong inner discipline. The more we develop, the necessity of outer discipline becomes less and less. The inner discipline takes over. Now for a child, we have to judge how much external discipline we shall impose on him and to what extent we should let him be free to do things as he wishes. If we just say 'freedom,' or we just say 'discipline,' neither one is right.

"Now the 8- and 9-year-olds I teach have freedom, can make choices within the class itself. There's a variety of activities that I present, and the child can choose among them. The older students I teach, they have a freedom in the choice of subjects."

"What if a child comes in," I ask, "with excitement about something that is not what is planned for the day? What do you do?"

"It depends," Dilip replies. "One may take it up or not. And the right choice will depend on if you have your inner guidance or not. One day it may be right to accept what he is saying. Another day it may be wrong. There is no rule."

"The word 'discipline' is often used in another way in schools, meaning controlling children's behavior. What do you do about children who act out in negative ways? Do you use punishment ever?"

"Oh, never. Never. We are forbidden to punish the child. We may have them sit by the door for awhile if they are too noisy. Or maybe in some extreme cases even call in the Registrar or send them home. But nowadays we try to avoid that, because a child doing mischief or troubling the class reflects on the teacher's inability to have provided something interesting for him. Or sometimes all a child wants is attention from you and your affection. So you call him over, you put your arm around him, and he is as quiet as a lamb. You see, you have to sense somewhat intuitively what he really wants."

"Let me ask you one last question. How is the school changing?"

"It is changing more or less constantly in the sense that we don't have a fixed way of working for our school. Every teacher has plenty of freedom given to him to work in his class in the way he understands best. Now it so happens that many of us, our way of working is rather old-fashioned. That means that in some fields, we do not consider sufficiently the interest of the child. Some feel there should a change in this, toward a freer way of working, externally. So, what amount of freedom the child should have is a constant point of discussion among teachers. And on these lines, there is change. That is, how better to really give the child his freedom.

"There is a continual exchange of views on these subjects, but there is no imposition of one person's ideas on others. Like the child should be free, so should the teacher be free. And for me, the method is really secondary. Which means that somebody who has got a developed inner being, he can teach a class in the most rigid, classical method with no freedom at all, and he will still be exerting a deeper influence on his students because of what he is than one working in the freest manner externally who did not have the corresponding inner development. So nobody can really say, well look here, what I'm doing is freer than you and therefore better. But still we are attempting to arrive at a greater external freedom at all levels, from kindergarten right up to the higher course."

The next morning I meet with Gauri Pinto. We sit on the edge of the large inner courtyard. Miss Pinto looks to be in her fifties. She has a lean, angular face, brown-black hair pulled back in a bun, and brown-framed glasses. She wears a white sari with a cream-colored top. She seems a little shy with me at first, but her expressions and her voice soon come alive as she talks about teaching and her students.

Miss Pinto explains to me that she was the first child ever to live in the Ashram. She came as an infant. All of her education was in the Ashram school, and she has been a teacher of English for many years. Now she teaches 12-year-olds, children who have just entered the secondary program. Her primary goal for them, she emphasizes, is to help them learn who they are as persons. "It's not the academics that are focus. We want to help them learn about themselves. What is the mind? The soul? How do you know what these are? We also want to help them develop their senses. In addition, we have our students spend time in nature, so they can learn to appreciate nature. If they are interested, we want them to learn about nature scientifically, too.

"The academics have value, too," she continues. "At this age we want to give children a taste of all of the different subjects, so they can choose well what to take when they are 14. We want a good balance now: to encourage their own interests but also to give them exposure to all different subjects and experience, so they'll have a better way to make their choices later on.

That afternoon I ride my bike out to the Ashram's sports complex on the north side of town. The sports complex includes facilities on both sides of the road, one side surrounded by a high stone wall and the other by a tall mesh fence. The gates to each area are open, but each is guarded by a man in uniform. Just within each gate are hundreds of bicycles, parked neatly in rows. One of the sports fields includes a large, competition-size swimming pool, track and field grounds, and basketball and tennis courts. There is also a weight and exercise gym. The other side has volleyball courts and soccer and field hockey fields.

As I enter the western field, I watch a group of about fifty young teenagers, the lower secondary group who are 12 through 14 years old, gather inside the track for a minute of concentration. They stand silently in formation. All of them wear identical white shirts and green shorts, and the girls' hair is tied up in white scarves. Then all of them, male and female, move through a series of track and field activities, including 100-, 200-, 400-, and 800-meter-runs, and discus, javelin, high jump, and long jump. The youths are relaxed but clearly focused. They're enjoying themselves and at the same time playing hard.

All of the other facilities are now in use, crowded both with groups of children and youths and with many Ashram adults. The young men from the higher or college program are swimming speed laps in the pool. The young women from the higher program are playing volleyball. I learn later that girls and boys play sports together until the age of 15 or 16. Then they separate into same sex groups.

Groups of younger children play soccer and field hockey, led both by teachers and by older students. Others play basketball and do gymnastics. Still others play games, such as freeze tag and something that looks a bit like "capture the flag."

All of the students take part in a wide variety of activities and sports. No one specializes in any one event for the purpose of competition. The purposes of physical education are enjoyment and the full development of the physical body, not winning.

At the end of the hour, I watch the crowd of students and adults collect their bikes and head through the gates before I follow them.

On Thursday morning I arrive at the building on St. Martin Street that houses the "Knowledge," or higher program, which is essentially at the college level. A four-story concrete structure, painted gray and white, it looks particularly modern in contrast to its surroundings. The "Knowledge" building is also one of the tallest structures in Pondicherry.

Inside the building is a collection of spacious rooms of various sizes, all with high ceilings and open windows. Many of the rooms are classrooms. Others include a computer lab, various science labs, a technology lab, machine shop, art studio, and offices and conference areas.

I climb the stairs to the fourth floor and find Jugal Kishore Mukherji, the supervisor of the higher program, in a small seminar room. We shake hands and sit down at a table. Mr. Mukherji is a brown-skinned man in his middle fifties. He is about five feet, eleven inches in height. His hair is white, but his face, though lined, is vibrant. He speaks with precision and enthusiasm, highlighting his points with vigorous hand and arm gestures. His expressions clearly convey the joy he finds in his work.

I ask Mr. Mukherji to tell me a little about his background, and he replies, "I was a student of nuclear physics in the University of Calcutta. And I came to join the Ashram in 1949, straight from my university campus. I have been associated with the Centre of Education since 1950. Now I am in charge of the higher course in the Centre."

I ask Mr. Mukherji about the name of the higher program— "Knowledge"—and he responds, "Yes, it is called Knowledge. But let me speak in a continuous way, and I will answer many of your questions.

"Now this Centre of Education has got a basic philosophy of its own. Here we are not so much interested in the externality of the child, but we consider that external manifestation to be an image, right through to the core, of what one is within. What we try to foster here is the growth of consciousness of the child. If that growth is well attended to, then we see that this external manifestation flows out smoothly, without any disturbance, along the lines of one's true nature.

"Now here we say that our method is the *free system*. Yet it is not a method at all. We have not stressed the word *system* because it is not a system as such. But we have stressed the word *free*. We want to turn our children into free beings. Then we must first understand what we mean by *free*; of course, not the dictionary meaning of the word.

"Most of our children come here at a relatively young age, so that they do not come with already formed ideas. With ideas ossified they will not be able to understand what you are aiming at, especially as we want to throw them into the sea of freedom. They should not mix up freedom and ordinary whimsical behavior.

"So what do we mean by *free*? Whenever children come to our program, we tell them our aim is to help them grow into free, deliberative beings. And they say, 'But we are already free. We are free to choose to be here in Knowledge.' And I say, 'No, you are not free.' And then I explain this to them. Before you manifest any psychological movement into action, and by movement we mean every piece of thinking, every piece of feeling and emotion, every piece of your evolution—Before you manifest, you have to step back in consciousness, and you have to ask yourself three questions: what, how, why? What's the exact nature of the movement that is occupying my field of consciousness at this moment? Next one, the how of the movement, from its genesis, how it rises to crescendo, how it goes down and disappears. As a detached scientist of the inner domain, you have to watch it without getting involved. Third question is the delicate question to answer, which requires great insight and honesty. Why? Why, at this particular moment, you felt like that, you react like that, you decided on this.

"This is the first element of education that you learn here: to ask the question 'why?' If you are sincere, you will discover that human behavior can function at any of five different levels, hierarchically arranged. . . . Our goal of education here is to help you rise, step-by-step, from the lowest plane to the highest plane. Rest of the things will automatically follow.

"On the lowest plane, as the impulse is coming, you give in to that one, you express that one. That is not freedom. Suppose, in the scorching heat of the midday on an Indian street, when the bullock driver is driving the bullock and putting the strings on the nose—The bullock is not free. And surely you won't like to be in the same condition as the bullock. You say, 'Of course not, but I am not.' Yes, all the strings are invisible. Through the arrangement of all the psychological factors involved in your consciousness in this moment, as you are conditioned, as you are impressed upon by all sorts of forces coming from the outside, all these are creating a resultant at every moment. Now it is this resultant which is inclining you along a course of action.

"Most people are functioning in that way without being conscious. So, we are made to think. We are made to feel. We are forced to act. At this lowest level, eighty percent of men are functioning, however beautifully cogent their reasoning appears to be.

But even their reasoning has been conditioned.

"Now the second level. At all moments a battle is going on in your field of psychological consciousness between two orientations. . . . One is toward what we call in a general way happiness, pleasure of all sorts. The other tends to what is true, the delight of what is true. . . . For many, the true remains as an ideal, just a mere intellectual concept, devoid of flesh and blood. Whatever comes with the prospect of some pleasure or immediate happiness, that looms large in my field of consciousness. That makes me act or react. But after all we are mental beings and therefore, on this second level, my mind seeks desperately to rationalize my action, to marshal specious arguments in its favor. But all of this, alas, is not freedom. It is the captive mind, the slave mind, that is functioning here, a mind that is altogether a slave to the pleasure-seeking, impulsive urges. On the second level, pleasure-seeking will make you act, but you look for arguments to legitimize this. This is not freedom.

"We now come to the characterization of the third level of human action. When one reaches this level, one's mind has already acquired the autonomy of right judgment but not the autonomy of execution. In other words, one has come to know what is right and true. Not only that—one does not seek any longer to justify one's weaknesses. But still when a temptation—temptation understood in the broader psychological sense of any weakness—when temptation presents itself, one fails to withstand it. One succumbs in action. One thus becomes a divided being: right in inner perception but wrong in execution. This, too, cannot be considered a state of freedom, as we understand it.

"So next comes the fourth level. Now on the fourth level, you are indeed truth-seeking, right-seeking, just-seeking. . . . Not only that, what is more significant is the fact that what you honestly consider to be right, that and that alone, you try to manifest in action. But the other part, the pleasure-seeking part, the impulsive vital part, is not yet converted. It goes on strike, and what's the result? You may do the sober, right thing but in a gesture of dry, dessicated duty. Life will be off-color. We don't want that type of freedom.

"So rise to the fifth level. On the fifth level, tables are turned, and the order is reversed. On the second level, one chose one's action under the spur of the pleasure-seeking tendency but sought to justify it as 'right,' whereas on this fifth level one decides one's action on the basis of what one sincerely considers to be right. What is more, one finds genuine peace and happiness only when one does this action. If you step off the track, you will immediately feel some sort of unease. And that is what you want to achieve, so that you will create in your own consciousness the right criteria for action, and none else has to dictate from outside, 'Do this and this, and don't do that and that.' A formal and artificial outer discipline will be replaced by a true inner one, for the being will be harmonized and one in thought and feeling and action.

"Each individual in his own situation, for his own development, being sincere to the utmost of his capacity, will know at this moment: for my growth I feel this is the right course of action, and only when I adopt that course of action in my daily life, it fills me with ease and happiness and contentment. And whenever I get derailed, there is a sense of subtle unease. So I tell the children, we want you to become like that. That is the real purpose of education. Your education doesn't end within the confines of the Knowledge building. Once you know how to do this here, then that will help you take the same course of action throughout your big, wide, unchecked field of life."

Jugal Kishore pauses for a few moments. I sit in silence, working at grabbing hold of what he has already said. "So usually, at all moments, step back. That's the first step for education here. Step back in your consciousness. Objectify whatever is executed. And in terms of your consciously held goals, try to live in the future as beings of aspiration, and not so much in the present. This is what we impress upon our students. We tell them, 'Whenever some impulse in action is arising in you, ask yourself first, if you express that one, if you manifest it, will it help you to take a step forward on the path of accomplishment of your goal? If yes, express. If not, seek to reject.'

"Then you say, 'Yes, I want to but I cannot. Lord, I know what not to do but I cannot but do.' Well, this situation probably will arise. And here comes the part of education. Then you see, from within you shall look out, and you will find out your instrumental nature, your physical nature, vital nature, mental nature, emotional, assertive, and what not. All this has been given to you for your happy growth—And also for the clouding out of the manifestation of your inner consciousness. So here you require, as Sri Aurobindo and The Mother have said, the five-fold education.

"There should be full development of the body but not for the body's sake. There should be full development of the emotional capacities, not for the sake of the vital nature's petty satisfactions. You should have a full development of your aesthetic faculties, not for the sake of petty sensations of pleasure. You should have full development of intellectual abilities, not for juggling with words and thoughts and concepts. Now each one can help you to become an integrated being, not only in the being within, living in peace, but as a well-rounded, fully formed manifestation. So here we have the total growth of the child.

"What we aim at is that each child should follow his own way, depending on his intrinsic abilities and the course of his true being within. And we give this a practical application in our system of education here. Children are taught slowly but progressively how to exercise one's freedom of judgment and action in the right way, in the way of the soul, and not in the way of a self-blinded, ego-driven creature of impulse. So when they come to the higher program, they can take up the challenge.

"Now I will tell you about the teachers. Here teachers do not think of themselves to be the teacher when they start this job. All here are engaged in the same task of growth. Here the teachers feel that, well, now by the accident of birth circumstance, I have come in a human body a few years earlier than the student. So, in age he may be younger than me, but the quality of his consciousness, the way of action and reaction in him, may be at a higher level than the level at which I am functioning. So how can I have this idea that I am the donating side and he is the receiving one? Not at all. I may have acquired some sort of external competence, some infusion of external knowledge. But so what? So every student is treated with great respect by the teachers here.

"And the students are made aware in the higher program, you will be given the challenging task. At each moment you decide on your own. You will be free to select your teachers. You will be free to select your courses of study, your subjects. You will be free to select the tempo and speed at which you pursue your courses. You are free in this program to study any subject at any level. You are free to suspend the study of any subject if momentarily your interest is concentrated on another line. But don't be pushed and pulled by the conditioning forces. At each moment, be conscious, be deliberate. Know fully that you are acting, you are deciding, that you are free. And in all cases, look within and see all this as a beautiful challenge. And you'll find out that there is no better joy than seeing oneself.

"Now let me move to the practical description of the Knowledge program. At the beginning of our session—you know, we are in session for all the year but for a month and a half—all of our so-called teachers introduce our subjects to the assembly of students. One day, two days, three days, we explain the scope of the subject, what is the level, what the teacher will expect from the student. Now for fifteen days, the students will move around. They'll go to this teacher, they'll go to that one, and others. They'll ask the questions to see how he is answering.

"In our school we have seventy students in the higher course, and sixty-five teachers. From these, the students choose. They are free to make the selection. Then they go to the teacher concerned and say, 'I want to do this. What are your expectations from me as a student? What am I supposed to do? How much time should I devote?' And so on. It is a question between teacher and student. A freely made decision. So, they also decide if a student comes individually or in twos or three or four, if they have an affinity for the same type of questions."

I ask Mr. Mukherji how many times each week most students meet with teachers. That varies considerably, he explains, depending on the agreement the student and teacher have reached. But on average, students spend about twenty-five periods a week meeting with teachers. School is in session every day except Sunday and the first day of each month, and there are seven hour-long periods each day.

Mr. Mukherji then explains to me that the higher program has a set of goals for the intellectual development of its students. There are four goals, he says: being an active participant; being able to express oneself in speech and writing with cogency and precision; being able to pursue the answers to questions and the solutions to problems; and being able to do research.

"Let me tell you one more thing about our teachers," Mr. Mukherji continues. "Our teachers have a very good rapport with their students. They are always watching them with a deep sympathy and love. A teacher represents a mirror in which the consciousness of the child is getting reflected. To be a teacher, it is not enough to have mere competence in the external field of knowledge. That will not equip him to be successful here. One has to become a true psychologist. One has to feel the pulse of the child. And one has to become a student of oneself. One has to seek to grow oneself. Then only will one be able to help the child. And if you don't do that, then in the free system next year you won't have any students with you."

Three young women stand at the door, looking in uncertainly. Jugal Kishore greets them warmly. He introduces us all and explains to me that they are scheduled to study with him this period. Would I like to ask them any questions about Knowledge? All three of the young women look to be in their late teens. Two wear saris, one red and the other purple. Bimala, the one who speaks the most, wears a bright print blouse and skirt. Her face is coffee-brown, and her eyes are intense. While her companions are quite shy in my presence, she is eager to talk.

"There was a time two years ago," Bimala says, "I didn't know what I wanted to study. I was very excited when I came to Knowledge but a little confused. Eventually I found out what was right for me to study. It was hard for awhile, but I looked inside.

"What's so important about the learning here for me," Bimala continues, "is that it's about who I am: not just the outside but what is inside, what is inner; not just things but the true person. And we learn with our teachers and with the other students. We can all learn from each other."

After thanking Mr. Mukherji and the three young women, I wander through the halls of the Knowledge building. I see classes of six or eight or ten students with a teacher, students meeting with each other in pairs or trios, a teacher with one student or two, and students working intently on their own. The feeling everywhere is relaxed and focused.

"I come from the state of Orissa. My father is a financial officer for a national project, so I never settled in my native village.

We used to go there for vacations. But I do keep contact with my relatives in Orissa, and I have that identity because my parents were so deeply steeped in Oriya (the language of Orissa) literature, in their mother tongue. And they gave that to us. We are a family of five sisters and one brother. My father was a student of Sri Aurobindo and Mother, and my parents brought us here to Pondicherry in 1966."

I am listening to Gayatri Mohaptra. She is twenty-eight years old, a graduate of the International Centre who now works in the Registrar's office and teaches Oriya, her native language, part-time. Gayatri is about five feet, three inches in height. Her skin is dark brown, and her black hair is tied back on both sides of her head. She wears a long green dress. She speaks with enthusiasm and precision, and her clarity and insight are both striking.

"I came to the Ashram on December 13, 1966. I was 9 years old. I had studied in outside schools before I came. Frankly speaking, as far as I can remember and my memory is quite vivid, I was never a happy child in outside schools. I was miserable. The teachers were not at all sympathetic to one's inner growth, to what one essentially is. However we projected ourselves academically, that was how we were considered to be.

"The most important thing I remember when I came to the Ashram's school, that feeling of being new wasn't there for me. I felt as if I had come to my own home. It's that homeliness that attracted me a lot. From our early childhood, we had accepted Mother and Sri Aurobindo as a sort of law. You see, in Indian families, it is a very important thing that apart from our parents and other philosophers and guides, we always look up to the saints and our family deities. And every evening we sit and pray, all of us together. Tis a natural thing for us. Since our childhood we had always worshiped Mother and Sri Aurobindo as somebody of our own, to whom we can always look up to and pray. So when we came here, I was extremely glad. I felt that I had come home."

Gayatri explains to me that she had always lived with her family during her years in school. Some families give all of their wealth to the Ashram and then live as an integrated part of the Ashram. But hers remained financially independent, although they were part of the Ashram community in many other ways.

"Can you tell me what you remember from your first years in the Centre?" I ask.

"I remember two teachers who helped me a lot in my formative years," Gayatri replied, "when we look up for guidance. There is an age in one's life when we look up for guidance to certain people. And I felt at that age I had really proper guidance.

"The most important thing for me in school was not the academics. I studied a lot in whatever subjects I was interested. But more, what this life taught me every moment, the values it taught me. You see, every moment here it must be seen that you are always transcending your limitations, your pettinesses. And you're always looking up to something higher. That is what has always appealed to me, and one of the reasons why I decided to stay here. I've been outside. I feel that the outside world is a continuous cycle of happiness, unhappiness. . . . But here I feel that we have cut away from that cycle. We are on our own. The freedom is there to choose if I want to be happy, if I want to be unhappy. In fact, when I have been under some circumstance that made me unhappy, in my growing stage, there is something here that mostly makes you conscious, which makes you go back and see what are the real difficulties."

"So when you think back to being in school in those years, the academics were a part of it," I say. "But the central part was?"

"My own growth: growth towards ability, towards light, towards new knowledge. Always the knowledge to know something more. Actually it's all the refinement of my nature. That's why I was more tuned towards literature and arts than mathematics and science. In fact I've ignored quite a lot of subjects frankly speaking.

"Now you see the freedom given to us here, the tremendous scope to learn anything we wanted to, provided with all the facilities. And give us so much scope for developing our inner being, and all of our selves, not just the inner being. In the outside world, they will impose on you that this is what you should do within this time limit. You have to study, this is the syllabus. Here it is totally different. I have a particular interest, and I have the complete freedom to go on intensifying, studying more and more in that subject. And that gives me tremendous joy. And I could also choose the method I wanted to study, the pace I wanted to go, the avenues I wanted to take."

"When you were 10 or 12 years old," I ask, "did you also have so much freedom?"

"Actually," Gayatri responds, "our Ashram school is a constant experimentation. When I came here, it was different, the experiment, than what it is now. When I came here, I did not know French, and French is a compulsory subject as well as the medium of instruction for science and mathematics. So my first year was completely taken up in the accelerated French course. After that year when I had come to grasp the language a little better, a lot of freedom was given to the students, to me. We could do it our own way, take certain subjects if we wanted to. There was nobody to tell us no. No one to tell us to take up subjects that were important, even if we were not interested. So, over the years, we have realized that a child may give himself to the whims of his fancy. If he is interested in the arts like I was, I gave my total amount of time to those subjects and ignored completely mathematics and science, which are difficult for me. If I loved a subject, I will give more to it. . . . Looking back, I know academically I've made a great mistake, because that other side of me is not developed. And I suffer now due to this."

"But nobody came to you and said, 'You should do this.'"

"No, nobody. But now things have changed. Now all the time the child is encouraged to follow all of the subjects for a good foundation, for your own broadening of horizons. Now there is more guidance. . . . But I had some teachers who were really helpful to me. They went on giving me more and more time, as much as I demanded from them. And I worked very hard in those subjects, English and French literature and Indian literature as well as Mother's and Sri Aurobindo's writings, not the very difficult books but some of the passages explaining what life is. What is the meaning of death? Why are we born? What is the soul? I had a questioning mind in those subjects."

"When did you start reading these passages?"

"Before coming here I read some of Mother's books, because my parents were reading them out to us. But more and more I started reading around 13, I'd say."

"Can you tell me about the Knowledge program?" I ask.

"There is total freedom," Gayatri explains. "In the beginning in the higher program I felt inadequately prepared. I felt I had a lot more to do before going there. My condition was not yet strong, I felt. But I started doing the projects that they were giving to me. As usual, I chose to intensify in literature, French and English, and more and more Sri Aurobindo's books. And it took me almost two years to settle in there. In the first year and last year I worked a lot. In the second year I slackened off. You see, this is what happened. This is the period when we had to decide whether to go out and follow a career or do our further studies or whatever, or choose to stay in the Ashram. I have spoken to many of my friends, and for many of them, this is a time of conflict. Because we have to decide. So this was a haunting question for me. I was quite disturbed for many months, what should I do?"

"Do most people leave the Ashram when they finish the higher course?"

"It's about fifty-fifty. Half stay here, and half leave. But when they leave, they never disconnect themselves from the life here. This life helps them a lot outside. And they come back often, as they say, to recharge their batteries."

"I want to return to the topic of freedom in the lower years. I'm interested in your perceptions about how well children learn to use their freedom."

"Well," Gayatri says, "to give you a clear fact of this place, every child does not succeed in utilizing freedom in the proper way. That one should be aware of. There were students that were at a loss at a certain age to use that freedom. And then it gives them license. Some will choose to play. They don't want to sit and draw, sit and think, sit and read. It needs a lot of effort and patience by the teachers to guide them, guide them in the proper channels.

"Yet there are students here who are very conscious at a very young age. If we observe them, you see they know what they want, what they will study. They will be regular in habits and discipline and take most advantage of the system here. But now when children are lost at whatever level, the teachers are always there to guide you. And gradually those children are left more and more on their own. Yes, this is a problem that we teachers discuss quite a lot, all the time experimenting with different methods, how it's possible to give freedom as well as be firm and give proper guidance.

"Still the point is, treat each child individually," Gayatri emphasizes. "Give him the freedom but guide him within his lines. It is important for the student to have freedom, but one has to make him feel what freedom means. First of all, you ask, 'Okay, what do you want to do?' And gradually, by observing, you see that the child is interested in one particular subject, say, natural life. He loves, he adores plants. So, through plants, we can bring in other subjects, like English and French and science. It's through one subject that you can diversify his interests. There are teachers who have tremendous skill in this, and others who are not managing as well.

"With all this, as a teacher one has to remember the central thing: to treat the child not as a machine but as a soul, as a living flower. He can blossom by encouragement; by love and warmth; by a relationship which is not distant but becoming more of a friend. Teaching is not only contact in a classroom, but it can be anything whatsoever: in a garden, in visiting together, in a walk, in playing together. And that is what is always happening in our school."

"Let me talk now about the true nature of our school," Paru Patil says to me on Friday morning as we sit in her office at the end of my visit to the International Centre. "Its purpose is for the child to develop himself and find his true inner being. Mother has said that usually when people turn to spirituality, they are already quite old. And it's usually after having some knocks from life or some frustrations or disappointments. Then they want a little place of peace and quiet, so they turn to an ashram. But this ashram is not for the purpose. You see, it's not really for peace. It is really for working, for perfecting oneself. We can't run away from difficulties, we have to face them. So this ashram is not a haven from troubles, although, you can see, there is peace around us.

"Mother said, instead of having only old people on the path, it would be nice if children could be made aware of the true aim of life. Then perhaps they wouldn't have to waste so much time over futilities. Then they would be able to come to grips with the main things. So that is really why this school was started, not to be like hundreds of other schools in the world but mainly to make the children conscious of the true being, to make them conscious of themselves. Know thyself, so that this is the thyself in the more compelling description of Sri Aurobindo. The true self is the psychic or spiritual self, but around that there are also the other layers of consciousness. So, to become aware of all that and to become master of oneself, these are the high ideals. How to realize them within an academic pattern is the challenge."

"I've learned that you base the school on what you call the free progress system," I say, "Can you tell me about this?"

"You see," Miss Patil replies, "we feel that at the age of 14 or so, a student is able to assume the responsibility for his whole education. Til then he is a little young to know exactly how to orient himself, how to plan out his program. But at 14 or so, he really becomes more conscious of himself, and he is able to choose for himself: his own subjects, the rhythm of his own learning, and so on. But we find that unless the students are prepared for responsibility, when they assume that responsibility, they are really at sea. So there has to be a period of preparation, where children are helped to learn how to become responsible for themselves.

"Now we don't all agree on exactly when and how this is done. Some of us still believe in total freedom at a certain age. And some of us feel that too much freedom may not be good for the children. So, you see, we are still finding our way. We are still searching. But right now, the students in Knowledge have almost complete freedom: the choice of subjects, the choice of teachers, the choice of periods for their subjects, and so on. The students in the secondary program have much freedom, particularly within the framework of their classes. Our classes are very small, usually eight or ten students. So a teacher can closely observe each child, find out his individual interests, and help him to develop those interests. So, many of our teachers, though they may seem to be working in a structured, traditional pattern, are helping students to follow their interests and be self-motivated.

"But then the outer structure is not that important. There is a dynamic interest of the teacher in his subject. And there is what each subject can give on two different levels: the outer, the practical, and the inner work. Now, take language. It is a medium of expression. So it's very important to know how to express oneself, both in writing and orally. To do that, one has to have vocabulary, one has to have spelling, one has to have grammar, and all the rest. But that's not the only thing a language can give. It can give a lot of sensitivity, a lot of self-awareness, a lot of imagination, a lot of self-analysis. So many different things. So, each subject teacher has to see what his particular subject can offer to the child in these two ways. And, of course, seeing the bent of the child, he could stress one thing more than the other.

"We are organized by subjects, but there are some teachers who disagree, who feel that this is an antiquated way of going. There should not be any subjects at all, they say, just so many teachers available, so many disciplines, and let the student find what he wants to do. But we are still working on these questions. We all agree that we need to help the child know himself, but there are all these ways to go about it. We are still exploring them."

Miss Patil glances at the clock, and I know that our allotted time is almost over. "One last question," I say. "Can you tell me how you go about helping children to know themselves, about the different levels of consciousness and different aspects of the self, and so on?"

"The most important thing in this regard," she replies, "is to help the best in the child to come forward, particularly in the kindergarten and primary sections. In these years, the children are much too small for any kind of conscious awareness of the parts of being or anything like that. But at this time very good work can be done to help the best in the child come forward, what Sri Aurobindo calls the psychic being. Now this can be helped because, you know, it's much in the forefront when they are still children, when the mind has not come and clouded it, when other emotions have not come and covered it up. You see, it's much in the front, and the children are always full of joy.

"So, if we can help the children to become aware of that something that is so beautiful and loving—And this can be done through all of the beautiful things: nature, art, music. And then one's own behavior with the children in dealing with adverse situations, the values that we put before them. And it's not merely lecturing to them. They are very, very observant little children, and they see, you know. If a person loses his temper and lectures for two hours on remaining calm, it's not going to have any positive effect on the child. But if the child notices that in a very difficult situation, the teacher was fully master of himself, that leaves a lasting impression on the child's life.

"So, I think, in the earlier stages, it is really the examples we give them. Then, of course, there are the stories we can tell them, beautiful stories that truly inspire them, inspire their faith in good, in beauty, in truth.

"Then, as they grow, naturally there are other movements that start coming in to them. They become more aware of their emotions, and of their thoughts. They have their own problems. Maybe they're personal problems which every growing youngster has. We don't focus so much on these directly, but while studying, say literature, a teacher can do a lot to help the child understand himself. Our teachers are aware of what Sri Aurobindo has written about human psychology, about the aspects of the personality, the various parts of the being. Since the teachers are aware, they can help the child when he is facing a difficulty. They can have an intimate, friendly relationship with the child and help him to see what it is that is going on. When a child is facing a problem in his own life, however childish the problem, it is a problem for him at that time. It's a big battle that's raging. So at this time he can understand the meaning of life: that life is not a battle, and yet each step has to be won consciously. Then there is progress. So each teacher can help the child to become aware. Each teacher can bring it differently, can help the child in his own way.

"And, you know, a child can't start studying Sri Aurobindo's philosophy at the age of 12 or 13. It would be too heavy a thing for the child. But he can have something from Sri Aurobindo's teaching. For example, there was this one boy who had a problem. He talked to a teacher, and the teacher didn't advise him much, didn't lecture him, just gave him a sentence from Sri Aurobindo. The boy read it. He was very happy. He thought about it much. Then he asked questions about it. You know, children really ask questions, they want to know certain things, and then a teacher can throw light on that, can help him to understand. And then when they are older, they can learn more about Sri Aurobindo's teachings."

I thank Miss Patil for all of her help. She wishes me good fortune, and we say goodbye.

7

THE VISION OF INAYAT KHAN

Inayat Khan's Vision of Human Nature

Central to Inayat Khan's understanding of human nature is a conception of the universe as consisting of many different planes of being—the physical plane, the mental plane, the astral plane, the spiritual or soul plane, and the divine—that are composed of vibrations of varying amplitude and character. Inayat Khan explains, "One speaks of these planes as if they were places. In point of fact they are conditions, but what we call a place is also a condition. It is only because it is rigid in its physical appearance that we think of it as a place. . . . "[1] These planes co-exist in the same "space" and interact with each other.

In Inayat Khan's vision of human nature, human beings are whole systems that consist of four interpenetrated and interrelated sub-systems, each of which exists primarily though not exclusively on a separate plane: the **physical body**, the **mind**, the **astral body**, and the **soul**. The physical body is material and exists largely on the physical plane. The mind, which includes the heart, is a field of energy that exists mostly on the mental plane. The astral body consists of a higher level of energy and exists on the astral plane. (All of Inayat Khan's terms are explained below.) Finally, the soul exists on the spiritual or soul plane. It is composed of an even higher level of subtle energy.

Another key element in Inayat Khan's vision is his belief that an ongoing evolution is the primary process in the universe. In his view, the divine was enfolded into matter when the physical universe was created. Over the millions of years matter has evolved back toward divinity. Humans are the most evolved beings with a material aspect on this planet. The attainment of God-realization by human beings is the fulfillment of the stage of evolution in which human beings are actors. Evolution is a dual process of unfolding, as a species evolves as a whole through the actualization of involved higher potentials within individual members of that species. Now human beings are striving to unfold their inherent divinity both as individuals and as the cutting edge of the evolutionary movement on this planet.

A third element in this vision of human nature is that human beings include elements and qualities both of lower and higher forms of being. From the mineral kingdom, manifested primarily within the physical body, we have received stillness, hardness, and strength. From the vegetable kingdom, also manifested in the physical body, we have received fruitfulness and usefulness. From the animal kingdom, manifested in the physical body and in the mind, come our fighting nature and our tendency toward attachment. From the astral plane, manifested both in the mind and in the astral body, we have received invention, artistry, and genius. And finally, from the soul or angelic plane, manifested primarily in the soul, come illumination, love, and peace.

Put more simply, what constitutes the person, in sum, is light from the soul plane, knowledge from the astral plane, inherited qualities from his parents and ancestors, and various aspects of the mineral, vegetable, and animal kingdoms that are expressed through the physical body. Inayat Khan notes that it is the need of each person to "balance all these (aspects) knowing that he has been created neither to be as spiritual as an angel, nor to be as material as an animal."[2]

A fourth element of Inayat Khan's vision of human nature is his profound sense of human interdependence with each other and with everything else in the universe. "We are not fundamentally separate beings," Sirkar Van Stolk explains, paraphrasing the words of Inayat Khan; "we are each a part, a cell, in that tremendous cosmic being which we call God."[3] Inayat Khan himself notes that "every individual is dependent upon every other. . . . When we see how limited man is even at his best, we see that it cannot be otherwise than that one must depend on another."[4]

PHYSICAL BODY

The physical body is the element of the person that exists primarily on the material plane. Its aspects include the **limbs** and **trunk**, the **five senses**, the **seven body centers**, and the **interrelated breathing and circulation systems**. Several of its important characteristics are its health, which is largely dependent on the circulation and breathing systems, its balance, and its sensitivity.

Inayat Khan explains that each of the five physical senses is actually a different part of the same basic sense, that there is really only one physical sense that acts through five separate channels. The purpose of the senses is experience, not indulgence, mastery, not slavery. He calls what humans experience through the senses the **audible life** to distinguish it from the **inner life**, that which is experienced through concentration, contemplation, meditation, and realization, as described below. The fineness of the senses helps to determine the quality and extent of the audible life.

Each human body has seven physical body centers within it that correspond to and interconnect with the **seven chakras**, centers that are elements of the person's astral body. These centers include the base of the spine, the area below the navel, the solar plexus, the heart, the throat, the "third eye" in the forehead between the eyebrows, and the "crown" at the top of the head. The body centers interact with the chakras in the process of intuitive knowing.

The breathing system operates on the material plane to bring oxygen into the bloodstream. In this process, it also gathers **prana**, subtle energy, which it feeds to the higher systems of the person. The breath touches the life-current that runs through all of the systems of the human being—physical body, mind, astral body, and soul—and connects them to each other and to their respective planes of being. One of the major determinants of the physical body's health is the regularity and the fullness of the breath.

The physical body has a particularly intimate interrelationship with the mind, as each can powerfully affect the state of the other. As Inayat Khan notes, "the thought of illness brings illness to the body. . . . At the same time cleanliness of the body helps to bring purity to the mind."[5] The body also relates to the soul. When the body is cared for with an attitude of holy reverence, the energy that develops within the body supports the holiness of the soul.

MIND

The human **mind** is both an individual system within the person and a tiny part of the divine mind. The mind is not the physical brain within the body but a field of energy existing primarily on the mental plane, which employs the brain as one of its instruments. It consists of six separate but interrelated faculties: the **thinking mind**; the **memory**; the **will**; the **reason**; the **heart**; and the **ego**.

- The thinking mind includes both a consciousness and a subconsciousness and is the creator of imagination and thought. Imagination is the outcome of the autonomic action of the thinking mind. It involves the apprehension of mental vibrations from the astral plane that the thinking mind first receives and then translates into a form. Imagination is a free flow that often expresses beauty and harmony. In contrast, thought is the outcome of the intentional action of the thinking mind. It is self-directed and controlled imagination in that it includes an element of will within its process. The thinking mind gives a form to each imagining and thought. Once created, each thought-form takes on an existence beyond the mind of its origin as an *elemental*. Such forms can be received by others and can affect the physical plane. Inayat Khan teaches that on the plane of mind, what you sow with your thinking mind is what you shall reap.

- A second faculty of the mind is memory. The memory is a largely automatic system that records all that comes to it through the five senses as well as whatever it may receive from the link between the personal mind and the universal, divine mind. Memory is responsive not to the use of willpower—when you will your memory to remember, it is actually more likely to forget—but to the quality of attention. The clearer the attention through the senses, the more effectively the memory will operate. Inayat Khan describes three aspects of human memory: that which is easily retrievable; that which is at the bottom of the memory but may be recalled; and that which has not been perceived by the senses but has entered the personal memory through its link with the divine mind.

- Another faculty of the mind is will, which is an expression of the divine power within human beings. The will is both a power of the mind and an action of the soul. It is the will that enables people to choose their actions and thus be guided not by their desires, impulses, and feelings alone but by their higher nature, their minds and souls. Desire is the enemy of the will. Surrendering to desire weakens the will. In contrast, experiencing desire and overcoming it strengthens the will, as does an optimistic and self-confident attitude toward life. To build the power of will, we must first avoid unintentional actions, speech, and thoughts. Then we must learn to check our desires and impulses, at first only for a short time each day but then for longer and longer periods of time. In this way, we learn not to be ruled by the desires of the body but to rule them from the higher self. Finally, we must learn to rule the mind through meditation and concentration.

The will plays an important role both in the maintenance of health and in the development of character. When the will is strong, the mind is ordered, helping the body to function well. When the will is weakened, the mind is disordered, allowing the body to become ill. A weakness of the will can cause not only illness but moral failure as well, for it is the will that gives a person the power to choose his actions. Strengthening the will gives a person the choice to act ethically, and it is a consistency of ethical action that constitutes good character.

- A fourth faculty of the mind is reason. It is reason that gives us the power to discriminate and decide, to evaluate and measure, to see angles and connections. There are three kinds of reason: the **lower reason** is attached to the impulses and desires and is often limited and selfish; the **middle reason** is attached to thought and can vary from self-centered to divinely inspired; the **heavenly reason**, which emerges from the soul, unfolds divine light within the personal mind through inspiration. To gain access to heavenly reason, we must be receptive and responsive, not always asking why but being open to receiving. "When one rises above what is called reason, one reaches that reason which is at the same time contradictory. . . . One sees death in birth, birth in death."[6]

Inayat Khan stresses both the value of reason and its inherent limitations and dangers. He describes reasoning as "a ladder. By this ladder one can rise and from this ladder one can fall. Reason is a great factor and has the possibility in it of every curse and of every blessing."[7] The lower reason is unreliable because it seeks to serve desire and impulse. The middle reason "takes the side of the ego. . . . The mind has only to turn its face to reason, and reason stands there as an obedient slave. It gives the mind a reason to do either right or wrong."[8] Yet the middle reason can be guided toward right when it is directed not by the ego but by faith. Reason must be the servant of faith, not the master. When reason alone rules, failure and harm follow. Finally, the heavenly reason, the deepest reason, is wisdom itself. It is knowing from the soul expressed through the channels of the mind. It often seems paradoxical to the lower or middle reason because it exists on a higher level of being.

For reason to be trustworthy as a guide, not only must it be the servant of faith but it must also be imbued with feeling. "Intellectuality cannot be perfect without sentimentality. Nor can the thinking power be nurtured, nor the faculty of reasoning be sustained, without a continual outflow of feeling."[9]

- The most profound faculty of the mind is the **heart**, according to Inayat Khan. Indeed he refers to the mind as the surface of the heart as often as he describes the heart as the depth of the mind. This interchangeability of reference clearly indicates the inextricable weaving of mind and heart as one central system within the human being. One aspect of the heart is the

physical organ within the body of matter. Another is the "little heart," the part of the body around the physical heart that receives emotion from the inner heart, feels the emotion most acutely, and transmits emotion throughout the physical body. This "little heart" is the vehicle of the **inner heart**, the third aspect, which is not matter but a subtle energy field, above substance. The inner heart is beyond the physical body and yet within it.

The energy of the heart is emotion. Emotion or feeling is a single energy that takes different forms. The vibrational level of emotion is higher than that of thought. The most powerful form of emotion is love, which can be felt as charity, generosity, kindness, affection, endurance, tolerance, or patience.

Inayat Khan teaches that to grow spiritually, we must open our hearts to feel all of our emotions without being overwhelmed by them. In particular we must open our inner heart to love. The more the heart is opened, the more we can be sensitive to the feelings of others and the more we can give to others, for to love is to give. While we must not repress or deny our emotions, neither should we allow ourselves to be controlled by them. Rather, we must feel our emotions fully yet still control their impact upon us. The emotions are not the person any more than the thoughts are.

Intuition, Inayat Khan explains, rises from the depths of the heart. While intuition and imagination appear in much the same way, we can learn to distinguish between them. Imagination is more active, more the doing of the person's mind. Intuition flows into the consciousness that is passive, open, and trusting of an inner guidance. Imagination can also be intuition if it is not corrupted by reason.

Intuition arising within the inner heart has five forms: **impression; intuition;** [10] **inspiration; vision;** and **revelation.**

a. Impression is dependent on an outer impression from something that leads to an inner knowing about that thing.

b. Intuition is an inner guidance that is independent of any outer impression. It is first expressed as feeling and then transformed by the mind into thought. Intuition is the sixth sense. When the mind is tranquil and receptive, wisdom rises from the depths of the heart and flows onto the surface of the consciousness. The more we can feel compassion and sympathy, the more open we will be to intuition.

c. Inspiration is a higher form of intuition from the divine mind down through the heart and into the consciousness as a stream of wonder and joy. Inspiration comes into the mind already organized into a complete idea. It can take five different forms: waves of thought; emotions; sufferings of the heart; a flow of wisdom; and a divine voice.

d. Vision is inspiration that comes through a clearness of the inner sight in the form of images.

e. Revelation is an even higher form of inspiration in which, through a fully awakened heart, the knower becomes one with everything in the universe, and every secret is revealed through the experience of identity of the knower with the known. Revelation, then, is the experience of fusion with the other.

- The sixth faculty of the mind is the **ego**, the limited self. The ego is formed in infancy when the soul identifies with the physical body. This identification creates the experience of duality: the "I" and the "other." The ego is the seat of desires and passions. It is the creator of disharmony through the manifestation of arrogance, wrath, attachment, and greed. The more the ego's desires are gratified, the more powerful it becomes.

For most humans, the development of the ego, the false self, is a necessary stage in unfoldment. As the child grows, the ego expands to include all sensation, emotion, imagination, and thought. The task of spiritual growth is to learn that body and mind are not the real self but only vehicles of the self, and then to disidentify with the ego and thus transcend its limitations.

Inayat Khan describes four levels of ego development that trace an awakening to a conscious identification with the higher self, the soul: (1) the automatic ego, characterized by "an eye for an eye" orientation to others; (2) the self-disciplined ego, characterized by the ability to choose one's actions; for example, wanting to strike back when struck but choosing not to do so; (3) the ego of inner calm, characterized by a profound inner calm that fosters deliberate control, allowing one to see others as their evolutionary stage; and (4) the ego of blessings, characterized by the ability to remain serene and radiate a blessing outward in all circumstances.

In his discussion of the nature of the mind, Inayat Khan also explains the steps by which the mind can raise its quality of concentration and evolve toward what he calls God-realization, bringing soul into the mind and thus transforming it into something beyond the mind. The first step is **concentration**, the experience of single-mindedness. The exercise of concentration involves fixing the thoughts on a single object by motion, repetition of a mantra, memory, or sight. It can also involve holding an image in the mind with the help of feeling or training the mind to watch its own process. The second step is **contemplation**, which is similar in structure to concentration except an idea is fixed upon rather than an object.

The third step is **meditation**, an opening to the silent life within and beyond which is the greatest teacher. Meditation involves going beyond the mind and awakening to wisdom by bringing soul qualities into the mind. It is experiencing "consciousness in its pure essence, which is not necessarily dependent upon the knowledge of names and forms."[11] Such experience brings access to the source of joy, peace, harmony, and power. The final step is **realization**, which is totally beyond the mind. With realization, the soul unfolds completely and what was the mind is transformed into an explicit expression of the divine consciousness.

ASTRAL BODY

The astral body is the aspect of the human being that exists on the astral plane, a higher and more subtle level than the mental plane. The seven chakras, the inner centers that are the seats of intuitive faculties, are elements of the astral body. Each chakra is a capacity that can be opened and brought into play. The astral body also brings higher levels of energy down into human life. This energy is manifested as genius, artistry, imagination, the creation of beauty.

SOUL

In the human being, the soul is the true self. The soul is a current, a spiritual ray, which exists first on the spiritual plane. The soul is the most essential manifestation of the divine. "The connection between the (divine) consciousness and the soul is like the connection between the sun and the ray (of light)."[12] The energy of the soul is light, love, beauty, and harmony.

Some souls remain on the spiritual plane; others descend to the astral plane. Still others move below the astral plane and incarnate as humans. Before the human being's birth, the soul travels through the spiritual plane and takes on a luminous body. It then journeys through the astral plane and creates an accompanying astral body, a body of impressions. When the physical body is born, the soul joins with it, and when the mind is created, the interaction of the soul and the mind creates a new field of energy called the **spirit**.[13]

Inayat Khan explains that when the physical body of a human being dies, the soul returns to the spiritual plane. But his teachings about reincarnation are paradoxical. In some of his writings, he notes that there is no reincarnation, that each soul makes the cyclical journey from the spiritual plane only once. As souls return to this plane, however, they leave an impress on souls that are journeying to their incarnation on the material plane. This impress or influence is the mechanism of evolution. In other passages, however, Inayat Khan describes reincarnation as a reality, indeed as the means of evolution. He says, "Reincarnation is a fact, but we do not teach it."[14] A resolution of this paradox is offered by Pir Vilayat Khan, Inayat Khan's son and also a Sufi teacher, who explains that reincarnation as it is commonly understood is not a literal truth but is a metaphor for a reality too complex for the human mind to comprehend.[15]

The soul has both an inner and outer experience. Its outer experience derives from its interaction with the mind and heart, as the soul and the mind and heart affect each other. The inner experience arises from the aspect of itself that becomes the spirit. The soul is motivated by five spiritual desires: (1) the desire to live with freedom; (2) the desire to gain spiritual knowledge; one manifestation of this desire is the child's intense curiosity; (3) the desire for power; the inner power of effacing the small ego and embracing the divine: (4) the desire for happiness; happiness is within the heart in the knowledge of the true self; and (5) the desire for peace within. Each of these soul desires is manifested in human life and helps to bring purpose and meaning to life, as does each soul's evolutionary movement toward the achievement of God-realization within the human person. Indeed, the power of the spiritual desires is a large part of the evolutionary motive force that propels humans to evolve toward increasing divinity.

Inayat Khan's Vision of Human Becoming

The teachings of Hazrat Inayat Khan offer a richly detailed vision of human becoming between birth and age 21. This vision is organized by three primary characteristics:

1. The evolution of the child and youth follows a path that is relatively consistent, regular, and foreseeable;

2. Yet the experience of individuals can vary considerably within the bounds of this path, and the most important growth need of the child and youth is to be allowed to unfold at his own pace. As Inayat Khan explains,

. . . there is a time, there is a day, an hour, a moment
fixed for the child to change its attitude: to learn to sit,
to learn to stand, to learn to walk. But when the parents, eager to see the child stand or sit or walk, help it,
the child will do it before the time, and that works
against its development; because it is not only that it
begins to learn to sit or to stand or to walk; there is a far
greater meaning in it. These are different stages which
an infant goes through in its spiritual life.[16]

3. The path of the child's unfoldment includes three eras:

a. from birth into the seventh year;
b. from the seventh year until 12 to 13 years of age: and
c. 12 to 13 years of age through 21 years of age.

While the child is involved in a spiritual unfoldment in his first
twenty-one years of life, his more central growth needs during
these years relate to the growth of his physical body, his mind,
and his character and personality. Inayat Khan defines character
as a learned form that the individual's nature takes on, a form
created largely in childhood and built from habit. Personality is
the finishing of character, the harmonizing of the individual's
nature and his character.

Another important aspect of the child's unfoldment is his relationship to faith. Every child is born with faith. Yet the child
learns doubt through the gaining of knowledge. The experience of
doubt is an essential part of growing up, yet the child must strive
to maintain his faith, because faith, "a trust even in the absence of
reason,"[17] provides an important energy for his growth.

FIRST ERA

Inayat Khan divides the first era of childhood and youth into two
periods: **infancy**, from birth to about two and a half years of age;
and what he calls **babyhood**, from about two and a half years of
age until into the child's seventh year of life.

In the first year of his life, the infant is still very much influenced by the energies of the spiritual plane. He really begins his earthly life only when he learns to creep. During the second year of life, the infant is powerfully influenced by the astral plane, and only after his second birthday does he become fully present in the material world.

When the child is born, the soul is unfinished.

> The soul of an infant is like a photographic plate which has never been exposed before, and whatever impression falls on that photographic plate covers it; no other impressions which come afterwards have the same effect.[18]

The soul's need for positive influence—and vulnerability to negative influence—is the infant's most prominent characteristic in the first year of life. Inayat Khan speaks of the "condensing" of the soul as an irrevocable process that presents the infant's parents with a profound responsibility.

In the first years of life, the child begins to develop his will, his heart quality, and his mind. He starts to manifest his will as soon as he can act in any way, and the expression of his will without harmful restriction is essential to the fullness of his unfoldment. "If in childhood the parents take good care that the will was not broken, then the will would manifest itself in wonders. The child would do wonderful things in life if its will was sustained, if it was cherished."[19]

The child's heart quality is developed through the experience of nursing from his mother. The interaction that occurs with nursing fills the child with love, and the mother's milk provides a naturally complete food for the nurturance both of the physical body and of the soul. The milk also aids the unfoldment of the physical heart and the inner heart directly.

The infant's mind begins to unfold when he is cutting his first teeth. "It is from that time that it [he] begins to take notice of things and begins to think. The coming of the teeth is only an outward manifestation; the inner process is that the mind is forming."[19] When the infant stands, his power is beginning to manifest through the development of the qualities of enthusiasm, courage, endurance, and patience. When he begins to speak, his spirit is forming as his mind connects with his soul.

During infancy, the child needs to learn his first lessons in discipline, balance, concentration, and ethics. When he first gives his attention to his parent, he starts to learn discipline by learning to respond to the parent. He learns balance through the experience of an even rhythm in the course of his days, a balance between activity and relaxation that is drawn within him and developed as an inner rhythm. His concentration develops as he learns to focus on a single object. Finally, his ethical sense begins to unfold as he learns to give as well as receive.

Inayat Khan describes babyhood, from about two and a half years of age into the seventh year, as a time of life when the child needs to experience **kingship**, the freedom and happiness of his own direction and the absence of worry, anxiety, competition, and ambition. The child's need in these years is to experience the fullness of his own initiative for play. He needs not to be directed toward the learning of language or numbers but to be encouraged to express himself through the means of his choosing. "In the children's play, in their hustle and bustle, in their crying and jumping and running and climbing, their soul is expressing itself."[20] If adults allow the child to experience this time of kingship fully, the child can unfold to his potentials on various levels of his being. In contrast, if they control the child's life to suit their own needs, expectations, or ambitions, his energy, enthusiasm, and spirit will be limited and narrowed.

During this period of babyhood the child learns primarily through imitation. Thus, he needs to have positive human and natural models that he can imitate. He needs to interact with adults who can offer him attitudes and behaviors that are worthy of emulation. He also needs to "be near to nature, where it [he] should absorb what nature gradually teaches."[21] Nature is a profound teacher for a child of this age, not through any intentional process of teaching but through the child's experience of immersion in the rhythms and cycles of the natural world. Also, by appreciating the beauty in nature, the child discovers the beginnings of worship. In bowing to natural beauty, he begins to satisfy the innate predisposition in every soul to experience love and express this feeling through worship. This unfoldment to the first step in worship has a profound importance for the child's spiritual evolution both in the present and in the future.

SECOND ERA

According to Inayat Khan's vision, for most children the first era of unfoldment comes to an end and the second era begins sometime during the seventh year of life. This year is a time of transition from babyhood to the second era, which he calls **childhood**. Often the child experiences conflict within himself at this time, sometimes expressed as restlessness or obstinacy. He can become much more active than he has previously been and less responsive to others.

Inayat Khan divides the era of childhood into two periods: **early childhood**, from ages 7 through 9 years; and **late childhood**, from ages 10 through 12 or 13 years. Early childhood is "like the soil that is just prepared for sowing the seed. It is such a great opportunity . . . to sow the seed of knowledge and righteousness in the heart of the child."[22] In the seventh year, the child's inner conflict dissipates as he enters this new era of his life. He grows calmer and more harmonious within and more responsive to influence from others. At this age he can grasp an ideal for the first time. The first ideal that he must understand is a respectful attitude toward his elders. It is essential that this respect flow from the child as an experience that gives him real joy, not just as the heeding of external convention or pressure.

The learning of respect for others is particularly important, because it is through such experiences of respect that the child learns to respect himself. Self-respect, not a false pride but a sense of honor, is another ideal that the child must learn in these years. A third ideal, which relates to the ideal of respect for elders, is a sense of duty to his parents and the feeling of joy in fulfilling his duty. A fourth ideal is the quality of thoughtfulness in speaking and acting and an accompanying awareness of what is appropriate for him as a child. A fifth ideal that he must learn is a feeling for the spiritual. "It is in childhood that the spirit is responsive, and if that God-ideal is inspired at that time . . . one has given the child a start on the path to God."[23]

In early childhood, the child is very much open to learning through aesthetic activity: drawing, painting, music, and dancing. The child's need for growth is not artistic training but, rather, the opportunity for free expression of his soul through the activities of the arts. It is a time to express as he wishes without a lot of direction and, through his own initiative, to experience gracefulness and lightness.

In these years the child also needs to learn patience, endurance, and perseverance. He is impatient by nature, and so it is important for him to learn to complete things, to wait when necessary, and to begin to develop a habit of patience. While adults should not force this, they can gently yet persistently encourage the child to be patient and to persevere.

Finally, the child's experience can grow from a generalized admiration of natural beauty to more evolved forms of worship. One of his tasks for growth is to find or develop specific ways in which he can experience worship at his new level of knowing and connect the ideal of the divine with his inner feelings.

In his eleventh year, the child unfolds into the second part of childhood. "This is a period when children drink in and assimilate any knowledge, and that knowledge grows with them in their growth."[24] One major way that the child learns is once again through imitation, though of a more complex nature than his earlier imitative experience. What his unfoldment requires is examples who are worthy of his imitation, wonderful personalities and heroes in history and myth, and caring and evolved adults with whom to interact in daily life. The child also begins to develop greater powers of concentration in these years and needs the opportunity to practice artistic and craft activities that require attention, patience, and fine coordination of his hands and eyes.

Another important aspect of the child's unfoldment is the evolution of his relationship with nature, for this relationship affects both his intellectual and his spiritual growth. He needs regularly to experience nature directly. As he learns to become knowledgeable about the natural world, he develops the intellectual capacities to classify, define, and discriminate. As his feeling for the beauty and wonder of nature deepens, he opens to his own spirituality. As Inayat Khan explains,

> In order to be spiritual . . . one must communicate with nature; one must feel nature . . . The faculty of communicating with nature . . . is the principal thing for every soul in his spiritual development . . . If the child is deeply interested in the knowledge of nature, that shows that it has taken the first step on the path of philosophical truth.[25]

In the second part of childhood, the child's inner bent begins to reveal itself, the first indications of what his strengths and proclivities will be as an adult. It is important that he both develop his strengths but also continue to work with tasks and challenges for which he has less natural inclination, so his growth does not become one-sided or narrowed.

At this time, sexual identity also begins to be important to the child. Inayat Khan describes the child's needs in this area as follows:

> It is the psychology of the boy and of the girl which makes it necessary to give certain things to the boy and certain things to the girl; but as they develop they take each others' qualities; with development it comes naturally. Balance is best, whether in the boy or in the girl; and balance comes through opposite qualities.[26]

Thus, while the child needs to develop the characteristics archetypally associated with his own sex, he also needs the opportunity to gain the balance that comes from developing characteristics that are usually associated with the opposite sex. This kind of balance in his experience will help him to unfold as a person who is not limited by societal sex roles but who has developed both the female and the male potentials within him.

THIRD ERA

The third era of childhood and youth starts in the thirteenth or fourteenth year with the ending of childhood and the beginning of youth. It is a time of inner conflict and struggle, of nervousness, agitation, and restlessness. The youth experiences an inner inconsistency that is manifested as inconsistent behavior. Sometimes he is clear and responsible, while other times he is absentminded and "impossible."

In the first few years of this era, the youth is no longer a child, but neither is he yet an experienced person. He does know the beginnings of adult comprehension, maturity, and development of the spirit. At the same time his struggle both to leave childhood and to mature is evident in his moodiness and self-absorption. During the middle three years of this era, the youth begins to establish a center and seeks balance and self-control. In the final three years, he clearly becomes more an adult than a child, establishing more consistently his clarity and his self-possession.

For the youth to unfold positively, he needs to be treated appropriately by adults. It is essential that adults not antagonize or alienate the youth but remain in relationship with him throughout this era. While the danger of estrangement is always present, adults can establish a nurturing relationship with the youth if they trust in his good attributes, appreciate them, and encourage him to continue to develop them. The adults must strike a fine balance, neither holding the youth in repressive check and inciting rebellion nor spoiling him by prematurely removing adult supervision. The youth needs firmness and consistency from adults to support his growth but always enough and increasing room to experience his independence and be responsible for it. The role of adults in the youth's unfoldment to maturity is critical, for only through the experience of interacting with adults who are caring, supportive, and consistently engaged with him in a balanced way can the youth grow into maturity without prolonging his adolescence into the next decade of his life.

The era of youth is a time when the young person is predisposed to self-absorption, to involvement with his "I-consciousness." While much of this focus is necessary for his development, he needs adults to help him experience life beyond the level of "I, me, mine," not with critical judgment or condemnation but through a gentle extension of his vision and reach beyond himself. His mind is still taking shape in these years, and he needs to be involved in experiences that open up and expand his feeling and thinking beyond his ego. Another way in which the youth's self-absorption needs to be softened is through his cultivation of a passive, in-taking attitude that he can practice for short periods of time on a regular basis.

The youth also needs to work consciously to develop his will. One way through which he can do this involves his articulation of a moral ideal, a natural activity for young people, and his conscious, ongoing attempt to embody his moral ideal. He can also help his will to unfold through the practice of will-related tasks and exercises.

Inayat Khan's Vision of Child Raising and Education

Inayat Khan teaches that conscious action by parents and teachers is essential to the physical, mental, moral, social, and spiritual unfoldment of the child and youth. While he strongly advocates allowing the child to develop according to his own inner law, he is equally forceful and clear in the case he makes for the child's need for education—for support, guidance, and help from adults—to grow up into the fullness of his potential.

The central focus of education, Inayat Khan maintains, is the study of unity: learning where and how things in the world unite and interrelate. The child must learn about the profound interdependence of all things on all levels as well as about the necessity of human interdependence and the unselfishness that makes interdependence work. With unity and interdependence as the focus, Khan describes the goals of education as

> the knowledge of oneself and of one's surroundings: the knowledge of others, both those who are known to us and those who are unknown and away; the knowledge of the conditions of human nature and of life's demands: and the knowledge of cause and effect, which leads in

the end to the knowledge of the world within and without.[27]

A second focus of education, almost as important as the first, involves helping the child to nurture a harmonious and positive attitude toward life. Attitude is a channel for effort. The right attitude brings the child's effort to the fore and helps him to accomplish what he seeks. The right attitude also helps the child to treat himself as a good friend, to respect himself and use his energies well.

The initial and most important phase of the child's education consists of the child raising he experiences with his parents during the first seven years. As the child learns primarily from example during these years, his parents are his first and most influential teachers. Their simple yet always demanding task is to be worthy of imitation. "The parents must themselves learn to be examples for their children. No theory has influence without practice."[28] Later on when the child goes to school, his parents need to connect his home experience with his experience of school.

FIVE ASPECTS OF EDUCATION

In his teachings about education, Inayat Khan first examines the five aspects of education: physical education; mental education; moral education; social education; and spiritual education. Then he explores the particular educational needs and potentials of the child and youth at each step in his unfoldment.

1. **Physical education** must begin in infancy. The child can learn to move his hands and feet rhythmically to music. When he is older, he can learn dance and gymnastics not as a chore but as play. Sound physical education includes a healthy yet simple diet and the experience of a harmonious rhythm in daily life, one that includes active play and exploration outdoors and indoors, a time for resting consciously—perhaps listening to a story or quiet music, or looking at pictures—and long and regular sleep.

2. **Mental education** involves helping the child to develop both the power and the fineness of his mind. Later on at an appropriate time in his unfoldment, it also includes helping him to develop his reason.

The education of the child's **mental power** must focus on the following:

- Helping him learn to concentrate by engaging him in activities that call for simple-minded attention.

- Helping him develop strength of mind by encouraging him to become self-confident in what he thinks, says, and does. The child learns self-confidence when he is allowed and encouraged to discover for himself and think and act from his own sense of rightness. The adult's role is to encourage him to explore on his own in this way, to support his efforts in doing so, and to resist the temptation to force beliefs upon him.

- Helping him gain a strong feeling for his own inner rhythm and the inner tranquility that living his own rhythm brings to his mind. Tranquility of mind brings the child balance, self-control, and self-confidence. The adult's role is to be aware of the child's rhythm and bring him back to it whenever he gives way to excesses of excitement or passion.

The education of the child's **fineness of mind** must focus on the following:

- Helping him evoke clarity, keenness, and subtlety in the perceptions of his senses.

- Helping him develop a sense of appropriateness in his speech and actions and to be guided by this sense.

- Helping him learn a gracefulness in his manner, which can evolve into good manners as he grows older.

Finally, when the child is ready to develop his reason, he needs to learn a receptive, responsive attitude that guides him first to be open to receiving and then to reasoning. He also needs appropriate practice in all of the aspects of reasoning and gentle guidance from an adult in applying his reason to the events and challenges of his life.

3. The child's **moral education** centers on his development of five qualities. One is the right quality of love as service to others. This quality of love is founded in consideration and often requires sacrifice. The child learns love first by being loved by an adult, yet this parental love must not be expressed in such a way that it spoils the child. The child who is loved will manifest the spirit of generosity, and the parent must nurture and support this spirit, as it is the opening of the heart. Such generosity cannot be taught, but it can be encouraged once it appears on its own. Generosity leads to the expression of other forms of love: tolerance, forgiveness, endurance, and fortitude. The spirit of generosity also leads to the expression of consideration for others.

In helping the child's quality of love to unfold, the adult must be careful not to compel but to guide. The adult's guidance of the child must come as positive support, not as criticism of limitation or failure. As Inayat Khan notes, "Teach consideration by praising the child when he shows consideration, not by accusing him of inconsiderateness."[29]

The second quality that the child must develop as a part of his moral education is a cluster of interrelated traits: humility, gentleness, gratefulness, and a sense of justice. When the child develops these traits, they help to purify his heart. And the energy of the heart as it becomes more pure helps the child to embody these traits even more.

A third quality is a keen sense of harmony. To foster this learning, the child needs to experience harmony in his daily rhythm and in the natural world. Another quality is a proper understanding of beauty. To gain this, he must regularly experience beauty both in nature and in the creations of human beings. A fifth quality involves becoming conscious of and having a feeling for his duty to every person in the world.

4. **Social education** engages the child in learning his relation and duty to everyone and everything around him. He needs to learn

what is expected of him in every relationship and the importance of fair dealing, give-and-take, reciprocity, and the honoring of one's word in relations with humans and the rest of the natural world. The child also must learn a sense of harmony in and of the world and a deeply felt appreciation of the ideal of the human community. As Inayat Khan teaches:

> For the world is a family, and the right attitude of a young soul must be to see in every man his brother and in every woman his sister; he must look on aged people as he would on his father or mother.[30]

5. **Spiritual education** involves the child in becoming aware of the ideal of the divine, of the oneness, both within and outside himself. It is not the learning of a religious belief but the apprehension of the essence of the divine, which he can learn to call upon for help and guidance and grow toward. The child must learn the habit of feeling and expressing his gratitude toward the divine within and outside himself at least once each day. He must also be encouraged to be sincere and genuine, for these qualities are the manifestation of the spiritual energy within him in the world of human relationship.

EDUCATIONAL NEEDS IN THE FIRST ERA

In his discussion of education, Inayat Khan details the educational needs of the child and youth in every stage of his unfoldment from birth through twenty-one years of age.

In infancy (birth to about two and half years), the best way for the parent to educate his child is to work with the child's own ongoing growth, particularly the development of his heart qualities. "The calmness, the quietness, the tenderness, the gentleness, everything the mother cultivates in his nature at that particular time when the infant is nursed, the infant will receive as a lesson in its cradle."[31]

The parent must learn to control the infant not by mastering him, which weakens his will, but by establishing a friendship with him. Experiencing a friendship with his parent sustains the infant's will and helps him to evolve. The parent also needs to be patient with the child and avoid annoyance as much as possible. The parent's annoyance harms the child's nervous and subtle energy systems, causing them to contract. The infant experiences this contraction both as depression and as fear, emotions that can take hold within him and endure as he grows up. The more patience the parent has with the child, the better, because the parent's patience both avoids the harm of contraction and strengthens the infant's will.

The parent must also be conscious and purposive in his interactions with the infant, particularly when he gives objects to the child. "Even from infancy every object that is given to the child must inspire him with its use. An object that has no use, that serves no purpose, hinders the progress of an infant."[32]

In his first three years of life, the infant's education should focus on the learning of affection, discipline, balance, concentration, ethics, and relaxation. He learns affection and love through his nursing and the consistent experience of loving care and attention from his parents. When the infant first gives his attention to his parent, the adult can begin to teach discipline to the child by calmly repeating the desired action before him.

> For instance, the infant wants something which it should not have, while the guardian wishes that it should play with a particular toy. This toy must be given continually into its hand; and when the child throws it away, or when it cries, give it again; and when the child does not look at it, give it again. . . . It is a wrong method when the guardian wishes to control an infant and wishes to teach it discipline by forcing a certain action upon it. It is repetition which will bring about discipline. It only requires patience.[33]

The parent can help the child to learn balance by consistently helping him to regain his normal inner rhythm whenever he loses it. Often when he becomes too excited, either laughing or crying, the infant cannot re-establish his own balance but needs help.

> When an infant is very excited, then the rhythm of its
> action and movement is not normal. By clapping the
> hands, or by rattling, or by knocking on something one
> can make the rhythm of the infant change. . . .
> However excited the infant may be, begin by making
> some noise in its rhythm, and then bring it to a normal
> rhythm. . . . The excitement will abate; the whole
> condition of the infant's mind, the blood circulation,
> the movement, the expression, everything will change
> to normal rhythm.[34]

Through the repetition of this inner balancing of the infant, the
adult can help the child learn to gain control of his own inner
rhythm and of his balance.

The child learns concentration by focusing his attention on
things that attract him: colored objects, fruits, flowers, and so on.
He needs to have ongoing access to objects that attract his interest. As he focuses his attention on these, he begins to develop his
concentration.

The parent can help the infant learn the beginning of ethics by
giving to him and asking him to give in return. It is essential that
the parent not force or compel the child to give but only persist
with calm and gentle requests. Eventually the spirit of generosity,
the essence of morals, will arise within the child, and he will begin
to give back for the pleasure of giving.

Finally, the infant needs to experience full and satisfying relaxation as a part of his daily pattern. He needs to be calm and
aware, to be resting and turning inward, and to be in a deep and
peaceful sleep. The parent must organize the child's day so he can
experience each of these conditions on a regular basis. At the very
end of infancy, the parent can teach the child to be silent for a
moment. Such a silence is the next step in the child's learning of
concentration.

In babyhood (from about two and half years into the seventh
year) the child learns most by imitation. Once again the greatest
responsibility of the parent is to work with his own unfoldment,
so that he can provide the child with examples that are worthy of
imitation. Inayat Khan strongly urges that the child not be

taught anything formally in these years nor even encouraged to learn letters and numbers. He explains that the learning of symbolic languages can wait until the next era of the child's life. Now his energy is better directed into his own play and expression, for it is through these activities that his soul can best grow and unfold. What the parent needs to "teach" the child is a regularity in the rhythm of life: eating, playing, sleeping, and sitting quietly. The adult can teach this most powerfully by example, though he can also direct the child by praising the child's accomplishments in living a balanced rhythm.

In these years the child needs to grow accustomed to sitting in silence for short periods of time. Once he becomes comfortable with this, he will soon learn to cherish its peace and warmth.

Inayat Khan suggests that the parent guide the child both with praise and with reasoning. As he explains:

> Never for one moment imagine that the child will not take in your reasoning. If not the first time it will take it in the second or third time. One must continue to reason with the child; and by doing so the guardian brings the child closer to his spirit, because the child feels a friendship between itself and the guardian.[35]

The parent should scold or punish the child only as a last resort. If he must scold or punish, the adult should do so with a spirit of gentleness, never with anger or any other intense feeling. The child needs to experience the scolding or punishment only enough to know that he is being punished. It is important that the parent not frighten the child, for the shock of fear hinders the enthusiasm of the soul to grow and evolve.

In babyhood the parent can begin to help the child learn manners, again by praising his good behavior rather than pointing out or punishing his limitations.

EDUCATIONAL NEEDS IN THE SECOND ERA

In his seventh year the child needs a good deal of attention as he experiences the conflicts that mark the passage from the first era of his life into the second. If possible, he should stay at home during this year and not go to school until after his seventh birthday, because what he needs is not the competitive life of the school but the comfort of his home. This seventh year is a particularly important time when the child can benefit most not from structure and competition but from freedom and happiness. Once he has moved through this transition into early childhood, then he will be ready for the wider and more demanding world of the school. When a child is faced with anxiety and competition too soon, he grows tight and restrained, unable to open to his full potential. In contrast, when he comes to the competition of the school at the proper time, his mind has matured and the challenges of school are not limiting but enlarging.

Inayat Khan explains that to teach the child in early childhood, the first half of the second era, the teacher must befriend the child and influence him with caring, praise, and inspiration. The teacher must not rule the child or try to compel his interests or enthusiasms. Nor must the teacher attempt to train him in particular skills other than the learning of language and numbers, as such learning is not appropriate for this age. Rather, the teacher must perceive the soul qualities already growing within the child and help him to express them.

One powerful way to guide the child is to offer him praise and appreciation for his own actions that are positive. Another is to encourage him to express himself through drawing, painting, music, and dance and to provide him with many opportunities for such expression. Once the teacher has become the child's friend, he can help the child overcome his natural impatience, learn to complete what he begins, and develop the habits of being patient and of waiting.

In these years the child also learns profoundly from stories that engage his interest and offer him a meaning to consider and understand.

> In no other way will the child absorb ideals as it will
> do in the form of stories. The stories told in its early
> childhood will remain with it all through its life . . .
> every year, as the child grows, the story will have
> another meaning; and so there will be a continual
> development of the ideal, which will become a great
> blessing in the life of the child.[36]

Late childhood, the second half of the second era, is a time
when the child is open, interested, curious, and hungry for knowledge. Although the teacher can be a little more direct in his instruction of the child, he still needs to limit his formal teaching to a
minimum and engage the child in learning through a rich and
varied array of informal activities that focus on conversation,
exploration and discovery, and imagination.

In these years the child needs to spend a good deal of time
exploring the natural environment, becoming familiar with nature,
and gaining a feeling for the natural world. "There is so much to
be learned from plant life, from birds, animals, insects, that once a
child begins to take an interest in that subject, everything
becomes a symbolical expression of the inner truth."[37] Such an
interest in and feeling for nature also provides a grounding for
later intellectual and spiritual development.

The child also must learn about his family origins and history
and about the characteristics, aspirations, and customs of the
people of his country. Inayat Khan suggests that the teacher introduce the child to the various customs, explain the psychology and
the meanings of them, and let the child "see for itself if it is a cus-
tom worth following or better forgotten."[38]

In these years the child can begin to learn metaphysics, "just
enough for it to know that there is a soul, that there is a mind, that
there is a body; that there is a relation between the soul and the
mind, and the mind and the body."[39] The teacher can also engage
the child's imagination in considering the nature of the world he
knows and how he would like to re-vision the world to make it a
better place. This kind of imaginative activity gives the child's soul
qualities an avenue of expression through his imagination and
involves the child in considering his own contribution to the evolution of human beings.

The child still responds powerfully to movement, music, drawing, and other artistic expression. He can begin to understand the role of skill in these activities and want to develop such. Any instruction in these skills must be balanced and not overbearing. The child is also still very much intrigued by the lives of heroes and heroines. The teacher can engage him in learning about the stories of worthy personalities from whom he can learn by example.

EDUCATIONAL NEEDS IN THE THIRD ERA

Inayat Khan describes youth as a season of blossoming, a time of rising physical and mental energies within the human being. It is also a time when the young person explores his own authority to know, feel, and do and, in the process, becomes less receptive to adults than he was as a child. Given this movement toward independence, the education of the youth must rely on presenting him with consciously selected impressions and encouraging him to explore and make sense of them for himself.

> The education of youth depends mostly on impressions. Sometimes you may make a youth read books and that will not help . . . once you show him the phenomena, the example of what you are saying, and let the youth see with his own eyes what are the effects of different causes, then the teaching is given in an objective way; and in this manner wise guardians educate a youth.[40]

In teaching the youth, the teacher must be careful not to force anything on him, for this will only motivate him to resist or rebel. Rather, the teacher needs to make the impressions of conditions, situations, and personalities available to the youth and suggest possible courses of exploration that he can pursue.

Inayat Khan discusses the education of the youth in terms of his five categories of education: physical, mental, moral, social, and spiritual. In his physical education, the essential quality that the youth needs to develop is balance: in sleep, diet, relaxation, and exertion. The youth's natural inclination is toward excess and imbalance. The teacher can help the youth learn balance by offering ways through which the young person can discover the effects of imbalance and balance for himself.

In his mental education, the youth must learn to use his reason with power and discrimination. The teacher can encourage the unfoldment of the youth's reason by asking him questions about everything that he says and does, not in a way that confronts him but, rather, in a way that gently draws out his processes of thought. The teacher must be sure to place this questioning at the level of the youth's thought, not at his own level.

While one way to help the youth develop his reason is to question him, another is to "make lines of thought and . . . place them before him, in order that he may use the lines as a track to follow."[41] In this way, the teacher provides the youth with models of clear and mindful reasoning that he can emulate, usually without even being aware of his emulation. These models of thought give the youth a way to feel clear thinking as well as conceive of it with his reasoning. As the teacher questions the young person and provides models of thought, he must also encourage consideration for others in the youth, for such consideration facilitates good, independent thinking.

Another aspect of mental education involves the imagination. The teacher can help the young person to cultivate his imagination by directing the young person's attention to what is beautiful, then asking him to imagine how he can make it even more beautiful and complete.

A third aspect of mental education involves concentration and receptivity. The youth tends to be more expressive than receptive in this era, yet it is important for him to cultivate his capacities for concentration and receptivity if he is to continue to evolve both now and later. The teacher can help the youth learn the ability to be passive and absorptive, not by urging this attitude upon him, but by engaging him gently in receptive experience. When presented with an opportunity to concentrate and be receptive as a suggestion rather than a demand, the youth will often welcome this experience and learn to treasure the calmness and peace of concentration and receptivity. This kind of experience also helps the youth to increase his mental strength, which is dependent on his capacity for single-mindedness.

The practice of concentration and receptivity through silence, breathing exercises, yoga postures, and simple meditations fosters not only strength of mind but also of will. The nurturance and strengthening of his will is a critically important task for the youth, and he can benefit from all the guidance and nurturance that he can receive from an adult. In these years his heart quality is still unfolding, and his emotions, like everything else about him, are ripe for the abuse of excess. The more that he can develop the clarity of his reason and the strength of his mind and particularly of his will, the more he will be able to open his heart without giving way to the potentially damaging excesses of emotionality that are too often the norm for youth.

In addition, the youth is highly sensitive to all the conditions around him. If there is sorrow, disharmony, and depression around him, these feelings go right to his heart and limit him, for he can feel it all but as yet do little about its causes. For this reason Inayat Khan explains that "it is not fair [for adults] to draw sympathy from the youth . . . for one's pains and troubles. . . . If pain is sown in the heart of the youth, decay develops at the root of his life, making him bitter all through life."[42] Thus, Inayat Khan urges that parents and teachers respect the specialness of youth, which is "the springtime of the soul,"[43] and as much as possible avoid burdening the young person with the difficulties of their own lives.

In his moral education, the youth needs to create an ideal for himself, not just accept one given to him by adults. Then he must strive to fulfill his ideal. The teacher can foster this process by engaging the youth in exploring and articulating his ideal and by supporting his efforts to live according to his ideal. The youth's ability to be guided by his ideal is largely dependent on the nature of his will, so the teacher must involve the youth in evoking and developing his willpower. Also, the teacher can help the young person to ground his ideal in dignity and honor by involving the youth in exploring what honor and dignity mean to him, in terms of both knowing and feeling. A final aspect of the youth's moral education has to do with his consideration for others. The teacher can help the youth learn about his duty to others by engaging him in exploring his sense and feeling of his obligations. The teacher's role in all of this, then, is not to offer an ethical standard to the youth but to help him to explore and articulate his own integrity.

In his social education, the youth needs to work on expressing sincerity in his relationships with others. A common tendency for a youth is to go along with the crowd, even if such is not genuine behavior for him. The teacher must help the young person learn to evoke sincerity within himself and be willing to take the risks of being genuine rather than superficial, for sincerity and genuineness are qualities of the soul that must be evoked and expressed, not held in by fear.

The fifth category of education is spiritual education. Youth is a time not of open and evolved spirituality but, rather, of experiencing religion while beginning to learn of an "inner stillness." Inayat Khan explains the difference between religion and spirituality as follows: "Often spirituality is confused with religion. . . . Religion for many is that which they know to be their people's belief; spirituality is the revealing of the divine light which is hidden in every soul."[44]

The adult can encourage the youth to participate in a religion, though, of course, without forcing him in any way but only responding to whatever interest he shows on his own. If he learns one religion in these years, then as he unfolds spiritually later in life he will understand the meaning of all religions for human beings and how religion relates to spirituality. While the experience of religion will support the spiritual growth of the youth, the adult needs to help him avoid adopting any of the vanity, bigotry, or fanaticism that are too often associated with religious groups.

Though the youth does not open fully to his own spiritual nature in this era, he can prepare for such an opening by learning to experience an "inner stillness." This stillness comes from opening his heart to his spirit. Related to this stillness is the youth's need to learn to "soften his heart," which will also help him to open to his own spirituality in later years.

> It is the constant softening of the heart of the youth
> that is necessary. There are two ways of softening the
> heart: one is by helping the youth to open himself to
> beauty which is shining in all its various forms. The
> other is to give him a tendency to righteousness, which

is the very essence of the soul. These things cannot be taught, but they can be awakened in the heart of the youth.[45]

Finally, the young person needs to learn about metaphysics, but only to the extent that such learning is prompted by his own feeling and thinking.

Inayat Khan's Way of Knowing

Hazrat Inayat Khan was a Sufi master whose primary means of knowing was the practice of his spiritual path. He explains that through his spiritual discipline he experienced various planes of being above the mental plane, which is the ordinary territory of the human mind. From these experiences, he notes, he gained knowledge and wisdom that is not directly available to human reason but that can only be apprehended through higher states of consciousness.

Inayat Khan describes these states in ascending order, as follows:

- Intuition is an inner knowing that is independent of any outer perception. It is first expressed as feeling and then transformed by the mind into thought. When the mind is tranquil and receptive, wisdom rises from the depths of the heart, a higher level of vibration, and flows into the conscious mind.

- Inspiration comes down from the divine mind into the heart and then on into the consciousness as a stream of wonder and joy. Inspiration comes into the mind already organized into a complete idea.

- Vision is inspiration that comes through a clearness of the inner sight in the form of images.

- Revelation is the experience of God-realization, as the knower becomes one with everything in the universe, and every secret is revealed through the experience of identity of the knower with the known.

Inayat Khan also describes in broad terms the four steps in his spiritual discipline: concentration, the experience of single-mindedness in relation to an object, sound, or sight; contemplation, the experience of single-mindedness in relation to an idea; meditation, an opening to the silent life within and an awakening to the soul; and God-realization, a oneness with the divine mind and with all of reality.

Through his spiritual practice, Inayat Khan experienced these various states and, he reports, learned to gain access to them whenever he entered his meditation. Sirkar Van Stolk, a student of Inayat Khan's as well as his secretary and traveling companion for several years, describes Hazrat Inayat Khan as embodying the highest of these states:

> He was an example of all those things he taught: of living in complete harmony with oneself and with one's surroundings; of being conscious of the unity underlying all forms of life . . . even while he talked of everyday things, he remained constantly in that state of highest awareness which the mystics call "God-consciousness." It was this consciousness which stood out most strikingly in the character of Hazrat Inayat Khan. From the moment of meeting him one felt enveloped in his radiance as in a mantle: completely safe, completely understood.[46]

A TALK WITH MURSHIDA VERA CORDA

I sit with Murshida[1] Vera Justin Corda in her living room and listen as she speaks of her life and her work. She grew up first in the foothills of the Sierra Nevadas in California, later in the San Francisco area. In her childhood she once corresponded with Hazrat Inayat Khan and also heard him speak. When her family traveled through Italy, she met Maria Montessori.

Mrs. Corda first worked with children in the Canon Kip Nursery when she was 10 years old. She was only 16 when she graduated from college. She was initiated into the Sufi Order by her longtime friend and teacher, Murshid[1] Sam Lewis, and has pursued her spiritual discipline and her study of Sufism for nearly fifty years. She also studied with Dr. Arnold Gesell and incorporated his work and that of other developmental psychologists into what has become her extension of Inayat Khan's vision of human becoming.

Murshida Vera worked first as an artist and designer of books and clothes, later as a teacher of exceptional children. In the late 1960s she founded and directed the San Francisco Seed Center, the first organized school of the Sufi movement in the United States. A few years later she did the same for the Marin Seed Center, which operated until 1982. She was described to me by members of the Sufi community in Boston as the foremost educator in the Sufi movement in this country, probably in the world.

Mrs. Corda lives in a small town in the Salinas Valley in central California. She is in her early seventies now, about 5 feet 3 inches tall, a woman clear of voice and mind. When she speaks, her face, already more youthful looking than her chronological age, seems even younger. Her animation lightens her, her vibrancy expressed most clearly in the openness of her eyes and smile. As I sit across the living room from her, I can feel her energy and the strength of her feeling. And I am warmed and supported by them, although I have met her for the first time only half an hour ago.

"I was born in 1913," she tells me. "When I was twenty-two I met Murshid Sam Lewis at the San Francisco Sufi Order headquarters on Sutter Street, where I was invited by the then secretary of the Order, Hazel Armstrong." Sam Lewis, a student of Inayat Khan, was one of the most prominent American Sufi teachers for four decades. While he was well known in the Sufi community for many years, he emerged into a wider recognition only toward the end of his life in the late 1960s when he became a major figure in the San Francisco counter-culture. "I had met Hazel on the Federal Arts Projects, where I was an illustrator. Her office was across the hall from mine, and we became immediate and close friends, though she was many years older than I.

"When I came into the Sufi Order that day, I had no idea that I was going to be initiated. But she said, 'Sam is in.' He was then a colleague within the Order. She said, 'Sam is in the next room.' She opened the door from the office, and he was standing at the altar with his back to me. As he turned around and met my eyes, it was an immediate recognition, and we, he embraced me. Hazel said, 'Sam, this is Vera. Vera, this is Sam.' He turned me around to the altar and initiated me. Didn't ask me if I wanted to be a Sufi or anything. Just initiated me, that was it. From that day, for thirty years following, ah, we were the closest of companions. When I married, my first husband was also a very close disciple of Murshid Sam's.

"Murshid Sam's idea of education began with me, in Fairfax, California, the large Sufi grounds and house where the so-called rock still exists on Hillside Drive today—a very sacred spot, ah, that Niajin Senzaki and Hazrat Inayat Khan both said when they stood on it was the most magnetic spot they had stood upon in America. So that is where, on every weekend, the Sufis came and brought their children with them. Some program had to be organized for those children so that the parents could do their Sufi work. And Murshid Sam and I did the work with the children involved in that.

"I had had great illness in my childhood and had not really completed those developmental levels. So at twenty two I was with kids who were of all ages from three through twelve. And I relived those levels, in hiking and horseback riding and exploring nature, and just walking and talking with Murshid Sam, and singing *The Pirates of Penzance,* which he loved—Relived again those developmental levels which I was totally lacking because of the health problem in that part of my life. So this is where I first came in touch with how the Sufi message was put to work in everyday living with children. And at that time, I didn't evaluate it for what it was.

"When Murshid Sam passed away, I was living in the Salinas Valley. I had lived a celibate life for sixteen years after the death of my husband. My children were then out and on their own in totally different areas of California. At about eleven o'clock at night, I finished my (Sufi) readings and was sitting in bed reading. And I decided my eyes were tired, so I turned off the lights. And, as I turned off the light, a sound of power came, as the sound is on the wires sometimes, the telephone wires. Or when a flock of birds is claiming a territory—the power sound—it comes out of them as a group, and it just—I immediately thought, is that a power line that's doing that? Or a flock of birds? And that was the first thought in my mind as I sat up in bed. It was still, the room was dark. And then at the foot of my bed, Murshid Sam appeared in the form of Shiva, all arms and legs dancing. He came in molecules of light through the wall, facing my bed, and manifested very clearly. And then he stopped dancing and looked right into my eyes with the same intense look that he gave me in real life. And he said to me, 'Guide my children, guard my children, protect my children.' And he repeated that three times, and then the pattern broke up again into little lights that disappeared through the wall.

"I just sat there and turned on the light. And I was just absolutely stunned, having never had such an experience in my life. I got out of bed, got my telephone book, and called Mentor Garden, Murshid Sam's home in San Francisco. I had the name of Walid Ali, whom I did not know personally, as being one of the heads of the Sufi society that Murshid Sam had formed. I called him, and I said, 'Please excuse me for calling you at this late hour, but I have had an experience I cannot explain.' And he said, 'Say no more. Murshid Sam passed away, fell down the stairs and passed away.'"

"He had come through to give me that message. I take that

very seriously in my life now, because I'm not the kind of person that receives this sort of stuff every day. It was an extraordinary event in my life, and I put it down, the dates and times and what was said. Then I went into seclusion. I went up to the Pinnacles and into the caves beyond the Pinnacles, where I stayed by myself. Took a leave of absence from my teaching in school. Went up there into seclusion to adjust to his passing and his guidance.

"After a time I came down to make contact with his children, the flower children of the Haight Ashbury in San Francisco whom he had taken off the streets into his home, had fed, had gotten off dope, and had given them the message that they were getting through drugs plus far more in depth. And so many personal realizations that did not come from taking drugs.

"So that is how my work began. These young women, all of them had babies that were very young, maybe fifteen, eighteen months of age, and some under that. And they were all burned out from childcare. They were really having it very hard financially and physically and certainly spiritually. They asked me, 'What shall we do?' And I said, 'Well, you've got to get together and get some kind of a little nursery school going, which I'll train you in so you can devote some time to that. But you'll also have days that you will be free of child care in the house, when you can go out and dance or do art or just be in nature. Time to rejuvenate yourselves and be away from that terrible drag that it is in the first two years when you have no help, no parents or no one to relieve you of childcare.'

"So that's how it began. We rented a store in the old Mission district (in San Francisco) that had katty-corner from it a small, a very small park. And there the first Seed Center began. Pir Vilayat's (the youngest son of Inayat Khan who became a teacher and leader in the Sufi Order in the 1960s) oldest son, now called Michael Serafil, was one of the children in that. All of the children of the members of the Sufi society were in that little Seed Center. So we probably had sixteen to begin with, then maybe twenty-six.

"Then we had to grow. But there was no place to grow, no play yard for one thing. So I taught the children right there. 'Walking on the line' and the work we did with movement they just learned on the marks on the sidewalk. We took them out, held their hands, and taught them to walk the line, how to balance, and how to get the fulcrum of their body straight.

"So then we developed into the larger school and then developed again, so that the Seed Center in San Francisco grew three different times. In the second school that we had, people were coming who wanted to know: how do you do the things you do? How do you put this to work? Can you teach it to us? And so the first training began there, and those people started other schools or worked within schools where they brought that teaching."

I ask Mrs. Corda about the Seed Center that she had started and directed in San Francisco, and she describes its structure for me. "We followed the teachings of Hazrat Inayat Khan about energy. We balanced activity with rest and relaxation. And that went on all day.

"When there was play, it was chiefly free play, except there were always two teachers on that playground or yard, wherever we were. One watched one direction, and one the other. The children had freedom within a controlled environment. That, of course, is the crux of the whole Sufi education system: to control the environment. Set up an environment that is controlled, and allow total freedom of the child within that environment.

"That's how it differs from Montessori schools. Montessori had learning tasks that were given to the child one after the other, in order. We do not do that, because our Seed Centers are made up of open learning centers. They were open space, like warehouse space or an auditorium that you started with and then built your centers around that. So there was an open circle where children would all come together, regardless of their developmental or age level. They'd all come to that circle of attunement in the morning. But beyond that, they went into their groups, into their own centers.

"During those thirteen years that I worked in the Seed Centers, there were children who had been kicked out of three schools, and not allowed in the public school system anymore. I didn't know you could do this by law, but they managed to get them out, they were too much trouble. Those children, we took in. And our method is to test before we begin with the child. There's nothing too original about our testing. Some of it you'd say is Gesell. Some of it was taken from methods that worked for me in the public school classroom, working with exceptional children. We tested the children to find out where they are. When we found out that a child by developmental placement could enter at a totally different level than his age would suggest, we then placed the child at that level.

"Every learning center was set up at three levels. The very beginning one was always tactile. And then developing into the second level, and then finally into the third level, where there were papers and matching and more intellectual things that children could choose. But everything was set out at the child's level, so they could walk in and wait on themselves. They were taught, the only things they were taught were how to set up your work area and how to clean it up. And we expected every child to put down their newsprint, use their little foam containers and the cups when they needed water. All of that set-up was put at their level, so they could walk along, pick it up, and set it up. They were taught that, and they were also monitored to get them to clean it up. That was not hard, because the children were always monitors. As soon as possible, they took over the organization of their own areas of work, their own classrooms, set up and clean up."

Mrs. Corda pauses, and I ask her, "In your working with children, what is your sense of who they are as beings?"

"I refer to the different parts as bodies," she replies. "I don't think that's exactly Hazrat Inayat Khan's way of saying it. First there's the physical body that one must be aware of. If the child has a certain build or a handicap, it's obvious. It's visual, and you pick it up right away. You have a picture, an impress on your mind of the physical quality of that child. That doesn't take very much insight. Anybody can see that. In fact, it's sad that they do, because they peg the child on that physical body alone.

"Next is the mental body. There are children who are alert, tuned in, are looking at everything in their surroundings the first day they come in. And then there are children who are emotionally still very much connected to the psychic umbilical cord of the mother. And they cannot part from the mother. The first two weeks in the Center are traumatic for them. And mothers who hang around make it worse. You finally have to say, 'You must go. We can handle this alone better than in your presence, where the child is going to cling.' So there's an emotional body, too, along with the physical and mental.

"Our first lesson at the Seed Center is to hang up your own clothes at your own cubby. And you have a photograph at that cubby, so if you don't know your name, you know your picture. And that is your job, not Momma's. It's very hard to stop mothers from doing that. 'No, this is your child's cubby. You do not take it off and hang it up for him. He does it by himself.' Self-reliance, right from the beginning."

"At what age does this take place?" I ask.

"Well, when they're coming to the Center, we say, 'When they are potty-trained.' In America this usually means around two and a half years old. But when we had our infancy center, we had children from six months up—When they were on their feet and running around, doors were always open. The child might be only 18 months, on his feet and interested in what's going on in the pre-school. He could walk through and observe the centers where the children would be sitting four to a table, with one guide, when the table work began. He came in, he was always offered a chair. There was always an extra chair there. He sat down and observed. When he could be timed, the timer was set. There was a timer in every learning center. When the child was sitting for five minutes—and that was consistent, he'd come in for three days and sit for five minutes—then he was invited to participate. He was ready, not by any testing but by his own demonstration that he was ready to learn in a small group. If you just came in to see what was going on and walked out, that was fine, too. So long as he didn't disturb learning materials, he could observe as much as he wanted to.

"We decided upon the four at a table because, physically the size of our tables in the first place and because we felt that we never wanted to make uneven numbers. Children pair up very soon, they make partners. And if you have five, there's always the spoke in the wheel that doesn't have anybody to meet with. We always tried to keep it to even numbers, two or four or six.

"From the time they started in the infancy center with their first projects—always with the hands, tactile—the child was encouraged as soon as he had basic forms in mind, as soon as he could make a ball out of his playdough or his clay. Roll it himself and make a whole bunch of them, and pat it down into a patty-cake. Then every day was a project. The projects were not something new each day, as it is in most nursery schools and kindergartens, but the child was given the opportunity of reinforcing until the concept became his own.

"I would say that geometry is probably the first thing we teach. Because we teach, first of all, making a ball and how to make all the basic forms. Out of those balls of clay—after those are all mastered—they learn to make the worm, or the column, and the sphere and the ovoid, or the egg. They'll say it's an egg, because that's what they associate it with. When they've learned how to make the cones and have got within their concepts those basic geometric forms, they can build anything. They can build animal, vegetable, man. And they've got freedom to create, and do create out of those basic forms.

"Now, let me get back to the bodies. How we educate physical bodies. Begin with the physical body, and place the child by what he is able to do. Now, we have physical, we have mental, and we have emotional bodies. There are children who can't take that many hours of other children a day. And we always had day care, so that the child who could not take that much organization or just body contact, physical body contact, would not be forced to make it for those long hours without falling to pieces.

"I feel that most aggression with young children in pre-school is because of body contact. The physical body is one thing, but for the emotional body—the electromagnetic field of some children's bodies is very strong. When they're placed too close to another child, there's aggression. They don't want that contact. It's energetic, and the child picks it up very easily. So we taught them to put their arms out so that the hands touched the breast, so that the elbows were straight out. If those elbows were touching, then they would move apart, so they were in their own space. Never another child involved in that space. . . . I don't know where you'd place that because it affects the emotional body very strongly. It's the electromagnetic field of the body which is disturbed by another field that enters it.

"Now, let me talk about the spiritual body. That is the training of the child in the goal, the ideal and the goal. And a recognition of the divinity within. The early introduction to concentration, contemplation, and meditation. At the Seed Centers, we had children of gypsy background and of Negro [sic] background who could go into—I guess you would call it—the beginning of samadhi in their first sittings. And I would have to bring them out of it, they would go so deep. But we don't find that much in Western cultures. A child can be taught to sit and contemplate on a flower, on a piece of colored paper. In our system we use the complementary colors. Hazrat Inayat Khan taught fruits and flowers as first contemplations, so we used that with children.

"But again, it is not a new project every day. We have charts in every Center that are just graphs and have a child's name on it, or a group's name on it. Whoever the guide or teacher or aide may be, all they're asked is to make a cross-line on that each day. If you have playdough or clay or cut paper or block building, there is a mark made. We found that it took fourteen to twenty-one consistent reinforcements before the child would have the concept. And that concept lasted. Because we had our children through sixth grade, they didn't lose it once it had been done. Whereas you see in public education and through all the companies that put out literature today—I found that there were never more than three reinforcements of any concept. And it is true that we have brilliant children who get it in three repetitions, but the great mass of American children do not. It takes fourteen to twenty-one. We've never known anyone who didn't get it in twenty-one reinforcements. If it were consistent. Not worked on a strand where if you don't get it this year, you're going to get it next year or the year after. And then you have this mass of humanity—dropouts in the fifth grade. No self-image, no success."

"The higher mind of man and the depth of his heart are one," Murshida Vera explains. "They are connected, they are not separate. You might say that every child comes with that realization. Every child knows that his feelings definitely affect that which he sees and that which he thinks. But by the time we get through with them in the first two and a half years, we have veiled that totally.

"A certain amount of that is self-protection, because the environments we expose them to demand self-protection. So the more the child puts up this protection, the more separated heart and mind become, until finally—he can have a good mental body, and he can have a good heart, but the heart is well hidden. And the desire to protect himself has brought in aggression. Fears, the fears grow into aggression, because there is never an aggression which does not have as its basis a fear in the child. And that fear makes him aggressive. It all goes back to self-protection.

"It's the spiritual training that opens the heart of the child, that teaches the ideal. Every day we introduce the child to prophets. We follow the holidays of the great religions of the world. At the Marin Seed Center, we tried to bring in for a day, a whole day, an outstanding spiritual teacher in his field—a rabbi, a lama, and others—who would come in and give the children the flavor of devotion to God through that particular religion.

"I remember we had one particular lama come who spoke very few words in English. He set up his altar in our Allah Circle space, which was a large alcove facing a window, where all the symbols of the great religions were painted upon that window. And he set up his own altar and shared his Tibetan Buddhist practices. Our little ones—we always had vases of flowers on tables throughout the Center. The children brought them and the parents, and I brought them. And the children went over and picked, each took a flower out of the vase without any tutoring whatsoever and marched up to the lama and gave him a flower. He said through the translator that he had never visited any Buddhist temples in the Western world where the children were as devotional and as recognizing of Buddhist tenets as ours. And our children were not taught Buddhist tenets. They were taught the unity of all religious ideals.

"We taught each religion in its time. When we had the High Holy Days of Judaism, the children were going through that period, every day they were having snacks and dances and songs and music, as well as the devotions. Ah, of course, we use Moses. The baby Moses, the child Moses were most inspiring to them. But any child who wanted to tell his story or his recognition of another prophet—we were always wide open to that. It's amazing how many young children, whose parents said they had never learned it at home, had that feeling, had that connection with a prophet that the family had taught them nothing about it. In fact, most of the families were not teaching religion in the home at all. But the children came with that devotion. And they found their connections to a prophet or saint.

"So, we feel that this kind of experience develops the heart very strongly. To have recognition of a master, a prophet, a saint that is close to your heart, that you recognize and feel connected with, this puts great power behind the child's concentrations and prayers.

"Understanding each child's path was also very important for us. Not every child would be turned on by the Sukkoth (the Jewish celebration of the harvest), but many would. Setting up the Sukkah (a specially constructed hut in which the celebration of Sukkoth takes place), and putting the fruits and flowers in there, and sitting in the little house were very thrilling for pre-school children. They really loved it and would find a time to sit in it. As at Christmas time when the same little framework was converted into a manger. Many of the children would go in there in their free time and sit there. They'd take the baby Jesus doll out of the manger and sit and hold it for awhile.

"To make devotion possible, available, and to cross the lines of different religions is not easy to do. But this brings the depth, this encourages the purity of the soul of the child, of the spiritual body. This teaches devotion that comes from the heart of a ritual instead of from a memorization that has to be done. Not that we didn't memorize. For every month, the religion of that month had a simple sacred phrase that every child memorized. But it had to be, as in the Sufi viewpoint, a universal message, not one that indoctrinated the child into a ritual religious form."

Mrs. Corda inhales deeply and looks away from me, out through the window to the shining of the late morning sun. "Let me tell you more about how the school was run. If a child was powerful, in physical build or in his mental body, we put him to work as a leader. If a child was reticent, was shy about doing anything in the group, we put him at the end of the line and made him a sergeant. In our schools, children line up children. Children lead children, not teachers or aides doing it for them. We work a lot with bells, so there are a lot of bells that are used for line-up time. The child who is the leader of the group rings the bell, and the sergeant sees that everybody is lined up. Until the sergeant gives the word, the sign to the leader, the line doesn't move.

"You don't come into the classroom yelling, jumping, screaming. You come into there in order, with your trip together. You know where you're going when you come in to an organized program. In the play yard, you are free to scream, yell, do whatever you want to do. But not when you come into the building. Then you have it together.

"Now the entire school had to be kept together by the people who are in that environment. And the little people all have tasks which they choose and like. They go to them without being assigned. . . . The time for organizing the materials in the learning centers is not a last-minute thing in the Seed Center. The children are definitely responsible for them, and time is given for clean-up. It's understood that it's important to do housekeeping and leave our centers in order. The children are not assigned to it. They go to it by themselves. Nor is there one person made responsible. No, it's the group's responsibility. If you use the center, then at the end of the day you get it in order for the next morning. And very little has to be done about this by teachers and aides, when you start off with that training from day one and follow it through."

"Let the child go as far as he wants to go. You can help him go along. And even show him the next step he's aiming for. But beyond introducing him to the next step, the child unfolds at his own rate and his own desire. We don't pressure the child to learn. We have an open environment.

"In the Seed Center, we had squares painted on the floor, the whole length of the building, starting always with the concept 'zero,' like a hopscotch. So the children can hop on it and, as they're hopping, count. Their first idea of number was done in that manner. But they won't come to that until they're ready. Nobody is forcing them to. When they're interested in numbers, they'll start counting. When the child was ready to do that, he'd come to it."

"What about Hazrat Inayat Khan's belief that children should not go to school until they are at least 7 years old?" I ask Mrs. Corda.

"That might have been right for England in 1910," she replies. "It might even have been right for America then. But in our time— It's a different time. Children need to go to school because of how our society is. And we make the school feel like a family. The child comes to feel that it really is another family for him. You can't just say that at 7 years, the child is ready. That's like the rules we have in public education, and you know the problems in that, especially for the little boy who was born close to the cut-off date and who is competing with girls who were born much earlier in the year. The boy is a year behind anyhow, and there's no way you're going to push him without making him lose self-image. It's undoing the very thing you're trying to do.

"At the same time you cannot hold back a child who's ready. The child who is ready will find a way, as I found a way to read out of a want-ad section when no books or teaching were given to me. Children find a way. They learn when they are ready to learn."

"So the educator's role is to help that finding of a way, to nurture it?"

"Recognize it," she replies forcefully. "The educator's way is to recognize the bodies that are developing within that child and to provide the open environment for the child's exploration and discovery of his own world. Let him explore where he is. If we don't get in his way, he'll stay on it until he has fully explored it, and it is a part of his being. And then he'll go on to the next step."

THREE VISIONS OF HUMAN NATURE: COMMONALITY AND DIVERGENCE

While Steiner, Aurobindo, and Inayat Khan describe a common vision of human nature in its overall contours, there are certainly differences of location and emphasis in their detailing of the various sub-systems, as explained below.

- **A physical being that exists on the material plane**: Steiner, Aurobindo, and Inayat Khan describe the physical being in nearly identical terms.

- **A life-force being that exists on the next higher plane, the plane of life-force or vital energies**: All three teachers describe life-forces consisting of subtle energy as an element within the human being. Yet they differ more in their descriptions of these life-force or vital energies—and in the related issue of the location and nature of the desires and the emotions—than in any other element of their descriptions of human nature.

Steiner calls these energies the **etheric body**, identifies them as subtle energies that humans have in common with other life forms, and characterizes them as the formative forces that help to organize and shape the growth of the physical body. Aurobindo names these subtle energies the **vital being**. He also describes them as life-force energies but explains that they are expressed through the four aspects of the vital being as instincts, impulses, desires, passions, and emotions. Inayat Khan notes that humans share a **subtle energy quality** with plant life. But he does not identify this energy as a major sub-system within the person.

As just noted, this lack of agreement about the life-force

energies extends to the location—and even to the nature—of both the impulses and desires and the emotions or feelings. Aurobindo locates the vital being as the seat of the impulses and desires and of the emotions. Inayat Khan places the emotions within the heart, which he describes as the inmost part of the mind, and locates the desires, impulses, and negative feelings like greed and wrath within the **ego,** a different aspect of the mind. Steiner describes the desires and impulses and the emotions as **faculties of the soul.**

All three teachers agree that the emotions are particularly interrelated with the physical heart and lungs and are felt most powerfully in these areas of the material being. Yet they differ about exactly what emotion and feelings are. Steiner includes desires, impulses, and cravings as well as emotions within his category of feelings. While he describes the feelings as a faculty of the soul, he does not specify what sort of energy they are. In contrast, Aurobindo organizes the feelings into three categories: the small desires and feelings of the **lower vital** such as likings, vanity, and cravings; the stronger desires and passions of the **higher vital,** such as anger, fear, ambition, and pride; and the higher emotions of the **emotional vital,** such as love, joy, sorrow, and hope. Aurobindo also identifies the emotions as energies without specifying what particular kind of energy they are.

Inayat Khan sees the emotions in a very different way. He describes emotion as the **energy of the heart,** a subtle energy that is of a higher vibrational level than thought. Yet he includes in the category of emotion only positive feelings, such as love, joy, and compassion. As noted earlier, he places the desires, impulses, and negative emotions within the ego, the false self.

While there is much disagreement among Steiner, Aurobindo, and Inayat Khan in regard to the life-force being and the emotions and desires, there is nonetheless more consensus than divergence in their descriptions of this sub-system. All concur about the existence of the life-force being as a body of subtle energy that activates matter into the form of life. All differentiate between desires, impulses, and cravings and emotions or feelings, describing desires as limits to unfoldment that must be transcended and emotion as a higher form of energy that calls for expression. Inayat Khan teaches that spiritual love, the highest form of emotion, is the path and the means to spiritual awakening. While neither Steiner nor Aurobindo uses this kind of terminology, the language they employ to describe spiritual awakening does not conflict with Inayat Khan's. Rather, it differs from his, relying on different kinds of images.

- **A mind or mental being that exists on the next highest plane**: Both Aurobindo and Inayat Khan describe the mental being as the sub-system that operates on the next highest plane of being. Both agree that the **mind** includes the following: the **memory**; the **element of the mind that receives sensory data and translates these data into thought forms, and that apprehends vibrations from higher planes and translates them into images;** and the **intellect,** the seat of reason. Steiner describes similar mental capacities but locates them within thinking as a faculty of the soul.

  Inayat Khan also locates the **inner heart** within the mind, describing it as a subtle energy center with a higher vibrational level than that of thought, a center that has access to the higher beings through the process of intuition. Aurobindo speaks of a very similar element within the mind, which he calls the **higher faculties of the mind.** This is the superconscient aspect of the mind, he explains, that has access both to the spiritual being of the self and to higher planes of energy and that can generate intuitive perceptions of truth from those sources.

  Finally, Inayat Khan also places the **will** within the mind. For Steiner, willing is the third faculty of the soul. Aurobindo speaks of the will throughout his teachings but does not locate it clearly within his description of the human system.

  Inayat Khan's and Aurobindo's descriptions of the mental being are quite similar. Although Steiner locates the mind as a faculty of the soul, his description of its functions is much like that offered by the others.

- **A spiritual being that exists on still higher planes**: All three teachers describe two levels of being that are spiritual. For Steiner, the first level of spiritual being is the **astral body,** the body of the soul. It is this body that includes the soul faculties—thinking, willing, and feeling—that make up the inner life. The second level of spiritual being exists on the highest plane that Steiner describes, the plane of spirit. This aspect of the human being Steiner calls the **body of the ego**. It is the element within the human being that is divine. The body of the ego joins with the soul to motivate human beings to evolve toward greater divinity. It is important to note that while Steiner describes the astral body as possessing spiritual qualities and descending from a plane of higher energies, the astral plane, its major faculties are those associated by Aurobindo and Inayat Khan primarily with the mind and, to a lesser extent, with the life-force being.

For Inayat Khan and Aurobindo, both spiritual levels of being are above the level of the mind. The first level of being above the mind, according to Inayat Khan, is the astral level, on which the **astral body** exists. Inayat Khan uses this term in a way that differs from Steiner's use of it. For Inayat Khan, the astral body helps to bring higher energy into human life, which is expressed as inspiration, revelation, genius, and imagination. The second level above the mind, the highest level of being, Inayat Khan explains, is the level of the **soul**. He describes the soul as the true self, the spark of the divine within the person. It is the soul that powers human evolution through the expression of its spiritual needs.

For Aurobindo, the first level above the mind is the level of the **psychic being** or soul. The psychic being is the element of divinity immanent within the individual identity. It is the psychic being that evolves. The second level above the mind is the level of the **spirit**. It is the grain of the universal being that is transcendent yet in connection with the psychic being. It is immortal and unchanging but supports the evolution of the psychic being.

In their descriptions of the spiritual levels, Steiner, Aurobindo, and Inayat Khan again differ somewhat but still convey a core of common vision. This vision describes a spiritual being that is an aspect of the divine immanent within the person. It is this being that motivates personal unfoldment and the evolution of the individual—and of the species.

While sharing this common understanding, each of the three teachers describes another spiritual level that does not seem to correspond with the teachings of the other two. Steiner talks of the astral body as the body of the soul. This being includes the thinking, feeling, and willing faculties that make up the human inner life. As noted before, Inayat Khan and Aurobindo locate these faculties in other beings. In contrast to Steiner, Inayat Khan describes the astral body as the body through which higher and more subtle energies are expressed in human life. These descriptions seem to refer to different elements that do not correspond with each other.

In his discussion of spiritual levels, Aurobindo describes a level of being and a related human aspect that are even higher than the immanent divine aspect on which all three teachers agree. This level is the divine consciousness itself. The human aspect on this level, the spiritual being, is a grain of that universal that is transcendent, immortal, and unchanging. This higher level of spirit is not discussed by Steiner or Inayat Khan as any part of the human being. Rather, they use this description to refer only to the divine consciousness or God.

Despite all the distinctions that draw the visions of human nature of Steiner, Aurobindo, and Inayat Khan apart, their common center holds fast. This commonality articulates a vision of human nature in which each of us consists of at least four separate yet integral sub-systems: a physical being, a life-force being, a mental being, and a spiritual being. Each of these sub-systems exists primarily, though not exclusively, on its own plane of being, each of which is composed of vibrations that grow higher and finer from the material to the life-force, from the life-force to the mental, and from the mental to the spiritual. Finally, their common vision describes the true self within each of us as the spiritual being. This true self is a spark of divinity that seeks to emerge into consciousness, for such an emergence is the next step in the evolution of our species.

COMMON VISION, UNCOMMON SENSE

What does the common vision *of Rudolf Steiner, Aurobindo Ghose, and Inayat Khan offer us now?* This *common vision* gives us much more than "common sense" understandings about who we truly are as beings. It tells us how we can raise and educate our children so that they can become more and more of their potential—and so we can evolve as a species through and beyond the dangers of our current paradoxical condition.

Applying the Common Vision

How should we apply the common vision *today?* Surely, even if we wanted to do so, we could not enact the *common vision* in its every detail today, because social conditions have changed so greatly during the past several generations. Nor, I believe, should we wish to enact this vision in its every detail as articulated in the first quarter of the twentieth century. Steiner, Aurobindo, and Inayat Khan all described an evolutionary process that included interrelated spiritual, mental, vital, and physical aspects. Human beings have continued to evolve since the years from 1910 through 1925 when Aurobindo, Inayat Khan, and Steiner offered their teachings, if not in the physical being then certainly in the other three. Were they alive today, these three teachers would be the first to note the critical significance of this ongoing evolutionary process and its inevitable impact on their own teachings.

The task of applying the *common vision* to our times requires that we distinguish between that which largely transcends historical time and place and that which is rooted in the historical and cultural moment of the early twentieth century. For example, when asked if children should not begin school until they are 7 years old as Steiner, Aurobindo, and Inayat Khan advocate, Vera Corda replies, "That might have been right for England in 1910. It might even have been right for America then. But in our time— It's a different time. Children need to go to school because of how our society is. And we make the school feel like a family. The child comes to feel that it really is another family for him." The essence of this particular aspect of the *common vision*, as Mrs. Corda explains, the part that transcends historical time, is the child's need during all of the first era for the emotional and spiritual qualities of a stable group of committed people who can create a feeling of family for the child. This need can be met by the family itself, or by an appropriate kind of pre-school in addition to the family.

So, we must consider the *common vision* in its original form, understand which of its elements transcend the historical and cultural moment of their origin, and learn to apply these elements to our own times. Given this understanding of the task, the question is: What are the major lessons from the *common vision* of Steiner, Aurobindo, and Inayat Khan that we can learn and use, today and tomorrow, and how can we apply them?

Major Lessons for Parents and Teachers

First, here are the major lessons for both parents and teachers, for child raising and for education.

- *The common vision's descriptions of human nature and of the course of human becoming in childhood and youth are as valid to-day as they were in 1920.* They provide us with an understanding of who we and our children are as beings—and of who we and our children can become. They also help us to understand the relatively predictable course of our children's and youths' unfoldment through the first twenty-one years of life.

However, we need to recognize that the timing described in the *common vision* of unfoldment is not absolute. Today, at least in North America and Western Europe, the onset of the third era of childhood and youth, the beginning of adolescence, seems to be earlier than was described by Steiner, Aurobindo, and Inayat Khan. Whether this is the result of spiritual or cultural changes, or some combination of both, is not clear.

Even with this change of timing, the three eras of childhood and youth continue to exist as they are detailed by the *common vision*, as do all of the many interrelationships among the unfoldment of body, emotions, mind, and spirit. As parents and teachers, we need to master an understanding of the nature and challenges of each of these eras of unfoldment and then use this understanding to inform the ways in which we parent and teach children and youth. Each child is unique, yes; but each child also moves through a relatively predictable course of becoming through the three eras. The more we know of this course, the more effective we can be as parents and teachers in supporting the unfoldment of the child.

- *The most profound element for child raising and education within Steiner's, Aurobindo's, and Inayat Khan's common vision is the understanding that we must have faith in the child's inner teacher to guide her own becoming.* Thus, we must provide the child with a safe environment and, within that zone of safety, as much freedom as possible to express and fulfill her own needs. While these three teachers agreed about this fundamental guideline, they differed considerably when they came to its implementation, particularly within the context of school.

Steiner espoused this principle in his teachings, and yet he created and supervised a school in 1919 in which the teacher both organized the learning environment and much of the child's activity within it. Indeed, as illustrated in Chapter Four, Steiner's pedagogy included a teacher-centered classroom and a detailed curriculum plan for every age. For example, this plan calls for children to learn, within the category of history and literature, about fairy tales in the first grade, fables and the legends of saints in the second grade, Biblical stories in the third, Norse sagas in the fourth, and so on. It contains similarly detailed subject matter for many other categories, including reading and writing, mathematics, science, geography, drawing and music, and handwork.

Steiner explained that although the teacher worked with a specified curriculum, she could learn about the needs and capacities of each child and engage each student in activities that were appropriate for that child. Using her knowledge of her students as unfolding beings, she could help them to draw out their inner knowing and encourage them to experience responsible freedom.

In contrast to Steiner, Mira Richard and several of Aurobindo's students followed Aurobindo's guidance about the role of the *inner teacher* from principle to practice in a more direct and literal manner. They created the "free progress system," in which the role of the teacher was never to act directly on the child but only upon her environment. It was never to teach directly but only to suggest and guide. Yet, as described in Chapter 6, educational practice at the International Centre of Education at the Sri Aurobindo Ashram has evolved over the past five decades, for much of that time under Richard's personal direction, to give the teacher a more active and directive role in her interactions with the child.

While Inayat Khan did not start or direct any actual schools for young people, he did address the questions of educational practice in his teachings. He asserted both the child's need for freedom to evolve and the teacher's primary role as helper and guide. While the teacher should not control the child, it can be appropriate for her to take a leading role at times in organizing and directing the child's activity within the learning environment. Inayat Khan stressed that when the teacher does take such a role, she must be careful not to compel or manipulate the child. Rather, she must obtain the child's involvement by engaging her interest, while always allowing the child the choice not be so engaged.

How do we make sense of this diversity of educational practice in relation to the very same principle of freedom and self-direction? We do so by seeing any contradictions as generated not by the ideal of freedom itself but, rather, by the attempts of limited, imperfect human beings to enact this ideal. What makes sense of these apparent contradictions is the understanding that we can only enact the teachings of the common vision with integrity to the extent of our own unfoldment as whole and integrated persons, and no more. We can only give the child as much respect for her *inner teacher*, as much freedom for her becoming, as the state of our current unfoldment empowers us. If we extend beyond that limit in our enthusiasm or pride, we will inevitably betray the understandings of the *common vision* and act out hypocrisy or contradiction, most likely through indirect or unconscious authoritarian behavior.

Thus, we must understand the *common vision* both as an ideal, a goal toward which we strive, and as a practical map toward achieving that goal. As a map, the *common vision* informs us of the steps that lead toward the ideal. Each step that we can enact successfully brings us closer toward the manifestation of the whole. In taking these steps, we must always stay aware of the intimate connection between our own growth as unfolding persons and our ability to nurture the growth of children and youth. The more we unfold, the more we will be able to move toward enacting the ideal of the *common vision*.

My belief is that it was this understanding of the relationship between the freedom of the child as an ideal and each teacher's own unfoldment as a limitation that led Steiner to develop the original Waldorf School as he did. The teachers in his school in 1919 needed a teacher-centered pedagogy and a detailed curriculum, given their levels of unfoldment, and Steiner provided them with both.[1] This same understanding also helps to make sense of the movement toward a more teacher-directed pedagogy at the Sri Aurobindo International Centre of Education. Over time the teachers in the school learned about how much freedom they could offer to students, given their own levels of unfoldment.

In summary, the *common vision* tells us today that while each parent and teacher must seek to give the child as much freedom as possible for the child's *inner teacher* to guide her, a parent or teacher can only provide the child with as much freedom as that adult's own unfoldment allows her to enact and value with adequate comfort. Only through a parent's or teacher's own spiritual evolution can she increase the amount of freedom that she can give to the child. Every step the parent or teacher can take toward the ideal, every motion toward greater trust in the *inner teacher* and greater freedom for the child, is worth taking. Every step in this direction is a significant step in the evolutionary process. So the issue is not all or nothing: freedom or its absence. It is as much freedom as possible, with clarity and integrity and enough comfort. This is our most important lesson from the *common vision* as parents and teachers.

Just for a moment, draw up an image of a 4-year-old you know or have known who is an engaged, determined, focused, creative, confident, and excited learner. Now imagine what children in the second era of childhood, or youths in the third era, could be like if they could bring this same energy for learning into their lives. If we don't limit or push or mold or direct or confine or terrorize children, there's no reason they can't be as whole, or even more whole, at 10 years or 15 years as many are today at 3 or 4.

• The timetables of the *common vision* are not absolutes. They are guidelines and norms. *All children and youth unfold at their own rates, and some do so much more slowly or quickly than most.* In addition, it is very common for a child to unfold at different rates in different aspects of her being.

• *Each era or stage in the unfoldment of the child and youth must be lived fully.* Each must be explored for what it can be and valued for itself, not rushed through quickly or seen only as a step on the way to somewhere else. Each era or stage has its own ultimate value. The principle that guides human growth is not haste or acceleration but the completeness of the un- foldment of the individual's potentials in each era of her life.

As parents and teachers we must understand this principle of becoming and respect its mandate. Sooner is not necessarily bet- ter. Each child has her own timetable. What is best for each child is the opportunity to live each era or stage fully, without pressure or compulsion to move on before she is ready to do so.

• *The common vision explains that children learn most profoundly from who their parents, care-givers, and teachers are as people, from the wholeness and rightness of these adults' qualities and actions.* To nurture our children more effectively, to help them grow and unfold, we need to work on our own growth as much as that of the next generation. We must strive to become as good examples for them as we can be, for the future is born in the present.

• *The common vision tells us explicitly that everything that children and youth experience has an impact on who they are and who they become.* The system is a seamless whole; nothing experienced by the child is without influence. This understanding informs us that children's experience of media matters tremendously. If children watch thousands of hours of violence and advertising on television, these images and messages affect who they are and will become.

As a society we have acted with profound irresponsibility in terms of the electronic media experiences that we create and allow for children and youths. If we seek to support the healthy unfoldment of young people, we must transform our media so that they support growth and becoming, not pervert it. In the short run parents and teachers must act to shield the child from destructive media experiences. In the long run we need to transform our electronic media so that they promote our ideals, not our greed.

- *We must always recognize our children as beings who have the potential to—indeed, who are likely to, if we are successful as parents and teachers—evolve beyond us.* Given this understanding of evolution and unfoldment, we must truly be open to learning from our children, from the very moment of their birth and in every subsequent moment, as well as helping them to learn.

Lessons for the First Era

Here are the lessons in particular for parents and teachers of children who are in the first era of life.

- The *common vision* tells us that the child in the first era belongs not in school but in the family. And yet, as noted earlier, we live in a culture in which more and more of our young children spend considerable amounts of their lives in daycare and preschool environments. How do we reconcile this teaching with our social reality?

There is nothing ultimately natural or necessarily desirable about the isolated nuclear family, or even about the multigenerational family. For most of human history, children grew up in tribal or clan groups, interacting intensively with other children and adults within the group. So the central element offered by the *common vision* in its essence is not the nuclear family as such, or even the multigenerational family. Rather, as noted before, it is the description of the child's need in the first era of life to be in a family-like context, a social setting of love, safety, stability, consistency, and a high quality of care. Within this context, she needs to have as much freedom and opportunity for self-direction available to her as possible, with little competition or pressure to achieve. This teaching of the *common vision* gives us a model for the kind of day-care and pre-school settings we need to create for our children.

• The *common vision* tells us that every child and youth learns from her interactions with the adults in her life. We need to understand clearly that the child in the first era of life, the first seven years or so, learns most profoundly from an often explicit imitation of those around her. If a child spends most of her conscious time in day care or pre-school, she will learn profoundly from her caregiver(s) or teacher(s) in that environment. There is nothing inherently wrong with this, but it is a reality that so-called *quality time* cannot change. *Quality is important in the relationship between adult and child, but quantity is undoubtedly more powerful with a child who learns through imitation.*

The *common vision* requires this of us as parents: if we put our child in day-care, we must place her with an adult who will provide her with as good a basis for imitation as we can find and who will stay in relationship with the child over time. This is a minimum requirement. The step beyond this requires social change so that both mothers and fathers can spend much more time with their young children without sacrificing their prospects of obtaining satisfying work. This change demands a more flexible workplace in which the needs of children and parents are more highly valued. It also calls for a society less concerned with material goods and more able to find satisfaction in human relationships.

Lessons for the Second and Third Eras: What Schools Can Become

Here are the lessons for teachers and parents of children who are in the second and third eras of life, particularly in relation to the nature and role of the school.

- The *common vision* speaks clearly and powerfully to the needs and potentials of the child and youth in the second and third eras. It tells us that much of what goes on in our schools today is antithetical to the growth and unfoldment of the child and youth. Conventional schools work primarily for the purposes of limiting consciousness and reality to the current norms and defining power relations among the next generation. If we wish to nurture and educate our children more effectively and more profoundly, we need to transform our schools: to align them with the needs and potentials of the child and youth as revealed by the *common vision*. We can accomplish this transformation only if we change the goals, structures, and processes of schooling as teachers engage themselves in growing and evolving as persons and educators. Both of these kinds of change, change in goals and structures and change in people, must come not only at the same time but as integrated elements of each other.

As a start, let me suggest three relatively simple steps that any school could take to begin its transformation:

1. One step we can take is simply to change our cultural expectations about when children will learn to read and write. Right now most parents and elementary teachers expect children to learn to read and write by the end of first grade. Yet a glance at the normal distribution of when children enter the second era of childhood informs us that somewhere from 20 percent to 40 percent of the

children are not developmentally ready for reading and writing until some time during second grade. Indeed perhaps 10 percent to 15 percent are not ready until third grade. Nevertheless we label millions of 6- and 7-year-olds as failures when they arrive at the end of first grade without initial reading and writing skills. The simple remedy of pushing back our expectations to the end of second grade or even beyond would profoundly transform millions of children's experiences of school—and their ability to learn effectively and feel good about themselves.

2. A second step is to free ourselves from viewing education as an industrial process in which we must ship the child from one teacher to the next, either every year in the elementary school or every forty-five minutes in the secondary school. If children and youths learn more from the teacher as a person through her example than from what the teacher knows, then we must organize the school to facilitate the growth of enriching relationships between young people and adults.

Perhaps keeping a class with a single teacher for eight years, as Steiner suggests, is too limiting for our society. But there is absolutely no reason why a teacher in elementary school cannot teach the same group of children for three or four years, or co-teach a larger group of children with another adult(s) for the same period of time. At the secondary level, teachers can work together in teams to teach the same group of youths for two or three or four years. When we create school structures that support the development of strong, caring relationships between young people and adults, we'll find that teachers become much more able to support the unfoldment of their students in personal and individual ways, because they will both know them much better and care more about them. As both Steiner and Aurobindo explain, the teacher must have a vision of the child as a process, in the past, present, and future. Only multi-year relationships allow the teacher to gain that kind of sense of who the student is as a person and who she can become.

3. A third step is to direct more focused, systematic attention in the education of young children to developing the senses, compassion, and the control of awareness. The development and

education of children's senses is already a goal in many pre-school and primary grades programs. So is the development of children's awareness of and compassion for others. What could be done within existing school structures to begin the work of transformation is to place far more emphasis on nurturing these capacities and qualities in young children.

Helping children to develop control of their awareness is more problematic, both because little is done now with this task in most schools and because there are some in our society who object to these kinds of activities as being religious. Learning to control one's awareness really has nothing to do with religious belief or practice. When parents and teachers understand more about this, the vast majority of them will support these educational activities. Gaining control of awareness involves the child's mastery of concentration and attention and her recognition that she is not her thoughts or feelings but, rather, is a being who has thoughts and feelings. It is a key step in the development of self-knowledge, self-awareness, and self-discipline. Learning these disciplines of concentration and attention also helps children to think with greater clarity and creativity.

Transforming Schools

Beyond these three steps, each of which leads in the right direction, the *common vision* tells us that we must literally transform schools. The key to this task is the recognition and honoring of the child's and youth's *inner teacher*. First, teachers of young children need to gain an understanding of and faith in the integrity and efficacy of the child's *inner teacher*. When they do so, they will create learning environments of freedom, self-direction, and self-discipline. Once we have such learning environments all across North America in which young children are motivating and guiding their own learning and growth, with the support and nurturance of teachers, we will extend this approach—indeed children and their parents will demand that we do so—to these same children as they grow into older children and youths.

In the free school movement of the late 1960s, some teachers tried to begin this evolutionary process by giving freedom to high-school-age youths. This is the wrong way to start. While we can certainly encourage adolescents to reconnect with their inner knowing and to become self-directed, we are much more likely to be successful on a broad scale with young children who have never experienced repressive, authoritarian, adult-centered schools. So, our transformational efforts must begin with the very young—and we must change the systems for them as a cohort as they move up through the years.

For many, many teachers to understand the true nature of human beings and to teach accordingly will require the beginning of an evolutionary leap. Any teacher who understands the *common vision* and values it must commit herself to beginning this task of transformation in her teaching and to communicating the common vision to her colleagues.

Three Final Lessons

Here are three final lessons from the *common vision*.

- The *common vision* of Steiner, Aurobindo, and Inayat Khan is founded on a spiritual understanding of reality. If you accept the spiritual character of human beings but do not believe in the fact of reincarnation, do not reject the *common vision* for this element alone. I am an agnostic when it comes to reincarnation. I have no way of knowing if it is literal truth, mythical truth, truth beyond my understanding, or fantasy. And yet I am convinced that even if there is no truth at all in reincarnation as a mechanism of evolution, the transcendent truth of the *common vision* as a description of human nature and unfoldment retains its essential validity. Why? Because I have directly experienced the truth of the *common vision* as a description of human nature and human becoming and as both an ideal and a practical guide for parenting and teaching.

- Those of us who understand the truth and power of the

common vision for parenting and education need to make a commitment to sharing this understanding with others. During the past several decades most of the conscious, spiritually based growth work undertaken by people in North America has focused on ourselves: on our own healing, on our "inner children," on our own spiritual unfoldment. Undoubtedly we adopted this focus because we needed to do this work. But now it is time for us to reach out beyond ourselves and make a commitment to educating many, many parents and teachers about what the *common vision* can tell them about children and youths and how they can use these insights to support the unfoldment of their children and students. Our evolutionary crisis demands that we take this new path, now.

- The *common vision* is not perfect or finished or complete. We can always learn more. We must draw on our knowledge of the *common vision* but always in relation to our own insight, discrimination, and common sense. We must not make it "an answer" but keep it as an ideal and a guide in relationship with our own unfolding selves.

The Common Vision and the Role of Culture

The *common vision* speaks about the nature and potential of all children, all human beings. Yet culture also plays a significant role in the growth and learning of children and youths. Culture gives each child a set of understandings for making sense of her world and powerfully affects each child's perception, meaning-making, and behavior. In the United States, despite the historic image of the "melting pot" as the forge for a single mainstream culture, many racial, ethnic, social class, and regional groups continue to embody and enact their own distinct versions of American culture—for example, African-American, Chinese-American, and Appalachian cultures—which exist along with mainstream culture. In addition, both mainstream culture and the various ethnic, racial, social class, and regional cultures define and create roles for young people based on gender.

As parents we must become as conscious as we can of our own cultural values and norms. We must honor and offer to our children the elements in our own home cultures that enrich life and unfoldment. At the same time we must identify cultural elements that inhibit or remove our children's exercise of appropriate freedom and self-direction, and if we truly seek the unfoldment of our children's potential, we must abandon these inhibitory cultural elements as much as we can.

As teachers we must recognize that each child brings her own home culture to the learning environment, a culture likely to be influenced greatly by her ethnicity and race, social class, and gender. We need to educate ourselves about the values and effects of the various cultural heritages of our students, so that we can understand the role that home culture plays in each child's experience. While we as teachers must respect the home culture of each child, we must also bring the insights of the *common vision* into our work with each child's unfoldment. Often the child's home culture and the *common vision* will be in harmony and will support each other's goals. Yet it is likely that a child's culture will also be in conflict with at least some aspects of the *common vision*, since many elements in our mainstream culture and in various ethnic, racial, social class, and regional cultures are repressive to the unfoldment of children and youth. In the case of such conflicts, teachers must act from a place of paradoxical or dual consciousness. We must respect the child's home culture, *and* we must nurture the child's unfoldment. We must hold both insights, both perspectives, at the same time, just as we must feel compassion both for the child and for her parents.

Of course, it is much easier to articulate this concept than to embody and enact it. The key to appropriate and effective action, I believe, lies not in a set of rules for oneself but rather in a quality of consciousness. When we can simultaneously understand and respect the child's home culture and her membership in that cultural group *and* support her unfoldment as a unique individual with a unique potential for becoming, we can often, though undoubtedly not always, know how best to serve her growth as her teacher.

The Common Vision: A Path to Coevolution

The *common vision* of Rudolf Steiner, Aurobindo Ghose, and Inayat Khan is a set of directions for coevolution, for our conscious participation in the process of ongoing evolution on this planet. It is also a set of directions for human survival if we choose to recognize and act upon it. We must grow and evolve, or we will surely perish. The *common vision* gives us a path to follow that will nurture this growth for ourselves and our children, a path that leads both to survival and to coevolution.

CHAPTER 1

1. There are so many striking similarities between the common vision of Steiner, Aurobindo, and Inayat Khan and the teachings of Maria Montessori that I can only conclude that all four of these teachers were drawing on the same apprehension of reality and truth. Indeed Montessori even publicized her vision at the very same time as her three "colleagues." Her first training course for teachers in Italy began in 1909, to be followed by publication of her various books and articles during the next decade. Her first international training course began in 1913. Yet by the late 1920s Montessori was no longer engaged in the research of new perspectives and methods. Rather she devoted her efforts to the preservation of the existing Montessori movement. So, as with her "colleagues," Montessori's period of discovery came to a close before the end of the 1920s.

Some of the most important ways in which Montessori's vision is identical with or similar to Steiner's, Aurobindo's, and Inayat Khan's common vision follow:

• Montessori described the newborn child as a "spiritual embryo" and understood the child's nature as a whole system, including the sub-systems of vital energy (what she called *horme*), physical body, and mind. She described these sub-systems as interrelated and interpenetrated.

• Montessori taught that each child contains vital energy or horme that directs her growth by motivating her to meet her growth needs during each period of development. This vital energy serves as an inner guide for the child. Parents and teachers must give the child freedom to follow her inner guide. When the child can do so, she develops both her will and her concentration.

• Montessori defined three periods of development in the life of the child and youth: from birth through age 6; from 6 to 12 years; and from 12 to 18 years. (She also defined a fourth period at the end of adolescence, from 18 to 24 years.) Each period contains *sensitive periods*: times at which the child is developmentally ready for a particular kind of growth and must accomplish this growth if she is to develop to her potential.

• Montessori maintained that the will of the child must be nurtured, and never broken.

• Montessori described the child's primary means of learning during the first period of growth as her "absorbent mind." Absorption and imitation are two ways to describe the same process of learning.

• Montessori taught that the function of education is to give the child opportunities to express her inner guide within an appropriately prepared and safe learning environment. An education based on this principle will help the child to develop independence, self-discipline, concentration, motivation, and sensitivity.

• Finally, Montessori taught that the role of the teacher is not to control or direct the child but rather to prepare the learning environment and then nurture and support the child. For this work, the teacher must focus on the development of her own spirit, character, and imagination. She must understand that her work is to be of service to the child's spirit and that the child will reveal who she is becoming over time.

All of these significant understandings of Maria Montessori are identical with or similar to those of the common vision of Steiner, Aurobindo, and Inayat Khan. And, of course, I would be the first to agree that there is much more in common between Montessori and her three "colleagues" than between Montessori and more traditional educational models. Why then have I not included her as an author of what I call the common vision? I have made this judgment for the following reasons:

• Although she calls the child a "spiritual embryo" and employs some of the language of the spirit, Montessori's vision does not describe or detail the spiritual elements of human beings. Thus, it omits significant aspects both of the description of human beings as whole systems that include spiritual energies and of the spiritual context in which we live.

• Although Montessori's vision does deal with some issues of the emotions, it does not provide a systemic exploration of the sub-system of the vital being. Thus, her vision does not deal in a comprehensive way with the whole realm of the emotions, desires, and feelings, an important set of elements in describing human unfoldment and in articulating principles and practices for child raising and education.

• Montessori's vision does explore the relationship between the physical body and the mind as the child grows. However, it does not contain the richness of description of the interrelationships among the physical, vital, mental, and spiritual sub-systems of the child and youth that is offered in the common vision of Inayat Khan, Steiner, and Aurobindo.

• Finally, Montessori urges that the child be encouraged to develop her cognition during the second half of the first era of unfoldment. She argues that these years are a sensitive period for the development of writing skills and for the learning of vocabulary, grammar, and numbers. While, of course, she would not teach any of this directly, she prepares the learning environment in such a way that the materials there encourage the child to embark on this kind of learning. Steiner, Aurobindo, and Inayat Khan strongly disagree with this approach. While they note that the child can learn all of this effectively during these years, they maintain that it is profoundly undesirable for such topics and skills to become the focus of learning. Rather, these years should be a time of imaginative, self-directed, noncompetitive play. Such play helps the child to develop her spiritual nature in its fullness and to prepare for her transition from the first era into the second.

Maria Montessori's teachings are clearly a visionary work of genius. So I mean no disrespect for Montessori by omitting her from authorship of what I call the common vision. Obviously she articulates significant sections of this common vision in her work. Yet I have chosen not to include her (1) because she does not provide significant sections of this vision, none of which are left out by Steiner, Aurobindo, or Inayat Khan, and (2) because she characterizes the needs of the second part of the first era of childhood in a profoundly divergent way from her colleagues.

So far Montessori's work has had a much greater impact on the world of schools than that of all three of her colleagues together. Perhaps her teachings will help to bring parents and educators to those of Steiner, Aurobindo, and Inayat Khan, so they can learn from the visionary teachings of all four of these teachers.

CHAPTER 2

1. Langley, *Sri Aurobindo: Indian Poet, Philosopher, and Mystic*, 13.
2. Motwani, *Three Great Sages*, 24–25.
3. Mitra, *Sri Aurobindo and the New World*, 49.
4. Gandhi, *Contemporary Relevance of Sri Aurobindo*, 327.
5. Bruteau, *Worthy Is the World: The Hindu Philosophy of Sri Aurobindo*, 31.
6. Ghose, *Sri Aurobindo on Himself and The Mother*, 6.
7. *Hazrat* is a reverent form of address in the Sufi tradition, meaning saint. Its use by Inayat Khan's disciples conveys their perception of him not as an avatar, like Buddha or Jesus, the most holy of human forms, but as a great initiate who helps to bring disciples to an understanding of and feeling for the teachings of the avatars.
8. Van Stolk, *Memories of a Sufi Sage, Hazrat Inayat Khan*, 27.
9. Ibid., 28.
10. Khan, *The Sufi Message of Hazrat Inayat Khan: VIII*, 135.

CHAPTER 3

1. Steiner, *Education as an Art*, 23.
2. Harwood, *The Recovery of Man in Childhood*, 20.
3. Steiner, *The New Art of Education*, 118.
4. Steiner, *Lectures to Teachers: Christmas 1921*, 50.
5. *Education As An Art*, 107.
6. During Steiner's life, the average age at puberty was about 13 years. In the United States and other industrialized counties, the average age at the onset of puberty has decreased in the years since Steiner's death. Now it is common for girls to experience puberty at the age of 11 or 12 years; for boys, at the age of 12 or 13. Many physicians have attributed this acceleration of unfoldment to improved nutrition. It is interesting to consider this phenomenon, however, in the light of Steiner's asser-

tion that undue early emphasis on intellectual learning in both the first and second epochs results in (1) a harmful acceleration of the processes of unfoldment within the child and (2) a diminution of his life of soul and spirit and a corresponding alignment toward a narrow materialism.

7. Harwood, *The Recovery of Man in Childhood*, 71.

8. Steiner, *The New Art of Education*, 106.

9. Ibid., 12.

10. Ibid., 107.

11. Steiner, *Paths of Experience*, 35–36.

CHAPTER 5

1. Ghose, *On Yoga I*, 257.

2. Bruteau, *Worthy Is the World: The Hindu Philosophy of Sri Aurobindo*, 438.

3. Ghose, *The Life Divine*, 2.

4. Ghose, *Sri Aurobindo Mandir Annual No. 23*, 258.

5. Langley, *Sri Aurobindo: Indian Poet, Philosopher, and Mystic*, 86.

6. Ibid., 73.

7. Ghose, *The Future Evolution of Man: The Divine Life upon Earth*, 28.

8. Ibid., 147.

9. Ghose, *On Yoga I*, 349.

10. Ibid., 341.

11. Purani, *Sri Aurobindo: Some Aspects of His Vision*, 144.

12. Ibid., 144–45.

13. Aurobindo's analysis of the over-development of the mind in Western cultures and the resulting excess of authority given to mental knowing was insightful in the second decade of this century. Today it is equally, if not more, accurate.

14. Purani, *Sri Aurobindo: Some Aspects of His Vision*, 145.

15. Ghose, *A System of National Education*, 11.

16. Ghose, *Sri Aurobindo Mandir Annual No. 6*, 40.

17. Ghose, *The Future Evolution of Man*, 68–69.

18. Ibid., 69.

19. Richard notes that the seventh year is not by any means an absolute. In some children, the psychic being is awake at birth. In others, it may awaken at times other than the seventh year. However, this time of awakening is far more common than any other. Aurobindo Ghose and The Mother, *On Education*, 121–131.

20. Gupta. *The Yoga of Sri Aurobindo. Part V*, 52.
21. Richard, *Bulletin of Sri Aurobindo International Centre of Education. February 1964*, 44.
22. Saint-Hilaire (Pavitra). *Education and the Aim of Human Life*, 84.
23. Sen, *Sri Aurobindo Mandir Annual No. 12*, 85.
24. Ibid., 93.
25. Joshi, *The Advent. Volume XXXII, No. 1*, 52.
26. Dowsett, *Psychology for Future Education*, 155.
27. Rishabhchand, *Sri Aurobindo Mandir Annual No. 11*, 89.
28. Ghose, *A System of National Education*, 3.
29. Ibid., 4.
30. Ibid., 5.
31. Saint-Hilaire, *Education and the Aim of Human Life*, 88.
32. Richard, *On Education*, 13.
33. Ghose, *Sri Aurobindo Mandir Annual. No. 23*, 260.
34. Dowsett, *Psychology for Future Education*, 19.
35. Sen, *Sri Aurobindo Mandir Annual. No. 12*, 97.
36. Dowsett, *Psychology for Future Education*, 20.
37. Sen, *Sri Aurobindo Mandir Annual. No. 12*, 262.
38. Prasad, *Education for A New Life*, 88.
39. Ghose, *A System of National Education*, 27.
40. Dowsett, *Psychology for Future Education*, 185.
41. Ghose and Richard, *On Education*, 100.
42. Ghose, *A System of National Education*, 59.
43. Richard, *The Advent. Vol. XXXV, No. 1*, 35. Richard recommends the interspersing of training in concentration with physical activities, such as games and sports.
44. Ghose, *A System of National Education*, 42.
45. Ibid., 40.
46. Ghose and Richard, *On Education*, 105.
47. Ibid., 104–05.
48. Ibid., 107.
49. Ibid., 109.
50. Ibid., 111–12.
51. Ibid., 112.
52. Richard, *On Education*, 56.
53. Ghose, *A System of National Education*, 18.
54. Ghose and Richard, *On Education*, 110.
55. Richard, *Bulletin of Sri Aurobindo International Centre for*

Education. February 1964, 33.

56. Ibid., 31.

57. Richard, *Sri Aurobindo Mandir Annual. No. 38*, 41.

58. Richard, *On Education*, 54.

59. Dowsett and Jayaswal, *The True Teacher*, 4.

60. Ibid., 67.

61. Ibid., 1.

62. Dowsett, *Psychology for Future Education*, 120.

63. Dowsett and Jayaswal, *The True Teacher*, 32.

64. Prasad, *Education for a New Life*, 95.

65. Saint-Hilaire, *Education and the Aim of Human Life*, 135.

66. Ibid., 80–81.

67. Ibid., 101.

68. Bruteau, *Worthy Is the World.*, 31.

69. Diwakar, *Mahayogi Sri Aurobindo*, 174.

70. Prasad, *Education for a New Life*, 121.

71. Langley, *Sri Aurobindo: Indian Poet, Philosopher, and Mystic*, 86.

72. Ibid., 87.

73. Ibid., 91.

CHAPTER 6

1. Personal communication. 1985.

CHAPTER 7

1. Khan, *The Sufi Message of Hazrat Inayat Khan: Volume III*, 135.

2. Khan, *The Sufi Message of Hazrat Inayat Khan: Volume I*, 145.

3. Van Stolk, *Memories of a Sufi Sage*, 89.

4. Khan, *The Sufi Message of Hazrat Inayat Khan: Volume VII*, 108.

5. Khan, *The Sufi Message of Hazrat Inayat Khan: Volume V*, 235.

6. Khan, *The Sufi Message of Hazrat Inayat Khan: Volume IV*, 140–41.

7. Khan, *The Sufi Message of Hazrat Inayat Khan: Volume II*, 245.

8. Khan, *The Sufi Message of Hazrat Inayat Khan: Volume V*, 20.

9. Ibid., 142.

10. It is not unusual for Inayat Khan to use a term both as a category and as a sub-category within that category. In this case, *intuition* is a category that includes the five ways of knowing that flow from the inner heart. This word is also used as the name of these five ways of

knowing.

11. Khan, *The Sufi Message of Hazrat Inayat Khan: Volume V*, 20.

12. Ibid., 84.

13. Inayat Khan uses the term *spirit* in three different ways: (1) a spirit is a soul that has not connected with a physical body; (2) a spirit is the interaction of a soul and a mind; and (3) a spirit is the soul of all souls, or God. Unless otherwise noted, I use the term spirit to mean the second definition stated above, as this is Inayat Khan's most common usage for this term.

14. Personal communication from Murshida Vera Corda, 1984.

15. Personal communication from Aostre N. Johnson, 1988.

16. Khan, *The Sufi Message of Hazrat Inayat Khan: Volume III*, 145.

17. Khan, *The Sufi Message of Hazrat Inayat Khan:Volume VII*, 96.

18. Khan, *The Sufi Message of Hazrat Inayat Khan:Volume III*, 1.

19. Ibid., 15.

20. Ibid., 29.

21. Khan, *The Sufi Message of Hazrat Inayat Khan: Volume X*, 58.

23. Ibid., 57.

24. Ibid., 10.

25. Ibid., 64–65.

26. Khan. *The Sufi Message of Hazrat Inayat Khan: Volume XII*, 32.

27. Khan, *The Sufi Message of Hazrat Inayat Khan: Volume III*, 66.

28. Ibid., 91.

29. Ibid., 95.

30. Ibid., 103.

31. Ibid., 10.

32. Ibid., 11.

33. Ibid., 4–5.

34. Ibid., 5.

35. Ibid., 42.

36. Ibid., 64.

37. Ibid., 65.

38. Ibid. 66.

39. Ibid., 67.

40. Ibid., 84.

41. Ibid., 108.

42. Ibid., 109.

43. Ibid., 109–110.

44. Ibid., 116.

45. Ibid., 118.
46. Van Stolk, *Memories of a Sufi Sage*, 76.

CHAPTER 8

1. *Murshida* is a title given to a Sufi spiritual teacher who has a profound spiritual development and understanding. It is the female form of the title. *Murshid* is the male form of the same title.

CHAPTER 10

1. This resolution of Steiner's apparent contradiction between principle and practice strongly suggests that modern-day Waldorf schools should explore whether or not it continues to be appropriate for them to apply both the curriculum that Steiner created in 1919 and the teacher-centered pedagogy that he taught to his Waldorf teachers in that and subsequent years.

BIBLIOGRAPHY

RUDOLF STEINER

Allen, Paul M., Ed. *Education as an Art*. Blauvelt, N.Y.: Steinerbooks, 1970.

Carlgren, Frans. *Education Towards Freedom: Rudolf Steiner Education*. East Grinstead, England: Rudolf Steiner Press, 1975.

Edmunds, Frances. *Rudolf Steiner's Gift to Education: The Waldorf Schools*. London: Rudolf Steiner Press, 1975.

Harwood, A. C. *The Recovery of Man in Childhood: A Study in the Educational Work of Rudolf Steiner*. Spring Valley, N.Y.: Anthroposophic Press, 1958.

————. *The Way of a Child*. London: Rudolf Steiner Press, 1979.

Kauffmann, George, Ed. *Fruits of Anthroposophy*. London: The Threefold Commonwealth, 1922.

Richards, M. C. *Centering: In Pottery, Poetry, and the Person*. Middletown, Conn.: Wesleyan University Press, 1964.

————. *The Crossing Point*. Middletown, Conn.: Wesleyan University Press, 1966, 1973.

————. *Toward Wholeness: Rudolf Steiner Education in America*. Middletown, Conn.: Wesleyan University Press, 1980.

Shepherd, A. P. *Rudolf Steiner: Scientist of the Invisible*. Rochester, Vermont: Inner Traditions, 1954, 1983.

Spock, Marjorie. *Teaching as a Lively Art*. Spring Valley, N.Y.: Anthroposophic Press, 1978.

Steiner, Rudolf. *The Gates of Knowledge.* Chicago: The Anthroposophical Literature Concern, Inc., 1922.

————. *Lectures to Teachers,* Christmas 1921. London: Anthroposophical Publishing Co., 1923.

————. *The Education of the Child.* London: Rudolf Steiner Publishing Co., 1927.

————. *The Story of My Life.* London: Anthroposophical Publishing Co., 1928.

————. *The New Art of Education.* New York: Anthroposophic Press, 1928.

————. *Paths of Experience.* London: Rudolf Steiner Publishing Co., 1934.

————. *Practical Course for Teachers.* London: Rudolf Steiner Publishing Co., 1937.

————. *The Four Temperaments.* New York: Anthroposophic Press, 1944.

————. *Study of Man.* London: Rudolf Steiner Press, 1966.

————. *Discussions with Teachers.* London: Rudolf Steiner Press, 1967.

————. *At the Gates of Spiritual Science.* London: Rudolf Steiner Press, 1970.

Unger, Carl. *Principles of Spiritual Science.* Spring Valley, N.Y.: Anthroposophic Press, 1976.

AUROBINDO GHOSE

Bainbridge, Robert. "The Teacher as Evolutionary Energy." In Norman C. Dowsett and Sita Ram Jayaswal, Eds., *The True Teacher*. Pondicherry: Sri Aurobindo Society, 1975.

Banerji, Sanat K. "Education for One World." *The Advent*. Vol. XXX, No. 4. November 1973.

Bruteau, Beatrice. *Worthy is the World: The Hindu Philosophy of Sri Aurobindo*. Rutherford, N.J.: Fairleigh Dickenson University Press, 1971.

Chaudhari, Haridas. *Sri Aurobindo: The Prophet of Life Divine*. Pondicherry: Sri Aurobindo Ashram, 1960.

Chaudhari, Haridas, and Spiegelberg, Frederic, Eds. *The Integral Philosophy of Sri Aurobindo*. London: Allen & Unwin, 1960.

Diwakar, R. R. *Mahayogi Sri Aurobindo*. Bombay: Bharatiya Vidya Bhavan, 1967.

Dowsett, Norman C. *Psychology For Future Education*. Pondicherry: Sri Aurobindo Society, 1977.

Dowsett, Norman C., and Jayaswal, Sita Ram, Eds. *The True Teacher*. Pondicherry: Sri Aurobindo Society, 1975.

———. *Education of the Future*. Pondicherry: Sri Aurobindo Society, 1976.

Gandhi, Kishore, Ed. *Contemporary Relevance of Sri Aurobindo*. Delhi: Vivek Publishing House, 1973.

Ghose, Aurobindo. *The Ideal of the Karmayogin*. Chandernagore: Prabartak Publishing House, 1921.

———. *Evolution*. Calcutta: Arya Publishing House, 1923.

———. *A System of National Education*. Calcutta: Arya Publishing House, 1924.

———. *Bases of Yoga*. Calcutta: Arya Publishing House, 1936.

———. "Letters of Sri Aurobindo." *Sri Aurobindo Mandir Annual*. No. 6, 1947.

———. *The Human Cycle*. Pondicherry: Sri Aurobindo Ashram, 1949.

———. *The Ideal of Human Unity*. Pondicherry: Sri Aurobindo Ashram, 1950.

———. *The Supramental Manifestation*. Pondicherry: Sri Aurobindo Ashram, 1952.

———. *The Synthesis of Yoga*. Pondicherry: Sri Aurobindo Ashram, 1957, 1958.

———. *The Hour of God*. Pondicherry: Sri Aurobindo Ashram, 1959.

———. *The Mind of Light*. New York: E. P. Dutton, 1953.

———. *Sri Aurobindo on Himself and The Mother*. Pondicherry: Sri Aurobindo Ashram, 1953.

———. *On Yoga I*. Pondicherry: Sri Aurobindo Ashram, 1957.

———. *On Yoga II*. Pondicherry: Sri Aurobindo Ashram, 1958.

———. *The Life Divine*. Pondicherry: Sri Aurobindo Ashram, 1960.

———. *The Future Evolution of Man: The Divine Life upon Earth*. (Compiled by P. B. Saint-Hilaire.) London: Allen & Unwin, 1963.

————. "Sri Aurobindo: His Life and Work (In His Own Words)." *Sri Aurobindo Mandir Annual.* No. 22, 1963.

————. "Sri Aurobindo: His Life and Work (In His Own Words) Part II." *Sri Aurobindo Mandir Annual.* No. 23, 1964.

————. *A Practical Guide to the Integral Yoga.* Pondicherry: Sri Aurobindo Ashram, 1971.

————. *The Essential Aurobindo.* Robert McDermott, Ed. New York: Shocken Books, 1973.

————. "Sri Aurobindo on The Mother." *The Advent.* Vol. XXXV, No. 1. February 1978.

————. Ghose, Aurobindo, and Richard, Mira (The Mother). *On Education.* Pondicherry: Sri Aurobindo Ashram, 1956.

Gupta, Nolini Kanta. *The Yoga of Sri Aurobindo, Parts I–X.* Madras: Sri Aurobindo Library, 1939, 1943, 1946, 1948, 1949, 1953, 1955, 1969.

————. "Editorial: A Review of Aurobindo's Life." *The Advent.* Vol. XXX, No. I. February 1973.

Iyengar, K. R. Srinivasa. *Sri Aurobindo.* Calcutta: Arya Publishing House, 1945.

Jayaswal, Sita Ram. "Personality of the Teacher." In Norman C. Dowsett and Sita Ram Jayaswal, Eds., *The True Teacher.* Pondicherry: Sri Aurobindo Society, 1975.

————. "Yoga and Education." *The Advent.* Vol. XXXIII, No. 3. August 1976.

Joshi, R. K. "Sri Aurobindo on Education during Childhood." *The Advent.* Vol. XXXI, No. 2. April 1974.

————. "On Education." *The Advent*. Vol. XXXII, No. 1. February 1975.

Joshi, Kireet, and Artaud, Yvonne. *Exploration in Education*. Pondicherry: Sri Aurobindo Ashram, 1974.

Kaul, H. K. *Sri Aurobindo: A Descriptive Bibliography*. New Delhi: Munshiram Manoharlal, 1972.

Langley, G. H. *Sri Aurobindo: Indian Poet, Philosopher, and Mystic*. London: David Marlowe, 1949.

Mitra, Sisirkumar. *Sri Aurobindo and the New World*. Pondicherry: Sri Aurobindo Ashram, 1957.

Motwani, Kewal. *Three Great Sages*. Madras: Ganesh and Co., 1951.

Nirodbaran. *Correspondence with Sri Aurobindo*. Pondicherry: Sri Aurobindo Ashram, 1954.

Prasad, Narayan. *Life in Sri Aurobindo Ashram*. Pondicherry: Sri Aurobindo Ashram, 1965.

————. *Education for a New Life*. Pondicherry: Sri Aurobindo Ashram, 1976.

Purani, A. B. *Sri Aurobindo: Some Aspects of His Vision*. Bombay: Bharatiya Vidya Bhavan, 1966.

Richard, Mira (The Mother). *On Education*. Pondicherry: Sri Aurobindo Ashram, 1952.

————. *Bulletin of Sri Aurobindo International Centre of Education*. February 1964.

————. "A Good Teacher." In Norman C. Dowsett and Sita Ram Jayaswal, Eds., *The True Teacher*. Pondicherry: Sri Aurobindo Society, 1975.

INAYAT KHAN

Corda, Vera Justin. *Holistic Child Guidance Course.* Gonzales, Calif. Vera J. Corda, 1981.

Khan, Inayat. *The Sufi Message of Hazrat Inayat Khan.* Vol. I: "The Way of Illumination." "The Inner Life." "The Soul, Whence and Whither?" "The Purpose of Life." London: Barrie & Rockliffe, 1961.

——. *Vol. II:* "The Mysticism of Sound." "Music." "The Power of the Word." "Cosmic Language." London: Barrie & Rockliffe, 1962.

——. *Vol. III:* "Education." "Rasa Shastra." "Character-Building and the Art of Personality." "Moral Culture." London: Barrie & Rockliffe, 1960.

——. *Vol. IV:* "Health." "Mental Purification." "The Mind World." London: Barrie & Rockliffe, 1961.

——. *Vol. V:* "A Sufi Message of Spiritual Liberty." "Aqibat, Life after Death." "The Phenomenon of the Soul." "Love, Human and Divine." "Pearls from the Ocean Unseen." "Metaphysics." London: Barrie & Rockliffe, 1962.

——. *Vol. VI:* "The Alchemy of Happiness." London: Barrie & Rockliffe, 1962.

——. *Vol. VII:* "In an Eastern Rose Garden." London: Barrie & Rockliffe, 1963.

——. *Vol. VIII:* "Sufi Teachings." London: Barrie & Rockliffe, 1963.

——. *Vol. IX:* "The Unity of Religious Ideals." London: Barrie & Rockliffe, 1963.

————. *Vol. X:* "Sufi Mysticism." "The Path of Initiation and Discipleship." "Sufi Poetry." "Art: Yesterday, Today and Tomorrow." "The Problem of the Day." London: Barrie & Rockliffe, 1964.

————. *Vol. XI:* "Philosophy, Psychology, Mysticism." "Aphorisms." London: Barrie & Rockliffe, 1964.

————. *Vol. XII:* "The Vision of God and Man." "Confessions." "Four Plays." London: Barrie & Rockliffe, 1967.

————. *Spiritual Dimensions of Psychology.* Lebanon Springs, N.Y.: Sufi Order Publications, 1981.

de Jong-Keesing, Elisabeth. *Inayat Khan.* The Hague: East-West Publications Fund N.V. in association with Luzac & Co. Ltd. (London), 1974.

Van Stolk, Sirkar, with Daphne Dunlop. *Memories of a Sufi Sage, Hazrat Inayat Khan.* Wassenaar, Holland: East-West Publications Fund N.V., 1967.

MARIA MONTESSORI

Hainstock, Elizabeth. *The Essential Montessori.* New York: Plume Books, 1978, 1986.

Lillard, Paula Polk. *Montessori: A Modern Approach.* New York: Schocken Books, 1972.

Montessori, Maria. *The Montessori Method.* New York: Schocken Books, 1912, 1964.

————. *Education for a New World.* Madras, India: Kalakshetra Publications, 1946, 1974.

————. *From Childhood to Adolescence.* New York: Schocken Books, 1948, 1976.

————. *Spontaneous Activity in Education*. New York: Schocken Books, 1965.

————. *The Secret of Childhood*. New York: Ballantine Books, 1966, 1991.

————. *The Discovery of the Child*. Notre Dame, Ind.: Fides Publishers, 1967.

————. *The Absorbent Mind*. New York: Dell Publishing, 1967, 1978.

⟨COUNTERPOINTS▶⟩

Counterpoints publishes the most compelling and imaginative books being written in education today. Grounded on the theoretical advances in criticalism, feminism and postmodernism in the last two decades of the twentieth century, Counterpoints engages the meaning of these innovations in various forms of educational expression. Committed to the proposition that theoretical literature should be accessible to a variety of audiences, the series insists that its authors avoid esoteric and jargonistic languages that transform educational scholarship into an elite discourse for the initiated. Scholarly work matters only to the degree it affects consciousness and practice at multiple sites. Counterpoints' editorial policy is based on these principles and the ability of scholars to break new ground, to open new conversations, to go where educators have never gone before.

For additional information about this series or for the submission of manuscripts, please contact:

Joe L. Kincheloe & Shirley R. Steinberg
637 West Foster Avenue
State College, PA 16801